The EdD and the Scholarly Practitioner

The EdD and the Scholarly Practitioner

The CPED Path

edited by

Jill Alexa Perry
University of Pittsburgh

INFORMATION AGE PUBLISHING, INC.
Charlotte, NC • www.infoagepub.com

Library of Congress Cataloging-in-Publication Data

A CIP record for this book is available from the Library of Congress
http://www.loc.gov

ISBN: 978-1-68123-541-7 (Paperback)
       978-1-68123-542-4 (Hardcover)
       978-1-68123-543-1 (ebook)

Printed in the United States of America

CONTENTS

SECTION I

TOOLS FOR CONSIDERING EdD PROGRAM REDESIGN

SECTION II

HIGHLIGHTS FROM CPED-INFLUENCED EdD PROGRAMS

SECTION III

IN THEIR OWN WORDS—
EXPERIENCES OF SCHOLARLY PRACTITIONERS

PREFACE

This volume highlights some of the efforts and learning that has come from the Carnegie Project on the Education Doctorate (CPED), a collaboration of 86 schools of education in the United States, Canada, and New Zealand, working to reenvision professional practice preparation at the doctoral level. In this volume, faculty and graduates from CPED-influenced EdD programs help readers to understand the distinctions being made in EdD program designs that improve the way practitioners utilize and engage scholarship to impact practice. These contributions are meant to offer ideas, tools, and examples of how changes to EdD programs can be made and what those changes result in—scholarly practitioners. The editor offers an overview of the CPED vision and the tools that have been developed by its members. Faculty from member institutions offer examples of how they have operationalized these ideas and what they have learned. Finally, several students reflect on their experience in a CPED-influenced EdD program and how they have become change agents as a result. This volume offers faculty who are interested in changing their EdD programs a unique look into how CPED's flexible framework for program design can be implemented in different contexts.

CHAPTER 1

THE NEW EDUCATION DOCTORATE

Preparing the Transformational Leader[1]

Jill Alexa Perry

Set the job descriptions of an assistant professor and a superintendent next to one another and what do you find in common? Nothing (see Figure 1.1).

The two career paths require distinct skills and knowledge, yet graduate schools of education have historically implemented a one-size-fits-all approach for those who wish to become academics and researchers and those who wish to become transformative leaders in educational practice.

Assistant Professor	Superintendent
• Be a productive scholar • Have an established program of research • Obtain external grants • Be an effective teacher and mentor • Serve the profession locally and nationally	• Be an effective leader • Operate a district • Oversee the administration of all instructional, business, and other operations • Advise and recommend action to School Board

Figure 1.1 Comparison of position descriptions.

The EdD and the Scholarly Practitioner, pages 1–10

Over the years, professional practitioners have reached out to me to express their frustration as they consider investing in a terminal degree. A sampling of this commentary includes:

> The debate of spending my hard-earned money on gaining *useful* knowledge has plagued me for the last year. I would rather learn about practical applications that can make me better at my job and serving society than theorizing about educational this or that. (Assistant Principal)

> I want to be a university president and have been told that I should get a PhD, but I want practical skills, not expertise in a discipline. (Senior advisor to a university president)

> I need better skills for my job. We are all struggling (but afraid to say so because we don't want to lose our jobs) because the training that people like me have received is either too simplistic or too theoretical. If I could get a similar level of education as a medical doctor I would be pleased. What I want is a degree that tells people, and especially my board, that I know a thing or two about how to make research on teaching applicable in our school district. (District superintendent)

All too often educational practitioners around the country are faced with the dilemma of wanting, or needing, a doctorate and choosing a program that offers them little more than a title and credential. In reality, practitioners return to the university because they seek enhanced abilities that will improve their practice and help them address the real problems they face daily (Zambo, Zambo, Buss, Perry, & Williams, 2014). However, in most programs, research preparation and traditional dissertations are theoretical exercises that leave practitioners struggling to apply learning to their contexts. In the end, these working professionals take on the burden; the expense and the time away from their family may be a means to meet demands rather than an opportunity to experience transformational leadership preparation. Seeking an EdD as opposed to a PhD may be one way to overcome this challenge.

When the Carnegie Project on the Education Doctorate (CPED)[2] came together in 2007, the consortium sought to better differentiate between the outcomes and expectations for EdD and PhD candidates. In particular, the consortium aimed to improve the EdD by asking, *What knowledge, skills, and dispositions should professionals working in education possess and be able to use?* In doing so, the consortium set out to redefine the EdD and the preparation that produces educational leaders who transform practice.

DOMAINS OF DEVELOPMENT

A colleague, Gordon Kirk from the University of Edinburgh, once asked me why the distinction between education's two doctorates was so complicated.

He suggested, "Clearly, the PhD is to understand the world and the EdD is to change the world." So simple yet so powerful a statement, which begs the question, How can doctoral preparation help practitioners change the world?

First, we must distinguish the type of doctoral preparation that is appropriate for professional educations. Deborah Colwill (2012) describes three categories of doctoral education. The first is the Professional Doctorate, which provides training through "lengthy internships and clinical experiences" (Gardner, as cited in Colwill, 2012, p. 13) and generally doesn't require a dissertation or thesis. Professional fields within the realm of medicine and law typically employ this type of doctorate. The second type of doctoral education is the Research Doctorate, which culminates in an original piece of research that contributes to advancing the field of study (Colwill, 2012). This type of doctorate typically prepares those who wish to conduct research or work as university-level faculty members. The final type of doctorate is the Professional Research Doctorate, which Colwill (2012) explains as focusing on both research and practice. A dissertation or thesis is required in such programs, however, the focus of the research is "investigating a particular professional topic or existing problem" (p. 13). Such profession-specific doctorates have arisen because of the lack of confidence that prospective students, employers, and other stakeholders have in traditional research as a means to adequately prepare graduates for the "pressures and challenges of an advanced level, nonacademic, professional context" (Gilbert, as cited in Colwill, 2012, p. 14; Usher as cited in Colwill, 2012, p. 14). The CPED-influenced EdD lies within this third group.

Next, Golde (2013) also helps us understand what student development in the CPED-influenced professional research doctorate looks like. Applying a theory she has developed for the PhD, Golde reviewed the CPED framework and proposed two domains for the development of the EdD candidate into a transformational leader: Development as a scholarly practitioner and reshaping a professional identity to Steward of the Practice.

Development as a Scholarly Practitioner

In the domain of development as a scholarly practitioner, Golde (2013) explains that students "learn to see important questions in the world of practice, frame those questions in terms of rigorous inquiry, answer those questions by generating and analyzing data, share what they have learned with other stakeholders, and directly apply what they have learned in settings of practice" (p. 145). She suggests that in this domain, the EdD candidate is developing from a novice of research to an expert who uses research to create change. CPED defines the Scholarly Practitioner as one who has been trained to

- blend practical wisdom with professional skills and knowledge to name, frame, and solve problems of practice;
- use practical research and applied theories as tools for socially just and equitable change; and
- resolve problems of practice by collaborating with key stakeholders and disseminating solutions in multiple ways.

Such knowledge and skills broaden the scope of a practitioner's toolbox by enhancing their understanding of problems and their potential to create impactful solutions.

Hochbein and Perry (2013) explain that the scholarly practitioner will engage three specific inquiry activities that support the solving of problems of practice: decipher, debate, and design.

Decipher

Historically, doctoral programs have assumed that practitioners need only the ability to "consume" research. However, as practitioner commentary above suggests, consumption of research does little for improving practice if the practitioners does not have the skills to properly understand and apply the knowledge gained from consumption. Rather, a scholarly practitioner should be able to decipher the methods, findings, and conclusions of research articles and be able to communicate such insights to stakeholders in practice (Hochbein & Perry, 2013).

Debate

Scholarly practitioners must also be able to advocate for their stakeholders and educational organizations. Research and empirical evidence offer means to build strong arguments as these leaders debate with policymakers and special interest groups who overwhelmingly impose accountability structures from the outside. Strong inquiry skills provide means to debate the ideological and methodological merits (Hochbein & Perry, 2013, p. 187) of outside policies.

Design

Scholarly practitioners must be able to apply the findings of research literature in the design of practical solutions to address pressing universal problems of practice (Archbald, 2008; Shulman, Golde, Bueschel, & Garabedian., 2006; Willis, Inman, & Valenti, 2010). Hochbein and Perry (2013) offer two primary types of design activities. The first is the application of knowledge from the research literature, both empirical and theoretical, toward developing a full understanding of a problem of practice and developing a solution for that problem. The second is the need to understand how to design interventions and evaluations of existing programs and new initiatives to avoid wasting resources and efforts.

As the result of such preparation in their CPED-influenced EdD program, the practitioner will now incorporate the use of inquiry as part of their professional practice, actively engaging theory and data (Golde, 2013) to solve complex problems of practice. They will also embrace their new identity as a scholarly practitioner and will utilize the skills in their toolbox to be transformational leaders. An example of this transformation is below.

An Example

David Cash is the superintendent of the Santa Barbara Unified School District and a graduate of the University of Southern California's EdD program. Upon arrival to his position, the Office of Civil Rights filed complaints regarding the disproportionate disciplinary practices on students of color in his district. After deciphering available data, he concluded that Latino males were six times more likely than white males to be suspended. He explains, "The data was easy to find, easy to understand. What was more difficult was working with staff and the community to arrive at solutions that would both meet the requirements of the OCR and change the culture of the district" (Perry, 2015, p. 23). Cash designed a study that gathered different data from the local community to learn how best to implement a more restorative approach to student-teacher and student-student interactions. As a result of his study, time expulsions for minority students moved from 50–75 per year to fewer than 15 per year. Cash attributes this success to his doctoral preparation that helped him blend research and practice and "provided [him] with the experiences necessary to identify and solve problems of practice."

Cash began his transformation to a scholarly practitioner during his doctoral program at USC, which helped him to see problems in new ways. This new skill continued to his dissertation in practice work in which he examined the processes and strategies utilized by superintendents to provide "defined autonomy" for school principals and resulted in changes to his own practice. More recently Cash employed his scholarly practitioner tools to develop a teacher-driven reform for the implementation of the Common Core in California. As a result of his program and evaluation of it, cadres of teacher leaders work within and across districts to design, implement, and evaluate the Common Core implementation. David Cash's experience exemplifies the formation of a scholarly practitioner. As a result of his EdD program, he embraces inquiry and to make better decisions and take actions that are positively impacting thousands of students.

Development as a Steward of Practice

Golde (2013) explains that EdD students are working professionals who "already have a well-developed professional identity" (p. 149). Most professional practitioners enter their EdD programs with at least 5 years of experience while many have much more. As strong professionals that are highly accomplished and respected, the EdD program must provide courses, experiences, and mentoring that will enhance their professional knowledge through new knowledge, skills, dispositions, and support as they refashion a new professional identity. Golde (2013) suggests this reshaping consists of "deciding what to let go, what to keep, and [learning] how to integrate new knowledge, skills, and dispositions into [their] professional life" (p. 149). Through this process, the practitioner evolves into a Steward of the Practice.

In 2006, Golde defined stewardship as the ability "to inculcate those we educate with the highest levels of competency and integrity" (p. 9). Writing on PhD preparation, Golde defined a steward of the discipline as "a caretaker who trains a critical eye to look forward and must be willing to take risks to move the discipline forward" (p. 13) through the generation, conservation, and transformation of knowledge (Golde, 2006). Building on Golde's (2006) definition of stewardship, CPED has applied the idea of stewardship to the preparation of practitioners, suggesting that the Steward of the Practice also maintains a caretaker role. The Steward of the Practice must generate and conserve knowledge that is composed of both theoretical and professional knowledge. Transformation of practice is the result of generating and conserving such knowledge. These ideas are articulated next.

Generation

A steward is "expected to conduct investigation according to accepted standards of rigor and quality" (Golde, 2006, p. 10). Such rigor and quality goes a step further for scholarly practitioners as they have the added responsibility of generating knowledge that both comes from the field and will impact their own practice, as Hochbein and Perry (2013) have noted above. On the one hand, given their daily confrontations with problems of practice, practitioners have the responsibility to conduct research in the field "at a depth that traditional forms of research might well not be capable, precisely because they are practitioners" (Jarvis, 1999, p. 24). On the other, applying inquiry and research to the practice setting requires some form of understanding of theory and research if their efforts are to result in improvement of practice.

Conservation

Conservation for Stewards of the Discipline involves "mastering the breadth and depth in the discipline" (Golde, 2006, p. 11), including historical and contextual landscapes. Berliner (2006) suggests conservation "requires understanding of how [a] field started and what it has become, so that the future of the field is both faithful to its origins and appropriate for its times" (p. 269). Stewards of the Practice understand the importance of having full knowledge of the field including the history, current events, and policy implications. As such, CPED-influenced EdD programs incorporate these aspects into the ways students investigate problems of practice—learning by doing as a means to become change agents. They are also taught that this knowledge needs to be shared both within and beyond their own boundaries. They are taught to design studies that include underrepresented voices and to communicate their findings effectively and clearly to various stakeholders, including the local and research community (Archbald, 2008).

Transformation

Golde (2006) defined transformation as the way in which a steward applies "knowledge, skills, finding and insights" (p. 12). Her definition builds upon the understanding of what a professional doctorate should be as established by the Council of Graduate Schools Task Force on the Professional Doctorate (2005); that is, preparation for the "potential transformation for that field of professional practice" (p. 7). The CPED consortium contends that the transformation of the field lies in CPED-influenced EdD graduates, stewards who apply their newly acquired skills and knowledge to impact their practice for the better.

EdD Students as Stewards of the Practice

Between 2010 and 2014, CPED received a U.S. Department of Education Fund for the Improvement of Post-Secondary Education (FIPSE) grant to study how EdD programs were changing at 21 of the original member Schools of Education. I conducted a smaller study (Perry, 2016) utilizing the larger dataset that analyzed existing student and alumni interview and survey data to understand how students saw themselves becoming Stewards of Practice.

In terms of generation, students and graduates noted two specific skills they developed as a result of their EdD programs—ownership and the ability and imperative to view problems of practice and solutions from multiple perspectives or lenses. In terms of ownership, students and graduates described having earned the skills to conduct research that resulted in change as part of their new identity. They further expressed owning the ability to debate or argue for change based on theoretical knowledge and expertise gained from their own inquiry work. Engaging multiple perspectives as part

of the inquiry and solution processes were described as means to intentionally move themselves "out of their comfort zone" to better lead and solve
problems. Such multiple perspectives were described as being global, diverse across groups of people, and broader, going beyond practical knowledge and opening theoretical frameworks.

Conservation in CPED-influenced EdD programs was described as the ways
in which students learned how to apply theoretical knowledge to practice—
learning by doing. Students and graduates described signature pedagogies
that taught them to apply data, historical knowledge, and academic theories
to problems they faced daily to better understand such problems and to develop solutions. Such exercises expanded their professional knowledge base.

Transformation was described in three ways. The first was the effect of
new knowledge, skills, and the application of one's own research on their
local context. Students and graduates frequently referred to this application as engaging research to "do" change.

Intellectual transformation was also a strong theme across the data. This
idea applied to the ways in which students and graduates described how their
minds and thinking had changed through the course of their EdD programs.
Finally, individuals described the personal changes they underwent during
their programs. Many felt they had broader perspectives and knowledge that
gave them the confidence they needed to become change leaders.

Golde's (2013) domains of development in professional practice doctorates offer a clear answer to the question asked above: How can doctoral
preparation help practitioners change the world? EdD programs must support the growth and development of practitioners through these domains.
The result of doing so is the preparation of a transformational leader, one
who blends practical wisdom with professional skills and knowledge as a
scholarly practitioner and one who has developed from practitioner to a
Steward of the Practice.

THE CPED PATH

The following volume consists of three sections that offer tools, examples,
and firsthand accounts of how CPED member institutions are redesigning
their EdD programs to support the development of transformational leaders.
The first section, "Tools for Considering EdD Program Redesign," shares the
learning from across the consortium on how to implement key programmatic changes. First, Hoffman and Perry offer an overview of the CPED Framework for EdD program design. The Framework, developed through collaboration of 80+ schools of education, provides members with a flexible way to
redesign programs while honoring their local context. The remaining chapters utilize data from the CPED-FIPSE study (2010–2014) or data recently

gathered from the consortium. Jones describes how leadership within the school of education plays an important role in undertaking the cumbersome EdD redesign process. Browne-Ferrigno and Maughan offer steps for creating a strong cohort relationship, a programmatic aspect that Golde (2013) notes as important in the domain of development as a scholarly practitioner. Ewbank describes that the faculty job of mentor has changed in CPED-influenced EdD programs. She suggests that traditional mentoring will not support the successful development of a transformational leader. Bengtson, Lasater, Murphy-Lee, and Jones provide an overview of how research courses have changed and how they need to continue to change if we are to remain true to the goals of professional research doctoral training.

In the second section, "Highlights From CPED-influenced EdD Programs," four examples of CPED-influenced programs are described. Chirichello, Wasicsko, and Allen describe the competency-based superintendent program at Northern Kentucky University offering descriptions of key components that have distinguished how superintendents are learning to improve their practice. Hochbein offers examples of University of Louisville student dissertations that have impacted one local school district. Buss and Zambo describe Arizona State University's signature pedagogy, Action Research, and provide guidelines for how to implement a similar pedagogy. Finally, Belzer, Axelrod, Benedict, Jakubik, Rosen, and Yavuz offer the experience of five students as they undertake the problem of practice dissertation and how their experience supports the Rutger's University EdD program goals.

In the final section, we hear from graduates of CPED-influenced EdD programs. In their own words, these practitioners tell us about how their programs have developed them into transformational leaders who exhibit traits of the scholarly practitioner and steward their profession. Jones and Campbell describe how a community college leader acquired the leadership and scholarly inquiry skills in the Texas Tech University's online higher education EdD to change her own practice. Kline explains how her dissertation in practice experience at Lynn University helped her roles as a superintendent to transform a district's attendance rate. Finally, Petrin, Artivita, and Belzer describe how two graduates of the Rutgers University program are using their dissertation in practice work to positively change teacher induction programs and ultimately improve the learning opportunities in schools.

NOTES

1. The March 2015 issue of School Administrator Magazine inspired this book.
2. See http://cpedinitiative.org

REFERENCES

Archbald, D. (2008). Research versus problem solving for the education leadership doctoral thesis: Implications for form and function. *Educational Administration Quarterly, 5*(44), 704–739.

Berliner, D. C. (2006). Toward a future as rich as our past. In C. M. Golde & G. E. Walker (Eds.), *Envisioning the future of doctoral education* (pp. 268–290). San Francisco, CA: Jossey-Bass.

Colwill, D. A. (2012). *Education the scholar practitioner in organzation development.* Charlotte, NC: Information Age.

Golde, C. M. (2006). Preparing stewards of the discipline. In C. M. Golde, & G. E. Walker (Eds.), *Envisioning the future of doctoral education* (pp. 3–23). San Francisco, CA: Jossey-Bass.

Golde, C. M. (2013). Afterward: Mapping the transformation of the EdD student. In J. A. Perry & D. L. Carlson (Eds.), *In their own words: A journey to the stewardship of the practice in education* (pp. 139–148) Charlotte, NC: Information Age.

Hochbein, C., & Perry, J. A. (2013). The role of research in the professional doctorate. *Planning and Changing, 44*(3/4), 181–194.

Jarvis, P. (1999). *The practitioner-researcher: Developing theory from practice.* San Francisco, CA: Jossey-Bass

Perry, J. A. (2015, March). The EdD and scholarly practitioners. *School Administrator Magazine.* 21–25.

Perry, J. A. (2016). The scholarly practitioner as steward of the practice. In V. Storey & K. Hesbol (Eds.), *Contemporary approaches to dissertation development and research methods.* Hershey, PA: IGI Global.

Shulman, L. S., Golde, C. M., Bueschel, A. C., & Garabedian, K. J. (2006). Reclaiming education's doctorates: A critique and a proposal. *Educational Researcher, 35*(3) 25–32.

Willis, J., Inman, D., & Valenti, R. (2010) Completing a professional practice dissertation: A guide for doctoral students and faculty. Charlotte, NC: Information Age.

Zambo, R., Zambo, D., Buss, R. R., Perry, J. A., & Williams, T. R. (2014). Seven years after the call: Students' and graduates' perceptions of the re-envisioned EdD. *Innovative Higher Education, 39*(2), 123–138. doi:10.1007/s10755-013-9262-3

SECTION I

TOOLS FOR CONSIDERING EdD PROGRAM REDESIGN

CHAPTER 2

THE CPED FRAMEWORK

Tools For Change

Rachael L. Hoffman and Jill Alexa Perry

The Carnegie Project on the Education Doctorate (CPED) began in 2007 with a group of education faculty members from 25 schools of education collaborating to ask questions and seek solutions for a problem that plagued the field of education for almost a century. In contrast to other fields, in education the doctorate came in two forms—the PhD and the EdD—and both had been used to prepare academic scholars and the highest level of practitioners (McClintock, 2005). This practice perpetuated a kind of confusion that left faculty members doing "neither [doctorate] very well" (Shulman, Golde, Bueschel, & Garabedian, 2006). In 2006, Shulman and his colleagues at the Carnegie Foundation for the Advancement of Teaching and Learning offered a challenge and potential solution. In their piece, *Reclaiming Education's Doctorates*, Shulman et al. challenged schools of education to reclaim both of their doctorates and improve them for the specific preparation of research scholars (PhD) and professional practitioners (EdD). Additionally, they outlined a "vision" for how this might be done by "networking of individual sites prepared to form consortia that

The EdD and the Scholarly Practitioner, pages 13–25
Copyright © 2016 by Information Age Publishing
All rights of reproduction in any form reserved.

experiment with such efforts [to redesign the professional practice doctorate] in collaboration" (p. 30). Thus, CPED was born.

With the support of 25 deans of education, CPED focused on engaging faculty to rethink the purpose and design of the EdD. These early faculty members were saddled with two tasks. First, they had to determine the purpose of the EdD, which the members overwhelming agreed would be practitioners only. The second task was to rethink how preparation would both differ from traditional EdD or PhD programs and be distinctly designed for practitioners. Members discussed the kinds of knowledge, skills, and dispositions educational practitioners need to be successful and impact practice. Furthermore, they identified ways in which EdD program components could support the development of these characteristics. This discussion detoured radically from the academic debate regarding the rigor, utility, and purpose of the EdD that took place throughout the 20th century (Anderson, 1983; Brown, 1966; Deering, 1998; Freeman, 1931). Overall, the field lacked a cohesive understanding of the purpose of the EdD, and scholarly inquiry into the status quo did little to alleviate confusion or define the degree. CPED's aim has been to clearly define the EdD as the terminal degree for professional practitioners and to do so by designing programs of study that are relevant and impactful.

A FRAMEWORK FOR PROGRAM DESIGN

CPED began in January 2007 when faculty members, administrators, and students from 25 schools of education joined in a conversation that would consider ways to develop models for programmatic and institutional change. Plans and thinking were shaped by the original four design ideas that Shulman presented at the first convening in June 2007 (signature pedagogy, capstone, scholarship of teaching and learning, and laboratories of practice). However, throughout the first three years of the project, a need for dynamic guidance to answer questions like "How can this be done at our institution?" remained. It was clear early on that a "one size" EdD program design would not fit all member institutions; that is, a universal prescriptive program model would be ineffective given the diversity of the Consortium membership. Rather, a dynamic framework that could be applied across contexts but which upheld a standard of excellence was needed. As a result, members decided that a set of guiding principles would provide flexibility while supporting excellence. They also agreed that such a set of principles would need to be a "working" set that could evolve as the consortium's membership, research, and network developed.

Defining the Working Principles

With the idea of establishing a set of working principles came several questions about their purpose and form. At the June 2009 convening, consortium members began to generate ideas of principles after having discussed defining a set of outcomes for EdD program graduates. However, as ideas began to take shape, so did questions. The three primary questions that members had were (a) What is the purpose of the principles? (b) Should the principles be defined within or across areas of concentration (e.g., K–12 administration, teacher leadership or higher education)? (c) How specific or general should the principles be? Through a series of discussions, the consortium reached the conclusions outlined below.

What Is the Purpose of the Principles?

Consortium members had decided that the EdD would prepare "doctoral students who graduate with the potential to transform the professional practice of education" (CPED, 2009). With this focus, the principles needed to distinguish the preparation of educational practitioners from that of scholars in education and further establish the rigor required for this preparation. Therefore, the idea of transforming practice was the criterion for which the principles would be aimed at and judged.

Should Principles Be Defined Within or Across Areas of Concentration?

Within the consortium, multiple areas of concentration were and continue to be represented. The focus of member institutions varies from developing school leadership programs to teacher education programs to institutional leadership/higher education programs. As the consortium has increased in size, the areas of concentration have also become more diverse. Many programs have an education leadership focus, with differences in settings (e.g., P–12, higher education, etc.), while others prepare practitioners in the area of curriculum and instruction. Still other programs offer multiple concentration options under one EdD program. The aim of the principles was to be universal enough to be applicable to the entire collective of programs yet specific enough to be purposeful. Therefore, members determined that the principles should be broad enough to be relevant to all EdD programs.

How Specific or General Should the Principles Be?

In the early stages of developing principles at the June 2009 Convening, many suggestions focused on a specific aspect of a program. For example, some ideas were specific to a process like admissions; others were specific to particular standards for a program component like the capstone project. A decision was reached to identify overarching themes that apply at a broader level to develop principles that could guide the overall goals and practices of a program.

The Process

The process for developing the CPED principles was a unique one that spanned a year of collaboration across the original 25-member institutional members. Members discussed the purpose and goals (outlined above) at the June 2009 convening. Those discussions were brought to the October 2009 convening where members were asked to submit sample statements that they believed to be consistent with optimal preparation of educational practitioners. Overall, 35 sample statements were considered after duplicate ideas were removed. More than 50 individuals from member institutions examined each statement and engaged in an iterative process of evaluation and improvement. Common themes across statements were identified as the original statements were narrowed and honed into the final six principles. Two days of collaborative analysis and discussions resulted in the following proclamation, which included a new definition of the EdD and a set principles to guide program design.

We, the members of CPED, believe

"The professional doctorate in education prepares educators for the application of appropriate and specific practices, the generation of new knowledge, and for the stewardship of the profession."

With this understanding, we have identified the following statements that will focus a research and development agendas to test, refine, and validate principles for the professional doctorate in education.

The Professional doctorate in education:

1. Is framed around questions of equity, ethics, and social justice to bring about solutions to complex problems of practice.
2. Prepares leaders who can construct and apply knowledge to make a positive difference in the lives of individuals, families, organizations, and communities.
3. Provides opportunities for candidates to develop and demonstrate collaboration and communication skills to work with diverse communities and to build partnerships.
4. Provides field-based opportunities to analyze problems of practice and use multiple frames to develop meaningful solutions.
5. Is grounded in and develops a professional knowledge base that integrates both practical and research knowledge, that links theory with systemic and systematic inquiry.
6. Emphasizes the generation, transformation, and use of professional knowledge and practice.

The definition and principles have become the foundation upon which 80+ member institutions have built or are building their professional practice EdD programs. In 2010, CPED received a U.S. Department of Education Fund for the Improvement of Post-Secondary Education (FIPSE) grant, which funded a 4-year research investigation of the impact of CPED membership on program redesign and the incorporation of these principles in 21 education doctorate programs. Results suggested that principles were being incorporated across all 21 programs, but to varying degrees. Though deans and the faculty member who served as the CPED principal investigator were the most knowledgeable of the principles, many faculty and students involved in the redesigned EdD programs could indicate (after reviewing a copy of the principles) that their programs were in fact grounded in the CPED principles (Perry, Zambo, & Wunder, 2015). An independent evaluator of the CPED-FIPSE study also discovered that CPED's principles were being adopted by nonmember institutions as they learned from outside of the consortium (Crowe, 2010). Still, one of the greatest findings of the study was that more needs to be learned about how these principles are being operationalized at member institutions. As new members were invited to the consortium in 2011 and in 2014, the aims have continued to focus on researching the impact of these principles on redesigned EdD programs.

Design Concepts

The principles provide the foundation for CPED. To build upon this foundation, member institutions use a set of design concepts as building blocks to develop effective and sustainable program components (see Figure 2.1). The CPED design concepts provide a common vernacular to refer to specific components present across programs and guidance on how these components can be implemented. They originated with ideas from Lee Shulman and the Carnegie Foundation but have advanced under collaborative thinking and research by consortium members. The design concepts include Scholarly Practitioner, Signature Pedagogy, Inquiry as Practice, Laboratories of Practice, Problem of Practice, and Dissertation in Practice. A brief overview of how CPED defines each of these concepts will be provided here in conjunction with examples of how several member institutions have implemented the design concepts. Additionally, several design concepts are discussed in closer detail throughout this book.

Scholarly Practitioner

The concept of a scholarly practitioner is present in many professional fields and may be known by several different names (e.g., Scholar-practitioner,

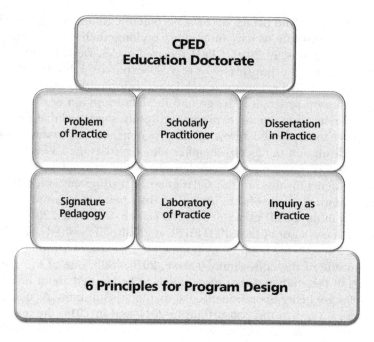

Figure 2.1 The CPED framework for program design.

Scholar of Practice, Practitioner-Scholar). Within the CPED Consortium a scholarly practitioner is defined as

> Scholarly Practitioners blend practical wisdom with professional skills and knowledge to name, frame, and solve problems of practice. They use practical research and applied theories as tools for change because they understand the importance of equity and social justice. They disseminate their work in multiple ways, and they have an obligation to resolve problems of practice by collaborating with key stakeholders, including the university, the educational institution, the community, and individuals. (CPED, 2010)

For many members, this definition serves to operationalize the principles for program design into an outcome of their program. On program websites, in program handbooks, on course syllabi, in orientation, and even as the topic of the introductory course, this design-concept provided an outcome for both students and faculty to direct their program intentions towards. Students enter programs knowing that the CPED-influenced EdD program is more than just a credential and will support their development in the use of inquiry and scholarship as a tool for impacting practice (see Perry chapter in this volume).

Signature Pedagogy

Shulman's work on pedagogies employed across several professional domains (law, medicine, clergy, engineering, nursing) was highly influential in the CPED design-concept signature pedagogy. Signature Pedagogy, as defined by CPED, is "the pervasive set of practices used to prepare scholarly practitioners for all aspects of their professional work: to think, to perform, and to act with integrity" (Shulman, 2005, p. 52). Signature pedagogy includes three dimensions, as articulated by Lee Shulman (2005):

1. Teaching is deliberate, pervasive and persistent. It challenges assumptions, engages in action, and requires ongoing assessment and accountability.
2. Teaching and learning are grounded in theory, research, and in problems of practice. It leads to habits of mind, hand, and heart that can and will be applied to authentic professional settings.
3. Teaching helps students develop a critical and professional stance with a moral and ethical imperative for equity and social justice (CPED, 2014).

In order to produce skilled professionals, programs need a cohesive, tailored approach to educate students. This approach must include the knowledge to be incorporated (i.e., what do students need to know?), methods of disseminating information, and ways for knowledge to be applied so that skills can develop (Perry & Imig, 2008). Though the original intention was to develop one overarching signature pedagogy for the EdD, like one would find in medicine or law, members reiterated the need to remain flexible to honor local context, which may include the skills and expertise of faculty as well as the needs of a regional student body. Therefore, the signature pedagogies employed across CPED member programs are diverse.

For example, at Arizona State University, Learner-Scholar Communities (LSC) of Practice (described briefly in the Chirichello, Wasicsko, and Allen chapter in this volume) designed in conjunction with Action Research methodology embody the Signature Pedagogy of their Leadership for Innovation EdD program. LSCs reinforce the skillset required for collaboration and group problem solving and support students in their completion of action research projects. The focus on action research develops in students the capacity to "address authentic problems and needs through innovation and action that is informed by scholarship" (CPED, 2015). As part of the Michigan State University signature pedagogy, annual Summer Forums "create arenas for public deliberation of leading issues and ideas, thus providing opportunities for multiple stakeholders to develop and disseminate strategies for improving schools and policies affecting schools" (CPED, 2015). Washington State University's Leadership in Education program also utilizes summer meetings, with a focus on action research training that "encourages students to conduct collaborative inquiry in their K–12 school settings to address problems of practice related to student learning" (CPED, 2015). Two common themes are noted across member's signature pedagogies—collaboration (via cohorts, communities of practice, or group dissertations) and developing solutions for problems of practice through scholarly inquiry.

Inquiry as Practice

Inquiry is an undeniable component of any educational process and crucial to doctoral study. In the case of the CPED-influenced EdD, however, inquiry has special meaning. Inquiry as practice is a process targeted toward improvement of practice through an examination of applicable questions and the development of relevant solutions. To this end, CPED defines Inquiry as practice in the following way:

> Inquiry as Practice is the process of posing significant questions that focus on complex problems of practice. By using various research, theories, and professional wisdom, scholarly practitioners design innovative solutions to address the problems of practice. At the center of Inquiry of Practice is the ability to use data to understand the effects of innovation. As such, Inquiry of Practice requires the ability to gather, organize, judge, aggregate, and analyze situations, literature, and data with a critical lens. (CPED, 2010)

Bengston, Jones, Lasater, and Murphy-Lee (2014) examined the ways in which programs approach the development of inquiry in students. These approaches feature hybrid courses with traditional research approaches blended with action research; mixed-methods coursework; an inquiry course sequence including data-based decision making, program evaluation, and action research; specially tailored coursework in specific research methodologies; and inclusion of coursework with a focus on reading, understanding, and analyzing scholarly work.

As discussed by Bengston et al. (2014), the implementation of structures, coursework, and experiences to facilitate inquiry at institutions varies. For example, Zambo (2013) describes the Direct Field Study course that is part of the Arizona State University course sequence for the EdD in Leadership and Innovation. This course requires students to engage in "elbow learning," a practice described by G. Stanley Hall in which the student completes an internship experience aimed at development of wisdom alongside mentoring and opportunities to practice skills. In this course, students select a mentor from a different setting. For example, a student with a position in the Department of Education might choose the Director of an Art Museum. By crossing discipline boundaries, students are encouraged to examine leadership from other perspectives and to learn from diverse experiences.

Ultimately, the lens through which students engage in inquiry and problem solving gains input and perspective from individuals outside of their typical environment (Zambo, 2013).

Laboratories of Practice

Laboratory of Practice is another concept that originated from Shulman and his work on the professions. In many fields, the laboratory is a kind of signature pedagogy, a place where students can practice what they are learning. For CPED, it is similar but remains a distinct design concept. According to CPED,

> Laboratories of Practice are settings where theory and practice inform and enrich each other. They address complex problems of practice where ideas—formed by the intersection of theory, inquiry, and practice—can be implemented, measured, and analyzed for the impact made. Laboratories of Practice facilitate transformative and generative learning that is measured by the development of scholarly expertise and implementation of practice. (CPED, 2010)

Given this definition, a number of settings can be appropriately identified as laboratories, but most often they are the student's place of employment. This point is important because the majority of EdD students remain employed during their program. In fact, most CPED institutions require that students are employed so that their organization can be the place where they "practice" their learning. Data from San Diego State University, for example, states, "All doctoral students concurrently hold full-time positions as educators. This full-time employment is an asset, providing opportunities to apply theoretical understandings covered in their coursework" (CPED, 2015). At California State Polytechnic, laboratories of practice are the "schools, school districts, or other agencies, organizations, or institutions that service or provide resources to the field of education" (CPED, 2015). Alternatively, at California State Fresno, laboratories are embedded as fieldwork into student courses. At Lynn University, case studies based on real situations are utilized as laboratories in which students can learn to apply learning.

Problem of Practice

Hochbein and Perry (2013) challenged CPED members to clearly define a term which is common in other professional fields but lacked clear and consistent understanding within the CPED consortium. As a result, this design concept was defined as, "a persistent, contextualized, and specific issue embedded in the work of a professional practitioner, the addressing of which has the potential to result in improved understanding, experience, and outcomes" (CPED, 2010).

Leaders in education are regularly faced with problems of practice (POPs), and in EdD programs, students frequently want to investigate these problems during their program. Across CPED members, however, it has been noted that students frequently confuse problems with issues. This confusion has led programs to rethink how they train students to clearly conceptualize problems, including understanding the roots of problems, how they are defined in their local context, by local stakeholders, and how they are understood in the broader academic literature. To illustrate, Archbald (2013) draws connections to the field of business, and the ways in which innovative leadership is needed to address problems and improve practice. He states,

> Vision is no less important for ordinary leaders in community organizations, schools, agencies, nonprofits, organizational departments and other roles like these. If a leader cannot identify problems and cannot conceive and communicate a vision of improvement, then that organization is without a critical lever for improvement. (p. 137)

In addition to preparing students with the tools needed to act as agents of change, students need an understanding of the transferability of those skills to their own practice. As the dean from one CPED member institution commented,

> [Students] are expected to bring their practice into this program in the hopes that what we are doing with them in coursework and the dissertation complements what they are doing as a regular part of their job and their work. . . . I would almost say that it is required. We want them to do that, otherwise I don't believe that they go through the program seeing that there is a connection between what they are studying and what their work is. (Bengston & Stacy, 2012, p. 16)

Dissertation in Practice

Originally conceived of as a "capstone," CPED members sought a name and definition of the culminating EdD project that would exemplify its purpose and goals. Thus, CPED developed and defined the Dissertation in Practice as "a scholarly endeavor that impacts a complex problem of practice" (CPED, 2014). In a dissertation in practice, conceptualizing and addressing problems of practice requires a much different skillset than in a traditional dissertation, which conceptualizes and addresses theoretical questions. Therefore, it follows that the culminating project of practitioner preparation programs should be distinct from that of research preparation programs. Equally, just as students who complete PhD programs in the field of education often develop three initial journal publications using their dissertation, thereby launching their professional careers, EdD students should have a foundation established on which they can build the next phase of their professional careers. This foundation should include relevant tools and plans of action with which a practitioner can incite real and impactful change.

Archbald's (2008) problem-based thesis idea has been influential on CPED member thinking about the dissertation in practice. He argues that a problem-based thesis is an alternative to the traditional dissertation that better serves professional practice degrees. His model proposes four specific qualities by which dissertations in practice should be considered: developmental efficacy, or the students' benefit from the training involved in developing the project; community benefit; intellectual stewardship; and distinctiveness in form and function. The problem-based thesis involves identification of a practical problem within one's own organization, collection of information, problem analysis, and development of an action plan. The resulting project should be crafted to persuade decision makers using evidence and arguments, and recommend actions and plans to move forward.

CPED members have admittedly had difficulty with this design concept. Tradition rules in higher education with policies and mindsets that have long steeped in "the way it has always been done." As such, members have struggled with changing the look and feel of dissertations to reflect the dissertation in practice design concept. Such struggle, however, is part of the CPED process of change. As a bottom-up effort, faculty members are pushing for change, and their push is supported by calls of practitioners (like those described in the introduction of this book) who want to develop products that will impact their practice. CPED has created the Dissertation in Practice of the Year Award, which has presented four awards that exemplify that change is happening.

CONCLUSION

This chapter serves the purpose of introducing and outlining the CPED framework for EdD program design. This framework is the tool upon which CPED members in this book and throughout the consortium have built, are building, and are evaluating their education doctorate programs. This framework is also meant to be shared beyond the consortium in the hopes of reframing the way all schools of education, their faculty and students, and professionals think about doctoral preparation for practitioners and the distinction of the EdD from the PhD. The framework, however is not fixed. It is fluid. As the consortium grows, as it investigates individual programs and programs across the consortium, learning will inform the improvement of this tool. As such, the CPED promotes an ongoing improvement model rather than a one-size-fits-all model as the way in which schools of education can support practitioners in their quest to improve education in the United States and abroad.

REFERENCES

Anderson, D. G. (1983). Differentiation of the Ed.D. and Ph.D. in education. *Journal of Teacher Education, 34*(3), 55–58.

Archbald, D. (2008). Research versus problem solving for the education leadership doctoral thesis: Implications for form and function. *Educational Administration Quarterly, 5*(44), 704–739.

Archbald, D. (2013). Vision and Leadership: Problem-based Learning as a Teaching Tool. *Journal of Leadership Education, 12*(2), 136–147.

Bengston, E., Jones, S. J., Lasater, K., & Murphy-Lee, M. (2014). *Research courses in the CPED phase I institutions: What's the difference?* Retrieved January 7, 2016, from http://www.cpedinitiative.org/files/bengston_jones_manuscript.pdf

Bengston, E., & Stacy, J. (2012). *Case report.* Unpublished manuscript.

Brown, L. D. (1966). *Doctoral graduates in education. An inquiry into their motives, aspirations, and perceptions of the program.* Bloomington: Indiana University.

Carnegie Project for the Educational Doctorate (CPED). (2009, October). Working principles for the professional practice doctorate in education. *CPED.* Retrieved from http://www.cpedinitiative.org/files/Working%20Principles%20 for%20the%20Professional%20Practice%20Doctorate.pdf

Carnegie Project for the Educational Doctorate (CPED). (2010). Design concept definitions. *CPED.* Retrieved from http://www.cpedinitiative.org/ design-concept-definitions

Carnegie Project for the Educational Doctorate CPED (Ed.). (2015). Consortium Members. Retrieved January 7, 2016, from http://cpedinitiative.org/ consortium-members

Crowe, E. (2010). *Redesigning the Professional Doctorate in Education Year 3 Evaluation Report.* Pittsburgh, PA: Carnegie Project on the Education Doctorate.

Deering, T. E. (1998). Eliminating the doctor of education degree: It's the right thing to do. *The Educational Forum, 62,* 243–248.

Freeman, F. N. (1931). *Practices of American universities in granting higher degrees in education: A series of official statements* (Vol. 19). Chicago, IL: University of Chicago Press.

Hochbein, C., & Perry, J. A. (2013). The role of research in the professional doctorate. *Planning and Changing: An Educational Leadership and Policy Journal, 44*(3/4), 181–194.

McClintock, R. (2005). Homeless in the house of intellect: Formative justice and education as an academic study. New York, NY: Laboratory for Liberal Learning.

Perry, J. A., & Imig, D. G. (2008, November/December). A stewardship of practice in education. *Change,* 42–48.

Perry, J. A., Zambo, D., & Wunder, S. (2015). Understanding how schools of education have redesigned the education doctorate. *Journal of School Public Relations, (36),* 58–85.

Shulman, L. S. (2005). Signature pedagogies in the professions. *Daedalus, 134*(3), 52–59.

Shulman, L. S., Golde, C. M., Bueschel, A. C., & Garabedian, K. J. (2006). Reclaiming education's doctorates: A critique and a proposal. *Educational Researcher, 35*(3), 25–32.

Zambo, D. (2013). Elbow learning about leadership and research: EdD students' experiences in an internship course. *Planning and Changing: An Educational Leadership and Policy Journal, 44*(3/4).

CHAPTER 3

CHANGE LEADERSHIP AND SUPPORT FOR THE CPED-INFLUENCED EDUCATION DOCTORATE

Stephanie J. Jones

Higher education organizations are historically slow to change. Steeped in longstanding traditions and the traditional philosophies of academe and the academy, the integration of a CPED-influenced education doctorate does not come without its challenges. The purpose of this chapter is to explore the experiences of the integration of the CPED framework into doctorate of education programs at Phase I CPED member institutions. This exploration will address change leadership, program specific changes and support, as well as the successes and challenges of implementing these programs.

Greenwald (2012) describes that many higher education institutions are "like Dorothy's house in the Wizard of Oz: they have been picked up by uncontrollable forces, are flying through the air and know not where they will land" (para. 1). This is due in part to decreased funding, which is forcing institutions to make budget cuts that affect programs and services as well as making necessary changes to the way they operate. Implementing

The EdD and the Scholarly Practitioner, pages 27–43

change in higher education can be unknown territory, but is a necessity due to more competitive technological and global environments as well as increased demands for accountability and productivity from external stakeholders (Fawson, 2012; Rich, 2006). Priest, St. John, and Boon (2006) note that as state and federal funding for higher education significantly declines, expectations for completion and employability of graduates rises. Yet higher education institutions continue to resist the need to change to address these external forces.

Though higher education institutions are challenged by external factors to change, the culture and climate of these institutions are often unresponsive to these pressures (Rowley & Sherman, 2001). Having institutional leadership who understands and who can communicate the importance of needed change, how the change can occur, as well as the likely outcomes of change is crucial for institutional success (Rowley & Sherman, 2001). According to Kotter (2012), communicating urgency in change initiatives is the first step toward gaining support for a change agenda in organizations where complacency is high. Higher education's history of deeply engrained complacency makes this first step crucial (Rowley & Sherman, 2001; Shugart, 2013). Kecskemethy (2012) argues that leadership has to effectively situate the organization for change, build consensus and support for goals, properly allocate and manage resources, and seek to impact decision-making at all organizational levels. Leaders who are flexible, responsive, innovative, and adaptable can influence changes in institutional culture and are a strategic necessity in higher education organizations (Kecskemethy, 2012).

The significant level of change facing higher education institutions requires a leadership philosophy and style that is proportionate to the challenges faced and who understand the support needed to affect change. Boggs (2012) notes that the defining characteristic of the leadership most needed in higher education today is being able "to instill a strong sense of purpose in all of the college's people" (p. 106). This is supported by Argia and Ismail (2013), who identify that "leadership focuses upon the attainment of organizational goals by working primarily with and through people" (p. 112). Effective leaders are those who are proud of the traditions of the organization but are not constrained by the past (Boggs, 2012). An organizational climate must exist that instills a common sense of purpose that encourages risk, rewards innovation, and does not punish failure (Boggs, 2012). The success of any change efforts in an institution ultimately depends on the willingness of faculty, staff, and administrators to risk failure. For change to occur in traditional organizations that are heavily steeped in culture and tradition, resistance to change and fear of the uncertain needs to be overcome so that the institution can embrace the opportunities and successes that are possible, even though resources may be constrained.

LEADERSHIP FOR CHANGE

Researchers have identified that higher education needs change leadership who have the skills and competencies to be able to (a) assess internal and external environments in order to be able to strategically position an institution, (b) understand the complexities of the organization, including its culture and climate, and (c) inspire others within the institution to be receptive to change and to be motivated to participate in it (e.g., Argia & Ismail, 2013; Ellington, 2009; Rich, 2006). Bolman and Deal (2008) define organizational culture as "the superglue that bonds an organization, unites people, and helps an enterprise accomplish desired ends" (p. 252). Cultures must exist that unite, promote dialogue, provide environments for collective learning, and collective action (Bess & Dee, 2012; Boyce, 2003); a culture that will "shape the change process" (Boyce, 2003, p. 120). This requires leaders who can shape and make meaning for the college (Bess & Dee, 2012; Northouse, 2013).

Northouse (2013) identifies that transformational leadership "changes and transforms people" (p. 185). When change is needed, leaders who have a transformational leadership style are successful as they develop and articulate a clear vision of the future, and value working with others within the institution to bring about needed success to position the institution for the future. Much of the literature on transformational leadership focuses on how these leaders position themselves, their people, and their organizations for change. Transformational leadership aligns with the preferred leader qualities discussed above by Boggs (2012), as it requires leaders to attend to a range of human concerns and realities (Northouse, 2013). Transformational leaders are heavily invested in the development of others. While this interactive process nurtures development and change within individuals, the overall effect is that it empowers people to effect positive change across the organization (Hendricks, 2014).

Executive leaders in higher education organizations have key roles in articulating a vision and purpose for the institution and the paths it should take toward realizing its vision and purposes. This is no different when articulating the vision and purpose of the CPED guiding principles and design concepts, and trying to integrate them into existing academic programs while trying to shift the organization's culture and philosophies. The articulation of the vision and purpose are instrumental to the success of any change is supported by Rowley and Sherman (2001), who argue that "it is the human core that actually gets the work done" (p. 218). Often resistance to change arises from valid human anxieties, concerns, beliefs, or situations.

Transformational leadership is instrumental to the success of integrating the CPED guiding principles and design-concepts into doctorate of education programs. Transformational leaders engage with followers and colleagues and form connections that intensify the motivation and moral purposes of both leaders and those with whom they interact. These leaders pay attention to what others need, their motives for following, as well as to help followers attain their potential (Northouse, 2013).

The transformational leader's openness to being transformed through the encounter with others is an important and unique aspect of this leadership model. It aligns with Quinn's (2000) work about changing a human system, such as a university or college. Quinn perceives that the first step in genuine transformative change in an organization is for those in the organization to transform themselves.

Higher education institutions are complex environments that are challenged to stay relevant (Hanna, 2003). They are challenged to react to changes caused by global, social, economic, political, and technological factors (Bornstein, 2007), as well as are faced with declining operating budgets and resources, an economy that has been in a downturn since 2007, a shift in student demographics, and employer demands for skilled workers (Basham, 2012; Boggs, 2012; McArdle, 2013). As Bunn (2011) claims, higher education organizations must respond to both internal and external forces, and this requires organizational transformation.

Transformational leaders take a holistic view of the people who work in their institutions. As leaders, they are invested in each person's needs, motivations, strengths, and ambitions (Northouse, 2013). While these characteristics are positive and quite likeable in a leader, being a transformational leader is not always this simple. Since they are called to be leaders of important change for their institutions, transformational leaders are known to disrupt a sense of what others consider normal, and their interest in developing others means pushing followers out of their comfort zones at times (Hendricks, 2014; Hogue, 2014). Change is uncomfortable, and transformational leaders understand there is a delicate balance between pushing the organization enough to effect needed change and alienating those who will help them execute their vision (Hendricks, 2014; Hogue, 2014).

Transformational leadership places an emphasis on the ability of a leader to anticipate change and then guide the institution successfully through the transition process. Kotter (2012) identifies that there is a distinction between managing change and leading change, and includes a strong sense of urgency, responsible risk-taking, and the empowerment of people to make things happen. However, change for the sake of change can be counterproductive, and followers can usually tell the difference. As noted by Shugart of the Aspen Institution and Achieving the Dream (2013), "the challenge is being the change, not just declaring it" (p. 5); people will follow leaders who live the change and who are not leading the change as part of a personal agenda.

In addition to transformational leadership, effective and efficient alloca-tion of available resources cannot occur without inventive and expansive stra-tegic thinking in today's competitive higher education environment (Bess & Dee, 2012; Rowley & Sherman, 2001). External stakeholders expect account-ability and that colleges utilize strategies in operations that connect them to their stakeholders (Bess & Dee, 2012; Fawson, 2012). Strategic thinking helps organizational leaders build capacity and infrastructure as well as respond in an environment that demands accountability. Leaders must have the skills and abilities to "convene allies and build coalitions" in support of leading institutions to transform (Pulley, 2014, para. 4).

As the review of the literature on change and leadership within higher education organizations indicates, these institutions are complex and are pressured by external factors to change. These external factors focus on ac-countability and productivity of higher education, which leads to pressures to assess current degree programs to ensure that they are producing gradu-ates who have the skills and competencies needed in the workforce. The guiding principles and design-concepts of CPED help institutions address some of these external factors with its focus on the practice-oriented doc-torate. To implement the principles and design-concepts of CPED within higher education institutions, it will take leadership that is well versed in change strategies and who possess the skills and competencies needed to encourage others to embrace change and who can motivate others to take part in the change process.

EXPLORATION OF LEADERSHIP, SUPPORT, AND CHANGE

The CPED consortium was developed to provide an avenue for educators and others to share change efforts and practices in transforming the education doctorate to a degree that produces graduates who can be stewards in the education profession. The Phase I consortium membership is composed of 21 higher education institutions: 11 are designated as very high research ac-tivity, 5 as high research activity, and the remainder as some research activity. Of the 21 institutions, 3 are nonprofit private and 18 are public institutions.

There are similarities among the 21 Phase I institutions as to why they became involved with CPED. All of the institutions were part of Colleges of Education in flux and who had already determined (for those that had existing EdDs) that changes were needed. Those that did not offer an EdD at the time were receiving pressure at the state and local levels to offer a practice-based doctorate to serve local, regional, and state school leader-ship needs. The discussions occurring about the education doctorate at the study institutions focused around four main points: relevancy, rigor, quality, and currency. The underlying reasons that these discussions of the need to redesign the EdD were occurring were tied back to underlying issues with College of Education academic programs:

- They had a number of students who were ABD and who were not completing;
- Indistinguishable differences existed between the EdD and PhD within a program and/or college;
- Pressures from state leaders who saw other states developing EdD practitioner-based programs were occurring; and
- The demands from the community/region/state for qualified practice-oriented educational leaders were increasing.

In addition to these areas, other discussions of transformation needs focused around reputations of research intensive institutions, low enrollments in existing EdDs programs, concerns with high faculty turnover in departments, inefficiencies of use of institutional resources or lack of resources (e.g., decreasing budgets; overlap in degrees), need to grow enrollments due to decreased state funding; serving the varying internal and external stakeholders' needs, and questions surrounding the relevancy of existing degree offerings to education practice challenges.

METHODOLOGY

In order to understand how Phase I member institutions were progressing in implementing the CPED guiding principles and design-concepts into their EdDs, a mixed-methods research study was conducted of the 21 institutions. A subset of this data was used to explore change leadership and what support structures were identified as necessary to implement effective CPED-influenced education doctorate programs, based on the lived experiences of CPED members who have implemented or are currently in the process of implementing their programs. Of interest was how college and faculty leaders at these institutions have effectively developed structures to support the implementation of their CPED-influenced EdD programs. In addition, of interest was how these leaders have addressed philosophical differences, workload calculations, and change resisters. The following research questions guided this study:

1. Who are the change leaders who set the vision and lead the redesign and implementation of the CPED-influenced EdD?
2. What are the processes of change that institutions encounter as they redesign and implement the CPED guiding principles and design concepts into their programs?

3. What support is needed to ensure successes and address challenges during the redesign and implementation of CPED-influenced EdD programs?

Data Sources

The sources for data for this study were 21 Phase I CPED member institutions that joined the CPED consortium in 2007. Phase I institutions were targeted for this study as they have the most experience in working with the CPED guiding principles and design concepts and are the most informed about implementing them. Of the 21 institutions, two had implemented or were in the process of implementing the CPED principles and design concepts through collegewide efforts, while the remaining institutions focused the transformation on specific programs. Subgroups participating as data sources for this study were program faculty of CPED-influenced programs ($N = 122$) and university/college administrators ($N = 31$).

There were two phases of data collection and analysis that were completed to answer the research questions for this study. The first phase entailed an open-ended survey that was sent to each CPED Phase I member institution. A portion of this survey was dedicated to obtaining information specifically about the support structures in place to support the CPED principles and design-concepts as they are being used to frame EdD programs. Only 6 of the 21 Phase I CPED institutions responded, for a 28.6% response rate.

The second phase of this study involved the analysis of qualitative data from a previous 2012 study of CPED Phase I institutions. Transcripts from 153 interviews were analyzed using the constant comparative method of coding, as well as open and axial coding. The constant comparative method was used to determine similarities and differences relative to the various participants (Merriam, 2009), and open coding of the data was used to develop major categories (Creswell, 2014; Merriam, 2009). Interview transcripts were closely examined to gain an understanding of the participants' perceptions. A list of emerging codes was developed as the data was reviewed numerous times, and the codes were grouped into broad categories that conceptually correlated to one of the three research questions (Merriam, 2009; Saldaña, 2013). Data collected from interview transcripts, the survey, and documents were used to establish valid, comprehensive themes (Creswell, 2014). After the first cycle of open coding was completed, axial coding was used to interpret and make meaning from open codes. During this cycle of data analysis, open codes were sorted, relabeled, reassembled, and condensed into a smaller number of broad conceptual categories based on similarities and differences (Saldaña, 2013). Data was grouped and regrouped until themes emerged that represented recurring patterns across the data (Merriam, 2009).

Though this study is bounded by the experiences of the 21 Phase I members of the CPED consortium, it is important to identify the limitations to this study. The survey distributed to CPED Phase I institutions yielded minimal responses (6 out of 21 possible participants). Because of the limited survey data available, findings of this study were primarily derived from the data collected in the 2012 CPED study and the perception and experiences of the participants. The 2012 survey was designed to measure changes in professional doctorate programs based on the CPED principles and not to specifically capture the participants' perceptions and experiences with leadership, institutional change, and institutional support.

FINDINGS AND DISCUSSION

Leadership for Change

The first research question explored who were the change leaders who set the vision and led the redesign and implementation of the CPED-influenced EdD at the member institutions. There were four main themes that emerged through the analysis of the data used to address this research question: (a) Deans of Colleges of Education; (b) CPED principal investigators; (c) other changes agents; and (d) administrative and leadership turnover.

In 2005, a presentation about the CPED initiative was presented at the Council of Academic Deans from Research Education Institutions (CADREI) meeting by Lee Shulman. It was at this meeting that many College of Education deans were able to obtain information about the CPED initiative, which stirred in some a possible avenue to obtain answers to their concerns of what to do with the EdD at their colleges. Prior to attendance at the CADREI meeting, some of the deans at the study institutions were already engaged in dialog about the need to distinguish between their PhDs and EdDs, or that their existing EdD lacked rigor and relevancy. The timing of the CPED presentation coincided with these discussions and was the impetus for many of these institutions to become members of the CPED Consortium. An additional point and need, and one that had state-level impact, was that state leaders were also charging their very high and high research activity universities to offer an EdD to meet the needs of constituents by providing a practice-based degree to ensure educational entities had qualified leaders.

CPED was introduced to the study institutions in a variety of ways but was mainly instigated through the College Dean. CPED had a proposal process for membership, and institutions had to submit a proposal to become a part of the Consortium. For some institutions, this proposal was submitted without faculty awareness. For others, department chairs or faculty of specific programs developed the proposal.

The decision to join the CPED Consortium was mainly driven by deans of Colleges of Educations. Many of the study institutions' deans strategically shared the information about CPED with particular administrators within the college for them to disseminate, or they chose to share the information personally with coalitions of individuals or groups of faculty who were part of the information dissemination processes. Their use of strategic thinking and processes to introduce the CPED initiative and to begin the process of disseminating the information throughout the college helped to build coalitions and develop allies around the initiative (Pulley, 2014). The role of the deans in leading the change and communications about the CPED initiatives was instrumental to the success at many of the study institutions. Rowley and Sherman (2001) and Kotter's (2012) assertions that effective change initiatives are tied to having institutional leaders who can communicate the importance of needed changes, explain how the change can occur, and visualize the possible outcomes of the change are supported by the findings of this study. In addition to the dean, the president or other executive level administrators were the determiners of their institution's involvement with CPED at some institutions. Only at a few institutions were the faculty the driving force behind participation in CPED.

The strength of CPED lies in its foundation and connection to the Carnegie Foundation. Institutional leaders and faculty perceive that this connection provides credibility to the initiative and since its dialog is occurring at the national level, these institutions wanted to be a part of the discussion. In addition, faculty valued being affiliated with a national group and for some institutions, having opportunities to interact with faculty from very high and high research activity universities. Being a part of the CPED initiative was seen as an avenue to be able to influence the discussions surrounding the redesign of the education doctorate in the following ways:

- Address higher faculty turnover in departments/programs
- Address inefficiencies
- Improve program quality and rigor
- Improve completion rates
- Avenue to stimulate ideas, share experiences and failures, and to help with program development
- Promote quicker change
- Provide strategies to distinguish the EdD from the PhD
- Provide a strong framework in which to transform the EdD

Though the deans of Colleges of Education were the main conveyors of the message about CPED at many of the study institutions, others took on the role as change agents, with their dean's support. Each consortium member institution was charged with identifying a Principal Investigator (PI) to lead their CPED-influenced program through transformation based on the CPED principles and design-concepts. Many of these PI's and other institutional members also played a role in the development of the CPED principles and design concepts as the founding members of the CPED Consortium. For the most part, the primary change agent identified was the project PI. These individuals had tremendous impact at many of the institutions and were seen as the main change agents in moving programs forward in the change process.

The study institutions that appeared to progress the most in their change efforts were those who identified a small number of dedicated change agents who were instrumental in leading and monitoring the progression of the transformation of the EdD, but who also had the support of the dean. Kecskemethy (2012) notes that leadership can influence a shift in institutional culture as well as argues that leadership has to be involved in opening up the organization to change, help build consensus and support goals, as well as properly allocate and manage resources. The need for a cultural shift to help support the change process was needed (Bess & Dee, 2012; Bolman & Deal, 2008; Boyce, 2003). In addition, participants noted how imperative the support of the dean was to the change efforts. The placement of an administrator as an oversight agent (e.g., associate dean and/or department chairs) as the "eyes of the dean" also appeared to be a strategy used, but there was no sense that this caused resentment among some of the faculty and was seen as administrative support. A small number of institutions noted that some had faculty who were dedicated to the project, either because they volunteered to be a part, it fit their philosophy of what they perceived the doctorate of education should be, or they simply held the passion to make the education doctorate a better product. As noted by Rowley and Sherman (2001) and what appears to have been instrumental in the change processes at these institutions is the "human core that actually gets the work done" (p. 218). They have been able to alleviate concerns and anxieties. These individuals were the primary change agents in a small number of the study institutions and appear to have been able to create a strong sense of purpose around the CPED focus as they do not appear to be constrained by the past (Boggs, 2012), which makes them effective as change leaders.

Several of the institutions experienced administrative and faculty leadership turnover, which at times affected their ability to progress in their change efforts. There was evidence at several of the institutions that a departing dean had been supportive of CPED involvement and principles, and had promised or allocated resources, and the incoming dean did not support this. As noted previously, the PI was an important position for the CPED change efforts. Many of the study institutions experienced turnover in this position; some multiple times. For those that have been able to have stability in their top leadership and PI positions, progress has been forward moving. For those that have had consistent change in leadership, the progress has been stalled. This supports the need to have stable and consistent leadership in the change agent role for the infusion of the CPED principles and design concepts into the change efforts. Most of the study institutions utilized college committees for specific areas such as curriculum redesign and implementation, which appear to have been instrumental in the change process. This is also where most faculty involvement was noted.

Supporting Change Processes

The second research question addressed what processes of change were encountered as institutions redesigned and implemented their CPED-influenced programs. There were three main themes that emerged through the analysis of the data for this research question: (a) institution size plays a role, (b) implementation and redesign occurred at the same time, and (c) need for rigorous practice-based doctorate drove the change. The study institutions experienced varying levels of successes and challenges related to the change process within their college and programs. Some institutions were able to redesign their existing EdD quickly due to the small size of the institution (identified as "nimble to change") and the willingness of those involved to participate in the change efforts in addition to having strong leadership in the PI position.

The type of institution played an important role in the ability for institutions to make progress through the change efforts. Many of the large, public research-intensive institutions appeared to face different concerns than those that are private or regional. Participants from these institutions had concerns of how being a part of the EdD is viewed in the tenure and promotion process, with many institutions focused on the prestige of the PhD and its role in the university's reputation. These institutions appeared to have more challenges with faculty and their participation and support in the EdD change efforts. It did not appear that these concerns had been resolved at any of the study institutions that participated in this study.

A number of the participants noted that the redesign of the EdD was occurring at the same time as it was being implemented. In this process, key faculty listened to student input and the program made adjustments. All study institutions reflected on the need to continually revisit and revise their programs—with some institutions identifying the program as a "living thing" that needed constant revision and nurturing. Though it appears that most of the institutional members involved in the change process wanted the CPED-influenced EdD to succeed, low enrollments, a lack of communication, and clarity of the change process appeared to have hampered progress in a time of budgetary and other challenges at some institutions. This was evidenced through constant revisions to requirements—the change process was in constant flux.

The main impetus for change came from those within the study institutions understanding that there was a need to have a practice-based doctorate that was relevant and rigorous as well as was distinguishable from the PhD. Those who were successful were those who had stable leadership, good communication mechanisms (Kotter, 2012), and program members who desired and supported the change efforts (Boggs, 2012). Though there were pockets of resistance from faculty (mainly at-large, public research-intensive institutions) the resistance was limited and was overcome by most. Most resistors who did not get on board with the change process were either allowed to engage in other programs such as at the master's level or with the PhD, or they left the institution. Faculty who remained engaged and involved in the change processes appeared to be generally supportive of the redesign initiatives.

Other strategies noted that supported the change efforts included providing training to develop faculty knowledge and skills, good communication, adding individuals with new perspectives, having the right people to lead and participate in the efforts, open and transparent dialog, and at times, help from other CPED consortium members and CPED representatives to share best practices and experiences in how to overcome challenges in the change process.

Support During Redesign and Implementation

The third research question addressed what support is needed to ensure successes and address challenges during the redesign and implementation of CPED-influenced EdD programs. The analysis of the data related to this research question produced three themes: (a) successes are easier for smaller institutions, (b) collaborations and partnerships are instrumental to change, and (c) barriers to change exist.

The participants in this study noted that they had experienced some successes in their change process as they worked as a college to transform their EdD. The change process was quick and barriers were easier to overcome for those institutions that were smaller in size, who had clear directives, and who had an established vision of the outcomes they wanted for the redesigned EdD. The outcomes of the redesign process based on the CPED guiding principles and design-concepts led to increased awareness and respect for practitioners. Key strategies used to overcome resistance in the change process included transparency through documentation, involvement through advisory councils, and leadership support. In addition, when programs had monthly meetings with clear agendas that addressed specific components of program change and that provided updates on the progress made, change efforts were more successful.

Transformational leadership, collaboration, and relationships have been instrumental to success in the change process, with institutions seeing increased interest in the redesigned EdD, and collaborations formed between the institution and school districts and other entities, and between faculty and students. These findings are supported by Hendricks (2014) and Hogue (2014), who state that transformational leaders have the skills to disrupt a sense of norm and to encourage others to step outside of their comfort zones so that they can consider, support, and be a part of needed change and transformation initiatives. Many of the study institutions show indications of transformational leadership throughout various levels of their redesign and implementation of their CPED-influenced programs, which has helped them to see some success. In addition, a majority of the study institutions have made progress in distinguishing their EdD from their PhD programs, creating distinct differences between doctoral preparation for aspiring academicians and doctoral preparation for scholar practitioners. There is evidence in some redesigned programs that supports that students' success and overall satisfaction have improved due to redesign efforts. As noted by some of the faculty participants, students had indicated to them that they perceived that their needs were being met and that, upon completion of the program, they would be well-prepared to have an impact on education needs.

Anytime a culture has to be changed and traditions are challenged, barriers occur in the change process. The challenges in the change process experienced by the study institutions spread across a wide variety of areas. Leadership was an identified challenge at all of the study institutions. Many experienced administrative turnover, which created a lack of support and/or unclear and delayed communication about the change efforts. There were several institutions that identified that the change process was a top-down directive, which caused concern for some faculty. In addition, the vision for change was not always transparent or clear. The abilities of leadership to lead change versus manage it (Kotter, 2012) are instrumental to the success of CPED-influenced programs.

Many of the participants noted how slow the change process was. Higher education organizations are known to change incrementally, and the change processes described in this study support that this continues to be a challenge with the redesign of the education doctorate. Another challenge noted was specific to communications and noted mainly that there was simply a lack of them. Failure to have clear communication processes and communications at all levels seemed to have the most impact on the buy-in to the change efforts. These communication issues led to environments of distrust at some institutions, and for others this resulted in the change efforts stalling.

Existing organizational structures also appeared to be a barrier to the change efforts. Within some of the study institutions, programs operated independently, and the program faculty made all curriculum decisions, while in others the programs were part of larger departments, and decisions were made more centrally. In some instances, programs were disaggregated into concentrations from independent programs in order to better affect the changes necessary to incorporate the CPED working principles and concepts into the college's education doctorates. The participants, both administrators and faculty, expressed concerns of how the traditional reward structures of higher education are not conducive to recognizing and supporting the increased workload caused by the redesign of the EdD. In addition, existing university policies on tenure and promotion were also noted as a concern to many of the tenured or tenure-seeking faculty at very high and high activity research institutions as they were unsure of how their work with the EdD would be measured.

Resources appeared to be a challenge at all of the institutions. Many of the institutions are state-supported institutions, and decreased funding continues to be a national issue in higher education. In addition, some of the institutions had existing inefficiencies among faculty and low enrollment programs, which affected the funding they could allocate to change efforts. This is supported by the work of Bornstein (2007), who identified that global, social, economic, political, and technological changes are confronting higher education institutions, and leaders must have the abilities to be innovative and flexible in these complex environments. As academic institutions continue to experience decreases in funding, a shift in student demographics, the rising impact of globalization and technology, and a growing demand to meet ever-changing employment needs, resources will continue to be a concern (Basham, 2012; Boggs, 2012, McArdle, 2013).

A final and major challenge noted throughout the study were faculty. Some faculty perceived that change efforts were mandatory and being directed from the top-down and were exclusionary. Some were unconvinced that change was needed and so they did not actively take part in the change processes or worked to stall change efforts. In addition, as noted previously, the increased workload for faculty involved in the EdD was a concern to many as well as how work with the EdD would be viewed through traditional tenure and promotion policies.

CONCLUSION

The findings of this study were based on data collected from the 21 Phase I CPED member institutions and must be contextualized from the perspective that the data collection tools were designed to collect data to measure changes in professional doctorate programs based on the CPED principles. The purpose of this specific study on change leadership was to extrapolate how change processes had occurred at these institutions through the analysis of the survey and interview data captured through the larger data collection process.

The participants at the study institutions portrayed a picture of faculty and administration being excited about being affiliated with a national group such as CPED with its tie to the Carnegie Foundation and that they would have the opportunity to interact with faculty from large, public R1 universities; opportunities to form new partnerships; and have opportunities to contribute to CPED and the debate surrounding the EdD. The membership in CPED was used as the impetus for change. In addition, being part of CPED brought recognition to the study institutions on the national stage.

CPED was also seen as a place to obtain guidance for colleges and faculty in their redesign efforts, as it provides a strong set of working principles and design concepts, which added credibility to the change process and helped to get the programs engaged in the redesign process. Faculty saw CPED's objectives as a means to help them make the program relevant to practice. Faculty and administration perceived that membership in CPED provided them avenues to seek advice, help them connect with like-minded individuals, allow them to see what other programs looked like, and offer support through the change process. Despite challenges, the faculty participants at the study institutions recognized the positives of being involved with the redesign of the EdD; as a group they wanted to make their program better and CPED provided the guidance and support needed to do this. In some cases, the study institutions had already developed a plan to transform their EdDs prior to joining CPED but utilized the CPED guiding principles and design concepts as support and confirmation of the change efforts as well as to refine their existing programs.

The power of the CPED consortium is attending biyearly convenings where institutions share their experiences of the redesign process. The CPED working principles, design concepts, and convenings were used to develop strategies to overcome challenges. Participation in CPED has led many of the institutions to hold monthly meetings to discuss the changes they wish to make and those they wish to reject and has enabled them to arrive at a place where faculty are able to function as a department as opposed to being fragmented.

While this may have been accomplished without CPED, CPED has been reinforcing to the study institutions. CPED provides the institutions a language that portrays the EdD as something of value. The biggest influence of CPED in the redesign of the EdD at the study institutions appears to be its role as an impetus. CPED provided a timely opportunity to redefine the education doctorate so that it is distinguishable from the PhD and establish it as a degree with value.

REFERENCES

Argia, H., & Ismail, A. (2013). The influence of transformational leadership on the level of TQM implementation in the higher education sector. *Higher Education Studies, 3*(1), 136–146. doi:10.5539/hes.v3n1p136

Aspen Institute. (2013). *Crisis and opportunity: Aligning the community college presidency with student success.* Joint publication of the Aspen Institute and Achieving the Dream. Retrieved from http://www.aspeninstitute.org/sites/default/files/content/docs/pubs/CEP_Final_Report.pdf

Basham, L. M. (2012). Leadership in higher education. *Journal of Higher Education Theory and Practice, 12*(6), 54–58.

Bess, J. L., & Dee, J. R. (2012). *Understanding college and university organization: Theories for effective policy and practice. Volume II–Dynamics of the system.* Sterling, VA: Stylus.

Boggs, G. R. (2012). Next steps—Looking to the future. In P. L. Eddy (Ed.), *Leading for the future: Alignment of AACC competencies with practice* (pp. 97–107). San Francisco, CA: Jossey-Bass.

Bolman, L. G., & Deal, T. E. (2008). *Reframing organizations: Artistry, choice, and leadership.* San Francisco, CA: Jossey-Bass.

Bornstein, R. (2007, Spring). Why women make good college presidents. *Presidency, 10*(2), 20–23.

Boyce, M. E. (2003). Organizational learning is essential to achieving and sustaining change in higher education. *Innovative Higher Education, 28*(2), 119–136.

Bunn, C. E. (2011). *Navigating change and leading an institution of higher education: A case study of the missional leadership of a university president* (Doctoral dissertation). Retrieved from ProQuest Dissertations and Theses database. (UMI No. 3445930)

Creswell, J. W. (2014). *Research design: Qualitative, quantitative, and mixed methods approaches* (4th ed.). Thousand Oaks, CA: Sage.

Ellington, L. (2009). A leadership deficit: The discipline of development. *Research in Higher Education Journal, 31*, 1–13.

Fawson, K. (2012). The global economic crisis: Winners and losers in higher education. *Journal of Research in Innovative Teaching, 5*(1), 2–13.

Greenwald, R. A. (2012, August 8). New kinds of leadership. *Inside Higher Ed.* Retrieved from http://www.insidehighered.com/advice/2012/08/08/essay-leadership-higher-education#sthash.EcIAjVaE.ws8ZSzeT.dpbs

Hanna, D. E. (2003, July/August). Building a leadership vision: Eleven strategic challenges for higher education. *EDUCAUSE Review*, 25–34.

Hendricks, D. (2014, January 27). 6 ways to empower your employees with transformational leadership. *Forbes.* Retrieved from http://www.forbes.com/sites/drewhendricks/2014/01/27/6-ways-to-empower-your-employees-with-transformational-leadership

Hogue, B. (2014, January/February). Leadership lessons from close encounters. *EDUCAUSE Review, 1*(49), 24–30.

Kecskemethy, T. A. (2012). *Leadership for change in two schools of education* (Doctoral dissertation). Retrieved from ProQuest Dissertations and Theses database. (UMI No. 3537411)

Kotter, J. P. (2012). *Leading change.* Boston, MA: Harvard Business Review Press.

McArdle, M. K. (2013). The next generation of community college leaders. *Community College Journal of Research and Practice, 37*(11), 851–863.

Merriam, S. B. (2009). *Qualitative research: A guide to design and implementation* (3rd ed.). San Francisco, CA: Jossey-Bass.

Northouse, P. G. (2013). *Leadership: Theory and practice* (6th ed.). Thousand Oaks, CA: Sage.

Priest, D. M., St. John, E. P., & Boon, R. D. (2006). Introduction. In E. P. St. John & D. Priest (Eds.), *Privatization and public universities* (pp. 271–284). Bloomington: Indiana University Press.

Pulley, J. (2014, March 17). Colleges compete with other worthy causes for financial support. *Community College Daily.* Retrieved from http://ccdaily.com/Pages/Funding/Colleges-compete-with-other-worthy-causes-for-financial-support.aspx

Quinn, R. E. (2000). *Change the world: How ordinary people can achieve extraordinary results.* San Francisco, CA: Jossey-Bass.

Rich, D. (2006). Academic leadership and the restructuring of higher education. *New Directions for Higher Education,* (134), 37–48. doi:10.1002/he.215

Rowley, D. J., & Sherman, H. (2001). *From strategy to change: Implementing the plan in higher education.* San Francisco, CA: Jossey-Bass.

Saldaña, J. (2013). *The coding manual for qualitative researchers* (2nd ed.). London, England: Sage.

Shugart, S. (2013, January/March). The challenge to deep change: A brief cultural history of higher education. *Planning for Higher Education, 41*(2), 7–17.

CHAPTER 4

BUILDING AND SUSTAINING A LEARNING COHORT

Tricia Browne-Ferrigno[1] and Bryan D. Maughan

The Carnegie Project on the Education Doctorate (CPED) focuses on "developing *stewards of practice*" (Perry & Imig, 2008, p. 44, emphasis in original) through Doctor of Education (EdD) programs uniquely different from traditional Doctor of Philosophy (PhD) programs primarily designed for research preparation (Golde & Walker, 2006; Schulman, Golde, Bueschel, & Garabedian, 2006). To achieve differentiation from traditional PhD programs, CPED-member institutions typically define a sequence of curricula delivered through laboratories of practice. These redesigned EdD programs also feature profession-oriented knowledge bases called signature pedagogies, research methods appropriate for use by scholarly practitioners, and unique dissertation formats for reporting practice-oriented findings (Gutherie, 2009; Loss, 2009; Osterman, Furman, & Sernak, 2013; Perry, 2011; Zambo, Zambo, Buss, Perry, & Williams, 2013). Because most EdD programs utilizing CPED design features are intended for educational practitioners who are employed full-time, they are often delivered through executive, cohort-based models that are carefully planned, fast-paced, problem-oriented, and applied (Browne-Ferrigno & Muth, 2012; Suleiman & Whetton, 2014; Taylor & Storey, 2011). Doctoral students participating in

The EdD and the Scholarly Practitioner, pages 45–64
Copyright © 2016 by Information Age Publishing

45

cohort programs thus develop not only new professional knowledge and skills (Amrein-Beadsley et al., 2012) but also collegial relationships that are sustained after graduation (Burke, Preston, Quillen, Roe, & Strong, 2009; Decker, Dykes, Gilliam, & Marrs, 2009).

Using cohorts for program delivery was initially introduced into postsecondary education during the 1980s as a convenient method for scheduling instructor assignments and organizing learning activities (Reynolds & Hebert, 1995; Saltiel & Reynolds, 2001; Yerkes, Basom, Barnett, & Norris, 1995). The term *cohort* does not however have a universally accepted definition. For example, some programs use the word cohort to describe a group of students enrolled in a program during a specific semester or selected from a particular local education agency or other organizational partner with the university. Students may begin (but not complete) their programs together as an intact community of learners. While progressing through their program, they engage with different students in self-selected classes, which results in transient learning environments that can influence group cohesion (Browne-Ferrigno & Muth, 2003; Swayze & Jakeman, 2014).

Conversely, when students remain together throughout their program as a single, identifiable group with few, if any, changes in group composition, the group is called a *closed cohort* (Norris, Barnett, Basom, & Yerkes, 1996; Saltiel & Russo, 2001). Closed cohorts typically include 10 to 25 students "who begin and complete a program of studies together, engaging in a common set of courses, activities, and/or learning experiences" (Barnett & Muse, 1993, p. 401). Changes in closed-cohort membership occur only through attrition: Students may exit, but new students generally do not join in-progress closed-cohort programs. Students participating in a closed-cohort program thus become an intact group of learners who study and work together for a set period of time, usually from 1 to 4 years, while completing required coursework. When EdD students remain together throughout their program, they can collaborate across semesters to explore research needs, develop theoretical frameworks, and conduct companion dissertations (Browne-Ferrigno & Jensen, 2012; McNamara, Lara-Alecio, Irby, Hoyle, & Tong, 2007).

Although this chapter focuses on strategies for developing and sustaining closed-cohort programs, those not using that model should nonetheless find the content informative and applicable. The first major section of the chapter presents comprehensive reviews on literature about using closed cohorts in higher education and learning theories relevant for delivering cohort-based programs via distance-learning strategies. The next three sections describe tasks required for faculty who assume responsibilities as designated cohort leaders, strategies that support cohort success, and benefits and opportunities gained by serving as a cohort leader. The chapter closes with a reflection by doctoral students in one of the first CPED-affiliated programs about the stages of group development they experienced during their first year of studies in a closed cohort.

LEARNING IN CLOSED COHORTS

Using the closed-cohort model of program delivery can enhance students' professional learning and skill development (Barnett, Basom, Yerkes, & Norris, 2000; Hebert & Reynolds, 1998; Witte & James, 1998) in three key ways. First, the structure provides continuity and opportunities for participants to learn and practice skills in group-developed goal-setting, community building, conflict resolution, and culture management (Bentley, Zhao, Reames, & Reed, 2004; Browne-Ferrigno & Muth, 2003, 2008; Muth, 2000b, 2002). Second, the closed-cohort structure supports utilization of long-term developmental activities and point-counterpoint discussions that are difficult to integrate effectively across individual courses (Cordiero, Boutiler, Panicek, & Salamone-Consoli, 1993; Guzmán & Muth, 1999). Third, through careful attention to group development, a cohort can transform into a professional community that enhances learning, develops group facilitation and leadership skills, and increases student retention and program completion (Butterwick, Cockell, McArthur-Blair, MacIver, & Rodriques, 2012; Floresh-Scott & Nerad, 2012; Nimer, 2009; Scribner & Donaldson, 2001; Suleiman & Whetton, 2014).

Benefits of Learning Cohorts

A successful closed-cohort program creates a learning environment where all participants experience a sense of belonging (i.e., feel valued and accepted), understand their collective purpose (i.e., share common commitment and goals), and actively and purposefully engage in group learning activities (i.e., recognize value of interdependence and interaction) (Barnett et al., 2000; Bentley et al., 2004; Butterwick et al., 2012; Decker et al., 2009). Further, a successful closed-cohort program can generate student persistence in degree completion (Dorn, Papalewis, & Brown, 1995; Lei, Gorelick Short, Smallwood, & Wright-Porter, 2011; Norton, 1995) and enhanced learning achievements (Browne-Ferrigno & Muth, 2012; Hebert & Reynolds, 1998) compared to programs delivered as a series of traditional, separate courses that students take whenever desired or available (Reynolds & Hebert, 1995). Research on student learning within cohorts also suggests positive outcomes on scholarship and reflective abilities (Barnett & Muth, 2008; Burnett, 1999; Mullen & Tuten, 2010; Witte & James, 1998), interpersonal relationships (Greenlee & Karanxha, 2010; Horn, 2001), professional networks (Bentley et al., 2004; Muth & Barnett, 2001), and transformative learning (Cranton, 2002).

Potential Impediments to Cohort Learning

Closed cohorts generally move through predictable stages of group development that generate unique group personalities (Maher, 2005; Tuckman, 1965) because cohort participants' beliefs, expectations, and experiences influence group dynamics over time (Donaldson & Scribner, 2003; Wesson, Holman, Holman, & Cox, 1996). Potential impediments to learning can thus emerge due to assumed or assigned roles among cohort members, communication or problem-solving styles, and use of ineffective instructional modalities (Muth et al., 2001; Scribner & Donaldson, 2001).

Group dynamics resulting in collusion and cliquishness, exclusionary group behavior, or breakdowns in communication can impede learning (Burke et al., 2009; McPhail, Robinson, & Scott, 2008). Counteracting such impediments to learning requires immediate faculty attention and intervention (Teitel, 1997; Tipping, Freeman, & Rachlis, 1995), typically accomplished through regular group reflections about cohort progress, candid discussions about what is happening or needs changing, and immediate implementation of needed changes. Despite efforts by faculty to mediate harmful group-dynamics effects, cohort members who prefer traditional educational settings or only working independently may withdraw from closed-cohort programs (Browne-Ferrigno & Jensen, 2012; Browne-Ferrigno & Muth, 2012).

Because using the cohort model "does not ensure a true cohort will develop" (Basom, Yerkes, Norris, & Barnett, 1995, p. 19), careful attention must be given to group processing at the beginning of and throughout a cohort program. Faculty must also remain attuned to group-dynamic issues within cohorts, addressing promptly interpersonal matters than can erode community cohesion and collaborative learning (Barkely, Cross, & Major, 2005; Browne-Ferrigno & Muth, 2004; Teitel, 1997).

Generative Learning Community

Because a distinctive difference between course-based programs and closed-cohort programs is peer collaboration (Barnett & Caffarella, 1992; Basom & Yerkes, 2001; Norris & Barnett, 1994), faculty teaching courses in a well-delivered cohort program often spend considerable time on initial and ongoing group-development and peer-interaction activities (Barkley, Cross, & Major, 2005; Bentley et al., 2004). Attending to group dynamics supports a cohort's progress through the predictable yet essential stages of group development—forming, storming, norming, performing, adjourning (Tuckman & Jensen, 1977). Group-building activities may need to be repeated each time a cohort experiences a change in instructors because the introduction of new faculty creates a different group dynamic, which could potentially threaten the cohort's learning culture.

With sufficient time and careful attention to group-development, a closed cohort can transform into a community of practice (CoP), which is defined by three fundamental elements: "a *domain* of knowledge, which defines a set of issues; a *community* of people who care about this domain; and the shared *practice* that they are developing to be effective in their domain" (Wenger, McDermott, & Snyder, 2002, p. 27, emphasis in original). CoPs evolve over time as participants develop expertise through shared learning and knowledge refinement "out of the raw material of [members'] experiences" (Drath & Paulus, 1994, p. 3). Engaging actively in a CoP can expand participants' opportunities for professional growth and career advancement through sharing of expert knowledge and development of collegial relationships. Closed cohorts functioning as a CoP in which both faculty and students actively participate set the stage for situated-learning opportunities in which novices work with experts to apply theories to practice, develop needed skills, and reflect about experiences and outcomes (Lave & Wenger, 1991; Wenger, 1998).

Technology Use in Cohort Programs

Growing in tandem with innovative EdD programs are advancements in technologies that assist doctoral faculty and students in achieving professional and research objectives through distance education (Kumar, Dawson, Black Cavanaugh, & Sessums, 2011; Palloff & Pratt, 2007; Parker, Lenhart, & Moore, 2011). Faculty using information technology to deliver doctoral programs should be aware of two network-centric learning theories (Anderson, 2010).

The first is heutagogy, a theory of self-determined learning developed by Hase and Kenyon (2003), which aligns well with the learning that occurs through CoPs. To create a heutagogy-based course, an instructor begins by preparing a draft syllabus that includes expected learning outcomes. During the first class meeting, the instructor seeks input from students about course features (e.g., readings, assignments, capstone project) and pace (e.g., assignment due dates). Leaners are typically provided assignment options (e.g., completed independently or collaboratively, recommended by instructor or designed by learners, achievement demonstrated via traditional academic paper or learner-determined creative format). Adult learners in a heutagogy-informed course are thus free to exercise self-agency and self-efficacy over their learning, which places the onus of knowledge and skill attainment on them. The instructor thus serves as facilitator, guide, mentor, and sometimes provocateur rather than an expert who lectures (Blaschke, 2012). Professionals working in the field may also engage with adult learners as they complete their self-determined learning experiences. Although heutagogy is becoming the learning theory of choice for instructors who use distance-education methods (Wheeler, 2011), it also is growing among instructors who design courses for face-to-face delivery. Although the theory provides a learning support structure where an instructor may engage more freely with adult learners, an instructor must remain ready to take supportive action as a protector, mediator, or advocate to assure optimal learning outcomes.

Connectivism is the most recently developed learning theory described by Anderson (2010) as being network-centric. First introduced by Siemens (2005), connectivism describes how learners discover and build knowledge by accessing information via technology and then processing and refining it before applying their new learning in different contexts. By repeating the cycle multiple times, learners determine what information is important and what is not. Connectivism becomes a knowledge-management activity as learners make group decisions about the value and veracity of the information.

Information technology provides diverse formats through which to deliver closed-cohort EdD programs (Kumar et al., 2011). Faculty and students involved in such programs need to remain cognizant that participating in CoPs is more than information gathering, assimilation of data, knowledge generation, and distribution of new knowledge—it involves people learning in community within unique situations (Lave & Wenger, 1991; Wenger, 1998). Using technology tools in cohort programs can however diminish individual and group learning if they are not used in meaningful ways (Chayko, 2008; Sproull & Kiesler, 1991; Wenger, White, & Smith, 2009). Thus, it is essential for doctoral faculty and cohort members to understand the mechanics of and purposes for various online networking tools and emergent innovative technologies as well as their proper uses. It is likewise critical for doctoral faculty to understand that establishing effective and sustainable online learning environments is complex, time-consuming, and challenging. Cohort leaders and faculty should explore what is available and honestly assess their needs to determine which technology tools meet program goals.

NEED FOR COHORT LEADER

Transforming a group of doctoral faculty and students into a CoP does not simply happen: The process must be carefully constructed, consciously nurtured over time, and carefully maintained through the collective efforts of all involved. Because creation of a well-functioning learning community is critical to a cohort's success (Browne-Ferrigno & Muth, 2012; Yerkes et al., 1995), at least one faculty member must be designated as a cohort leader. Responsibilities assumed by a cohort leader may include (a) working closely with program faculty to assure program is delivered as planned, (b) ensuring that students and instructors assume appropriate responsibilities for shared learning and goal achievement, and (c) monitoring student progress toward timely program completion (Barnett & Muth, 2008; Muth, 2002a; Muth et al., 2001; Saltiel & Russo, 2001). Cohort leader responsibilities may also include investigating collaborative learning techniques and digital technologies and then facilitating discussions about their appropriate uses for ensuring cohort collaboration and engagement (Barkley et al., 2005; Cyrs, 1997; Palloff & Pratt, 2005, 2007; Tisdell et al., 2004; Tu & McIsaac, 2002). Because faculty leadership is instrumental to the success of a closed cohort program, particularly if a goal is to create and sustain a CoP among program participants, the cohort leader's role is essential (Browne-Ferrigno & Muth, 2004).

Professors who assume responsibility for coordination of a closed-cohort program must be comfortable with high levels of ambiguity. They must understand from the outset that program plans serve as guidelines and that change is an omnipresent partner. Serving as a cohort leader also requires diverse organization and leadership skills (e.g., strategic thinking, visioning, patience, organization, diplomacy, advocacy), but most especially adaptability because program modifications will probably be required. The sections below describe various responsibilities assumed by a cohort leader as reported informally by professors who served as both cohort instructors and cohort leaders in programs that were successful.

Working With Faculty Colleagues

A major responsibility of a cohort leader is coordination of faculty activities. If using the closed-cohort model is new to a university, the dean needs to be informed of required faculty commitments. The department chair needs to be actively engaged in discussions during the program design and development phase and kept apprised of program progress throughout implementation. A cohort leader may be assigned the task of identifying and recruiting prospective faculty. Before committing to serve as cohort instructors, professors need to understand that they will be working as members of an instructional team that shares a common vision about desired outcomes and that student learning in a closed-cohort program is viewed across multiple semesters rather than during a single course.

During the planning and development phase, the instructional team must engage in candid conversations about relinquishing ingrained notions of individualistic academic freedom, typical for professors when delivering traditional courses. Thus, developing group norms to support their working together effectively is strongly advised. Involved faculty must commit to participating in all cohort-faculty meetings where they discuss openly what is working and what is not working and collaboratively make needed curricular or assessment changes. New faculty joining an in-progress closed cohort need a formal orientation that not only includes review of program goals, curriculum, and learning assessment but also review of the instructional team norms and cohort norms.

Prior to the launch of a new cohort program, the instructional team typically develops a broad program syllabus, which articulates the overarching program goals and objectives (i.e., what students are expected to know and be able to do at program end). Course syllabi thus become a sequence of developmentally appropriate units of study with expected learning outcomes, activities, and assignments that support achievement of the program goals and objectives. A cohort leader typically facilitates these activities and assures decisions are written in the program syllabus, distributed to all involved, and saved for future reference.

To achieve program goals, cohort instructors must conduct ongoing assessments of cohort progress and modify instruction or assignments, if necessary, to address the learning needs of cohort members. When programmatic changes are made, everyone must be informed in writing. Thus, maintaining regular and timely communication with the cohort instructional team and cohort members is another task assumed by a cohort leader.

Managing Virtual Learning Environments

Cohort-based executive models of program delivery that integrate traditional face-to-face class sessions and online learning activities are called hybrid or distance-learning programs. Successful utilization of diverse technology platforms such as learning management systems for course development and student engagement (e.g., Blackboard, Canvas, Moogle) and virtual meetings (e.g., Adobe Connect Pro, Google Hangout) requires faculty expertise. Depending on available support services for distance learning at a university, a cohort leader may assume responsibility for assuring faculty and students are prepared to use effectively the adopted or recommended technology tools.

Working With Institutional Partners

When a cohort program is delivered through a formal partnership (e.g., two postsecondary institutions, a university department and local education agency), a concisely written partnership agreement is required. Careful attention to distribution of responsibilities among institutional stakeholders and occasional appraisal to monitor completion of responsibilities help ensure that cohort program goals, objectives, and tasks are accomplished on a timely basis. Although these responsibilities are typically assigned to the cohort leader, some tasks can be distributed among university faculty, graduate assistants, and partner personnel. If tasks are assumed by others, a cohort leader must stay apprised of task accomplishment and maintain accurate records because accountability for a partnership-based cohort's success typically rests squarely upon the cohort leader.

Managing External Funding and Program Evaluation

When a cohort program is underwritten by external funds, a cohort leader may be designated as the individual responsible for budget accounting and performance reporting to the funding agency. Because both formative and summative evaluations (i.e., annual progress reports, final report) are generally required for funding, the cohort leader may assume responsibilities as the project's principal investigator, which requires adherence to the university's requirements for approved human subjects research.

When cohort programs are delivered through partnerships with other institutions or agencies, the cohort leader typically serves as the key liaison or frontline leader if the university is the host institution. Without careful management or oversight, a program's reputation can be damaged if learning and instructional experiences are viewed as haphazard or if program goals are not achieved. An unsuccessful cohort program can also jeopardize future partnerships or external funding.

STRATEGIES TO SUPPORT COHORT SUCCESS

Using the closed-cohort model for program delivery requires a cohort leader to attend to three critically important objectives:

1. Curriculum integration: the continuous focus on instructional components to ensure that they are developed and combined into an integrated whole;

2. Program coherence: the ongoing assessment of cohort progress to ensure that program parts are logically interconnected and delivered congruently and harmoniously; and

3. Shared responsibility: the collaboration of all cohort participants to ensure that learning goals and program objectives are achieved. (Browne-Ferrigno & Muth, 2004, p. 86)

The literature review below supports these three major responsibilities described by experienced cohort leaders presented in the previous sections and provides additional recommendations for designing and implementing a successful cohort program.

Curriculum Integration: Seamless Interconnections

The cohort leader guides the group—instructors and students alike—as they incorporate various instructional strategies, including integrated course content, team teaching, problem-based learning, reflective strategies, and case studies (Martin, Ford, Murphy, Rehm, & Muth, 1997; Yerkes et al., 1995). Use of online learning technology adds nuances to instructional strategies with which cohort leaders must become familiar, and program faculty and doctoral students may need training on how to use selected technology effectively. Another important consideration when designing an effective cohort program is the selection of "present experiences that live fruitfully and creatively in subsequent experiences" (Dewey, 1938/1997, p. 28). The program syllabus (i.e., written scope and sequence of curricula) developed collaboratively by the instructional team needs to be reviewed regularly to assure that learning activities align with program goals and that expected learning outcomes are being or can be achieved. Facilitation of these responsibilities are typically assumed by a cohort leaders.

By integrating group-conducted research projects into the curriculum, doctoral students learn the power of collaborative inquiry, importance of careful use of data, and value of group reflection and collective mentoring (Barnett & Muth, 2008; Churchill, 1996; Geltner, 1994; Mullen & Tuten, 2010). By developing small-group and whole-class activities, cohort faculty can help students learn the challenges of group dynamics and practice leadership skills (Browne-Ferrigno & Muth, 2012; Muth et al., 2001; Suleiman & Whetton, 2014). Longitudinal assignments (e.g., small-group projects, presentations, inquiry projects) require students to share resources and responsibilities, gain peer support and feedback, work through conflict, and seek agreement through consensus (Burke et al., 2009; Butterwick et al., 2012: Decker et al., 2009; Ford & Vaughn, 2011; Lei et al., 2011, Nimer, 2009). Authentic assessments that include peer and expert critique help attune learning to professional practice (Bransford, Brown, & Cocking, 2000; Bransford & Schwartz, 1999) and thus require cohort leaders and faculty to match assessments to practice expectations and, if relevant, relate them to state and national standards.

Program Coherence: Learning Objectives

Using the closed-cohort model effectively requires a cohort leader to engage faculty in identifying and implementing critical elements that generate optimum learning experiences (Barnett et al., 2000; Muth, 2002b; Saltiel & Russo, 2001). Cohort instructors often need to reshape their perceptions about content coverage within individual courses to focus on learning gained through a coordinated scope and sequence across the entire program. Collaborative program development requires faculty to explain why their content and assignments need to be included in the curriculum and substantiate how their contributions support program goals (Cordiero et al., 1993; Muth, 2000a, 2000b). The determination of desired cohort outcomes requires extensive deliberation during program development to ensure cohort activities are aligned with what is to be learned, how it is to be learned, what processes are to be used, and what faculty and students should do (Choy, Delahaye, & Saggers, 2015; Holloway & Alexandre, 2012). A cohort leader needs both formative and summative data to ensure that program goals are achieved, which requires engagement by cohort instructors in the design and utilization of group-determined formative learning assessments and ongoing progress checks.

Shared Responsibility: New Roles for Cohort Success

An effective cohort leader also cultivates shared responsibility for learning that typically requires dissolution of traditional instructor and student roles (Cordiero et al., 1993; Muth et al., 2001) and development of group-learning roles as members of a CoP that includes experts and novices. Over time, cohort members assume greater responsibility for their learning, both as individuals and as group members, and regularly make known their requests for changes in instructional delivery or learning assessments (Barnett et al., 2000; Blaschke, 2012). Cohort instructors thus serve as facilitators, mentors, and occasionally mediators during cohort meetings that more closely resemble professional-development seminars and workshops than traditional higher-education lecture classes (Browne-Ferrigno & Muth, 2012).

Group learning does not emerge simply by grouping students together (Basom et al., 1995; Browne-Ferrigno & Muth, 2008; Hannafin & Land, 1997). A cohort leader may need to guide and support program instructors in creation and maintenance of inviting, risk-safe learning conditions and in understanding the progressive stages of cohort transformation (Geltner, 1994; Maher, 2001). During the planning phase of a new cohort program, the cohort leader and faculty need to develop strategies and feedback mechanisms to assess the status of collaborative learning at various stages throughout program delivery.

SERVING AS COHORT LEADER: BENEFITS AND OPPORTUNITIES

Serving as a cohort leader may seem overwhelming, even for experienced cohort instructors, because the most difficult task is time management. A professor who assumes the role of cohort leader is seldom relieved from other teaching, research and publishing, or service obligations. The challenge thus becomes finding a workable balance across these professional responsibilities, ideally through creating opportunities to overlap professional tasks required of a cohort leader.

Several benefits from serving as a cohort leader can emerge and provide professional growth and new insights for a professor contemplating the role. One is the opportunity to work closely with colleagues, at one's university and perhaps at others, in examining and sharing experiences about using closed cohorts. Working in and studying about the effectiveness of cohorts and cohort leadership create unique CoPs within the academy, often generating critically important scholarship about using the closed-cohort model. Additionally, when professors work together to create and implement a new cohort program at their own institution, they often also change the culture of a department into one based on collegiality and shared responsibilities for all program outcomes. Such working coalitions, within or across programs, can produce research opportunities—funding proposals, research papers, publications—that can help professors address a primary expectation in university work.

Perhaps the most significant benefit of serving as a cohort leader is getting to work closely with all cohort members as they progress through their program. The regular interactions between cohort members and a cohort leader can develop into trusting, collegial relationships that enhance professional practice for both. When students feel safe to share honestly without repercussions on performance measures, they often disclose what works effectively to enhance their professional growth and what does not. A cohort leader can use the information to improve program delivery.

Serving as a cohort leader requires organizational skills, clear under-standing of the responsibilities necessary to coordinate long-term learning throughout a closed-cohort program, and strong commitment to assuring program success. That success, as measured by curriculum integration, pro-gram coherence, and shared responsibility, rests squarely upon the shoul-ders of a cohort leader. Although this work can be demanding, frustrating, and at times disappointing, the benefits far outweigh any disadvantages.

CLOSING THOUGHTS

The overarching purpose for our writing this chapter was to present a com-prehensive review of literature on using the closed-cohort delivery model in revitalized EdD programs. The intent of these new doctoral programs is to prepare scholar-practitioner leaders (Mullen & Tuten, 2010) who positively influence their work environments and broader educational systems. The quoted commentary below was written by five doctoral students participat-ing in one of the first CPED-affiliated programs. At the beginning of their second year of studies, they developed and administered a survey to their other 17 cohort peers to gather perceptions about the group's first-year experiences in a program that required them to complete companion dis-sertations as their capstone assessment (Browne-Ferrigno & Jensen, 2012). The text below appears in the closing section of the conference paper they prepared and presented. It highlights key elements about their cohort's transition through four of the stages of group development (Tuckman & Jensen, 1997). We perceived that their reflections on their learning expe-riences encapsulated key elements of building and sustaining a learning cohort.

> The value of cohorts, along with the multitude of ways that educators and learners can benefit from them, suggests implications for both the design of cohorts and the use of cohorts. Since cohort members gain value from the cohort experience in multiple ways and at different stages, active learning in a collaborative environment can be viewed as its fundamental influence and therefore warrants more study. The pedagogy of active learning used in the EdD program allows for more than educational attainment—it created an environment within which adult learners work and function as a multi-skilled group with an array of skills and abilities that over time complement each other....
>
> Experiences gained from participating in a cohort can be both challenging and rewarding. Each member of our cohort had to become an active partici-pant in her or his learning. With faculty serving as guides, we were forced to assume collective responsibility for our learning. Being placed outside our comfort zones helped us to learn each other's strengths and limitations, while

appreciating the value of differing backgrounds, perspectives, and positions on institutional topics. New relationship bridges were built, thus laying the foundation for respect and trust among the cohort members and building a network of colleagues from across the state. While the goal of this EdD program is to prepare cohort members for leadership positions at the two-year's colleges, the knowledge gained from the cohort experience reaches far beyond the goals of the program by bringing strangers together to form perfect partners....

Although the path was initially obscured with dust through the forming and storming stages, illumination settled the dust to allow norming and performing to emerge. Even though it is certainly true that each cohort member would have preferred to pick their own teams, it was productive when instructors used different methods for selecting the groups—whether by balancing group membership based on individuals' strengths, by positions group members hold at their respective institutions, or by simply counting off. The continuous regrouping helped us get to know one another and to develop close relationships. Our cohort provides its members support and encouragement needed to progress us together on our journey toward attaining the EdD degree and thus reaching the final stage of group development—adjourning. (Burke et al., 2009, p. 7)

NOTE

1. Portions of this chapter were adapted from publications appearing in the references that I co-authored over the years with Rodney Muth, professor emeritus at the University of Colorado Denver, where I completed my doctoral studies. My interest and subsequent research on cohorts emerged through participation in a doctoral laboratory on adult learning organized by Rodney and in which Bruce Barnett participated while he was a professor at Northern Colorado University. Those doctoral laboratory experiences and continuing collaborations with both men during my early career as a university professor supported my development as a cohort leader for two externally funded projects and as a cohort design team member and instructor in one of the first CPED-affiliated doctoral programs. References at the end of this chapter evidence the breadth of literature on closed cohorts contributed by Rodney Muth, Bruce Barnett, and their colleagues over nearly two decades.

REFERENCES

Amrein-Beadsley, A., Zambo, D., Moore, D. W., Buss, R. R., Perry, N. J, Painter, S. R.,...Puckett, K. S. (2012). Graduates respond to an innovative educational doctorate program. *Journal of Research on Leadership Education, 7*(1), 98–122.

Anderson, T. (2010) Theories for learning with emerging technologies. In G. Velesiano (Ed.), *Emerging technologies in distance education* (pp. 23–39). Athabasca,

AB, Canada: Athabasca University Press. Retrieved from http://www.aupress. ca/index.php/books/120177

Barkely, E. F., Cross, K. P, & Major, C. H. (2005). *Collaborative learning techniques: A handbook for college faculty.* San Francisco, CA: Jossey-Bass.

Barnett, B. G., Basom, M. R., Yerkes, D. M., & Norris, C. J. (2000). Cohorts in educational leadership programs: Benefits, difficulties, and the potential for developing school leaders. *Educational Administration Quarterly, 36*(2), 255–282.

Barnett, B. G., & Caffarella, R. S. (1992, October). *The use of cohorts: A powerful way for addressing issues of diversity in preparation programs.* Paper presented at the annual meeting of the University Council for Education Administration, Minneapolis, MN. Retrieved from ERIC database. (ED354627)

Barnett, B. G., & Muse, I. D. (1993). Cohort groups in educational administration: Promises and challenges. *Journal of School Leadership, 3*(4), 400–415.

Barnett, B. G., & Muth, R. (2008). Using action-research strategies and cohort structures to ensure research competence of practitioner-scholar leaders. *Journal of Research on Leadership Education, 3*(1), 1–42.

Basom, M. R., & Yerkes, D. M. (2001, April). *Modeling community through cohort development.* Paper presented at the meeting of the American Educational Research Association, Seattle, WA. Retrieved from ERIC database. (ED451814)

Basom, M., Yerkes, D., Norris, C., & Barnett, B. (1995). *Exploring cohorts: Effects on principal and leadership practice.* Evaluative report supported through minigrant from the Danforth Foundation, St. Louis, MO. Retrieved from ERIC database. (ED387857)

Bentley, T., Zhao, F., Reames, E. H., & Reed, C. (2004). Frames we live by: Metaphors for the cohort. *The Professional Educator, 26*(2), 39–44.

Blaschke, L. M. (2012). Heutagogy and lifelong learning: A review of heutagogical practice and self-determined learning. *The International Review of Research in Open and Distance Learning, 13*(1), 56–71. Retrieved from http://www.irrodl. org/index.php/irrodl/article/view/1076/2087

Bransford, J., Brown, A., & Cocking, R. (Eds.). (2000). *How people learn: Brain, mind, experience, and school.* Washington, DC: National Academies Press.

Bransford, J. D., & Schwartz, D. L. (1999). Rethinking transfer: A simple proposal with multiple implications. In A. Iran-Nejad & P. D. Pearson (Eds.), *Review of research in education* (Vol. 24, pp. 61–100). Washington, DC: American Educational Research Association.

Browne-Ferrigno, T., & Jensen, J. M. (2012). Preparing Ed.D. students to conduct group dissertations. *Innovative Higher Education, 37*(5), 407–421. (ERIC Accession Number EJ982740)

Browne-Ferrigno, T., & Muth, R. (2003). Effects of cohorts on learners. *Journal of School Leadership, 13*(6), 621–643.

Browne-Ferrigno, T., & Muth, R. (2004, Fall). On being a cohort leader: Curriculum integration, program coherence, and shared responsibility. *Educational Leadership and Administration: Teaching and Program Development, 16,* 77–95.

Browne-Ferrigno, T., & Muth, R. (2008). Generative learning communities: Preparing leaders for authentic practice. In R. Papa, C. Achilles, & B. Alford (Eds.), *Leadership on the frontlines: Changes in preparation and practice* (pp. 73–86).

Sixteenth Annual Yearbook of the National Council of Professors of Educational Administration. Lancaster, PA: Pro>Active.

Browne-Ferrigno, T., & Muth, R. (2012, July). Use of learner-centered instructional strategies in higher education: Doctoral student assessments. *International Journal for the Scholarship of Teaching & Learning, 6*(2). Retrieved from http://digitalcommons.georgiasouthern.edu/ij-sotl/

Burke, L.., Jr., Preston, N., Quillen, M., Roe, R., & Strong, E. (2009, October). *Stages of group development: From strangers to partners.* Paper presented at the annual meeting of the Southern Regional Council on Educational Administration, Atlanta, GA.

Burnett, P. C. (1999). The supervision of doctoral dissertations using a collaborative cohort model. *Counselor Education and Supervision, 39*(1), 46–52.

Butterwick, S., Cockell, J., McArthur-Blair, J., MacIver, S., & Rodrigues, J. (2012). Connectivity and collectivity in a doctoral cohort program: An academic memoir in five parts. *Alberta Journal of Educational Research, 57*(4), 446–459.

Chayko, M. (2008). *Portable communities: The social dynamic of online and mobile connectedness.* Albany: State University of New York Press.

Choy, S., Delahaye, B. L., & Saggers, B. (2015). Developing learning cohorts for postgraduate research degrees. *Australian Educational Researcher, 42*(1), 19–34.

Churchill, F. (1996). Collaborative inquiry: The practice of professional development. In Z. Donahue, M. A. Van Tassell, & L. Patterson (Eds.), *Research in the classroom: Talk, texts, and inquiry* (pp. 108–116). Newark, DE: International Reading Association.

Cordiero, P., Boutiler, L., Panicek, J., & Salamone-Consoli, A. (1993, February). *The roles of practitioners, students and professors.* Paper presented at the annual conference of the American Association of School Administrators Conference-Within-a-Conference, Orlando, FL.

Cranton, P. A. (2002, Spring). Teaching for transformation. *New Directions for Adult and Continuing Education, 93,* 63–71. Retrieved from http://onlinelibrary.wiley.com/doi/10.1002/ace.50/epdf

Cyrs, T. E. (1997, Fall). Competence in teaching at a distance. *New Direction for Adult and Continuing Education, 17,* 15–18. Retrieved from http://onlinelibrary.wiley.com/doi/10.1002/tl.7102/epdf

Decker, A., Dykes, M., Gilliam, J., & Marrs, S. (2009, October). *Being students again: Balancing ambiguities, expectations, and responsibilities.* Paper presented at the annual meeting of the Southern Regional Council on Educational Administration, Atlanta, GA.

Dewey, J. (1938/1997). *Experience and education.* New York, NY: Touchstone.

Donaldson, J. F., & Scribner, J. P. (2003). Instructional cohorts and learning: Ironic uses of a social system. *Journal of School Leadership, 13*(6), 644–665.

Dorn, S. M., Papalewis, R., & Brown, R. (1995). Educators earning their doctorates: Doctoral student perceptions regarding cohesiveness and persistence. *Education, 116*(2), 305–313.

Drath, W. H., & Paulus, C. J. (1994). *Making common sense: Leadership as meaning-making in a community of practice.* Greensboro, NC: Center for Creative Leadership.

Floresh-Scott, S. M., & Nerad, M. (2012, Spring). Peers in doctoral education: Unrecognized learning patterns. *New Directions in Higher Education, 157,* 73–83.

Ford, L., & Vaughn, C. (2011). Working together more than alone: Students' evolving perceptions of self and community with a four-year educational administration doctoral cohort. *The Qualitative Report, 16*(6), 1645–1668.

Geltner, B. B. (1994). *The poser of structural and symbolic redesign: Creating a collaborative learning community in higher education.* Ypsilanti: Eastern Michigan University. Retrieved from ERIC database. (ED374 757)

Golde, C. M., & Walker, G. E. (Eds.). (2006). *Envisioning the future of doctoral education: Preparing stewards of the discipline.* San Francisco, CA: Jossey-Bass.

Greenlee, B. J., & Karanxha, Z. (2010). A study of group dynamics in educational leadership cohort and non-cohort groups. *Journal of Research on Leadership Education, 5*(11), 357–382.

Gutherie, J. W. (2009). The case for a modern Doctor of Education degree (Ed.D.): Multipurpose education doctorates no longer appropriate. *Peabody Journal of Education, 84*(1), 3–8.

Guzmán, N., & Muth, R. (1999, Fall). Building blocks: Structures and processes for PhD student success. *Educational Leadership and Administration: Teaching and Program Development, 11*, 83–99.

Hannafin, M. J., & Land, S. M. (1997). The foundations and assumptions of technology-enhanced student-centered learning environments. *Instructional Science, 25*(3), 167–202.

Hase, S., & Kenyon, C. (2003, September). *Heutagogy and developing capable people and capable workplaces: Strategies for dealing with complexity.* Paper presented at the Changing Face of Work and Learning Conference at the University of Alberta, Canada. Retrieved from http://nferciindonesia.blogspot.com/2013/04/heutagogy-and-developing-capable-people.html

Hebert, F. T., & Reynolds, K. C. (1998). Learning achievements of students in cohort groups. *Journal of Continuing Higher Education, 46*(3), 34–43.

Holloway, E. L., & Alexandre, L. (2012). Crossing boundaries in doctoral education: Relational learning, cohort communities, and dissertation committees. *New Directions for Teacher and Learning, 131,* 85–97

Horn, R. A. (2001). Promoting social justice and caring in schools and communities: The unrealized potential of the cohort model. *Journal of School Leadership, 11*(4), 313–334.

Kumar, S., Dawson, K., Black, E. W., Cavanaugh, C., & Sessums, C. D. (2011). Apply the community of inquiry framework to an online professional practice doctoral program. *International Review of Research in Open and Distance Learning, 12*(6), 126–142.

Lave, J., & Wenger, E. (1991). *Situated learning: Legitimate peripheral participation.* New York, NY: Cambridge University Press.

Lei, S., Gorelick, D., Short, K., Smallwood, L., & Wright-Porter, K. (2011). Academic cohorts: Benefits and drawbacks of being a member of a community of learners. *Education, 131*(3), 497–504.

Loss, C. G. (2009). Building, sustaining, and expanding the education doctorate at Peabody College: An administrative view. *Peabody Journal of Education, 84*(1), 44–47.

Maher, M. A. (2001, April). *Professional living situations: Cohorts as communities of living and learning.* Paper presented at the meeting of the American Educational

Research Association, Seattle, WA. Retrieved from ERIC database. (ED451 796).

Maher, M. A. (2005). The evolving meaning and influence of cohort membership. *Innovative Higher Education, 30*(3), 195–211.

Martin, W. M., Ford, S. F., Murphy, M. J., Rehm, R. G., & Muth, R. (1997). Linking instructional delivery with diverse learning settings. *Journal of School Leadership, 7*(4), 386–408.

McNamara, J., Lara-Alecio, R., Irby, B., Hoyle, J., & Tong, F. (2007, May). *Doctoral program issues: Commentary on companion dissertations.* Retrieved from http://cnx.org/exports/b5cdd64d-0621-49c9-8cd4-ec17a9287b7e%401.pdf/doctoral-program-issues-commentary-on-companion-dissertations-1.pdf

McPhail, C. J., Robinson, M., & Scott, H. (2008). The cohort leadership development model: Student perspectives. *Community College Journal of Research and Practice, 32*(4/6), 362–274.

Mullen, C. A., & Tuten, E. M. (2010). Doctoral cohort mentoring: Interdependence, collaborative learning, and cultural change. *Scholar-Practitioner Quarterly, 4*(1), 11–32.

Muth, R. (2000a). Learning at a distance: Building an online program in educational administration. *Educational Leadership and Administration: Teaching and Program Development, 12,* 59–74.

Muth, R. (2000b). Toward a learning-oriented instructional paradigm: Implications for practice. In P. Jenlink & T. Kowalski (Eds.), *Marching into a new millennium: Challenges to educational leadership* (pp. 82–103). Eighth Annual Yearbook of the National Council of Professors of Educational Administration. Lanham, MD: Scarecrow Press.

Muth, R. (2002). Scholar-practitioner goals, practices, and outcomes: What students and faculty need to know and be able to do. *Scholar-Practitioner Quarterly, 1*(1), 67–87.

Muth, R., Banks, D., Bonelli, J., Gaddis, B., Napierkowski, H., White, C., & Wood, V. (2001). Toward an instructional paradigm: Recasting how faculty work and students learn. In T. J. Kowalski & G. Perreault (Eds.), *Twenty-first century challenges for school administrators* (pp. 29–53). Ninth Annual Yearbook of the National Council of Professors of Educational Administration. Lanham, MD: Scarecrow Press.

Muth, R., & Barnett, B. G. (2001). Making the case for professional preparation: Identifying research gaps, improving professional preparation, and gaining political support. *Educational Leadership and Administration: Teaching and Program Development, 13,* 111–122.

Nimer, M. (2009). The doctoral cohort model: Increasing opportunities for success. *College Student Journal, 43*(4), 1373–1379.

Norris, C. J., & Barnett, B. (1994, October). *Cultivating a new leadership paradigm: From cohorts to communities.* Paper presented at the meeting of the University Council for Educational Administration, Philadelphia, PA. Retrieved from ERIC database. (ED387877)

Norris, C., Barnett, B., Basom, M., & Yerkes, D. (1996). The cohort: A vehicle for building transformational leadership skills. *Planning and Changing, 27*(3/4), 145–164.

Norton, M. S. (1995). *The status of student cohorts in educational administration preparation programs.* Paper presented at the annual convention of the University Council for Educational Administration, Salt Lake City, UT.

Osterman, K., Furman, G., & Sernak, K. (2013). Action research in EdD programs in educational leadership. *Journal of Research on Leadership Education, 9*(1), 85–105.

Palloff, R. M., & Pratt, K. (2005). *Collaborating online: Learning together in community.* San Francisco, CA: Jossey-Bass.

Palloff, R. M., & Pratt, K. (2007). *Building learning communities: Effective strategies for the virtual classroom* (2nd ed.). San Francisco, CA: Jossey-Bass.

Parker, K., Lenhart, A., & Moore, K. (2011, August). *The digital revolution and higher education.* Washington, DC: Pew Research Center. Retrieved from http://www.pewinternet.org/2011/08/28/the-digital-revolution-and-higher-education/

Perry, J. A. (2011). The Carnegie Project on the Education Doctorate: Phase II—A quest for change. *UCEA Review, 52*(3), 1–3. Retrieved from http://www.ucea.org/resource/ucea-review/

Perry, J. A., & Imig, D. G. (2008). A stewardship of practice in education. *Change: The Magazine of Higher Learning, 40*(6), 42–49. Retrieved from http://www.cpedinitiative.org/files/Change%20Article%202008_0.pdf

Reynolds, K., & Hebert, F. T. (1995). Cohort formats and intense schedules: Added involvement and interaction for continuing higher education. *The Journal of Continuing Higher Education, 43*(3), 34–42.

Saltiel, I., & Reynolds, K. (2001, April). *Student connections: An integrative model of cohorts, community and learning.* Paper presented at the meeting of the American Educational Research Association, Seattle, WA. Retrieved from ERIC database. (ED451812)

Saltiel, I. M., & Russo, C. S. (2001). *Cohort programming and learning: Improving educational experiences for adult learners.* Professional Practices in Adult Education and Human Resource Development Series. Melbourne, FL: Krieger. Retrieved from ERIC database. (ED 457369)

Schulman, L. S., Golde, C. M., Bueschel, A. C., & Garbedian, K. J. (2006). Reclaiming education's doctorates: A critique and a proposal. *Educational Researcher, 35*(3), 25–32.

Scribner, J. P., & Donaldson, J. F. (2001). The dynamics of group learning in a cohort: From non-learning to transformative learning. *Educational Administration Quarterly, 37*(5), 605–636.

Siemens, G. (2005, January). Connectivism: A learning theory for the digital age. *International Journal of Instructional Technology & Distance Learning, 2*(1). Retrieved from http://elearnspace.org/Articles/connectivism.htm

Sproull, L., & Kiesler, S. (1991). *Connections: New ways of working in the networked organization.* Cambridge: Massachusetts Institute of Technology.

Suleiman, M., & Whetton, D. (2014, August). *Promoting team leadership skills in doctoral candidates.* Paper presented at the annual meeting of the National Council of Professors of Educational Administration, Camarillo, CA. Retrieved from ERIC database. (ED546632)

Swayze, S., & Jakeman, R. C. (2014). Student perceptions of communication, connectedness, and learning in a merged cohort course. *The Journal of Continuing Higher Education, 62*(2), 102–111.

Taylor, R., & Storey, V. A. (2011). (Re)designing and implementing the professional doctorate in education: Comparing experiences of a small independent university and a large public university. *International Journal of Educational Leadership Preparation, 6*(3), 1–16. Retrieved from http://www.ncpeapublications.org

Teitel, L. (1997). Understanding and harnessing the power of the cohort model in preparing educational leaders. *Peabody Journal of Education, 72*(2), 66–85.

Tipping, J., Freeman, R. F., & Rachlis, A. R. (1995). Using faculty and student perceptions of group dynamics to develop recommendations for PBL training. *Academic Medicine, 70*(1), 1050–1054.

Tisdell, E. J., Strohschen, G. I. E., Carver, M. L., Corrigan, P., Nash, J., Nelson, M.,... O'Connor, M. (2004). Cohort learning online in graduate education: Constructing knowledge in cyber community. *Educational Technology & Society, 7*(1), 115–127.

Tu, C., & McIsaac, M. (2002). The relationship of social presence and interaction in online classes. *American Journal of Distance Education, 16*(3), 131–150.

Tuckman, B. W. (1965). Developmental sequence in small groups. *Psychological Bulletin, 63*(6), 384–399.

Tuckman, B. W., & Jensen, M. C. (1977). Stages of small group development revisited. *Group and Organizational Studies, 2*(4), 419–427.

Wenger, E. (1998). *Communities of practice: Learning, meaning, and identify.* New York, NY: Cambridge University Press.

Wenger, E., McDermott, R., & Snyder, W. M. (2002). *A guide to managing knowledge: Cultivating communities of practice.* Boston, MA: Harvard Business School Press.

Wenger, E., White, N., & Smith, J. D. (2009). *Digital habitats: Stewarding technology for communities.* Portland, OR: CPsquare.

Wesson, L. H., Holman, S. O., Holman, D., & Cox, D. (1996, April). *Cohesion or collusion: Impact of a cohort structure.* Paper presented at the meeting of the American Educational Research Association, New York, NY. Retrieved from ERIC database. (ED398809)

Wheeler, S. (2011, July 8). *Learning with e's: Digital age learning* [Blog post]. Retrieved from http://steve-wheeler.blogspot.com/2011/07/digital-age-learning.html

Witte, J. E., & James, W. B. (1998, Fall). Cohort partnerships: A pragmatic approach to doctoral research. *New Directions for Adult and Continuing Education, 79,* 53–62. Retrieved from http://onlinelibrary.wiley.com/doi/10.1002/ace.7906/epdf

Yerkes, D. M., Basom, M., Barnett, B., & Norris, C. (1995). Cohorts today: Considerations of structure, characteristics, and potential effects. *Journal of California Association of Professors of Education Administration, 7,* 7–19.

Zambo, R., Zambo, D., Buss, R. R., Perry, J. A., & Williams, T. R. (2014). Seven years after the call: Students' and graduates' perceptions of the re-envisioned Ed.D. *Innovative Higher Education, 39*(2), 123–137.

CHAPTER 5

MENTORING STUDENTS IN CPED-INFLUENCED DOCTORAL PROGRAMS

Ann Dutton Ewbank

Choosing to obtain a doctorate is one of the most important decisions an educational practitioner can make. Based on my experience as an EdD program mentor, I discuss in this chapter how faculty members can best mentor from the beginning potential students (those who are considering pursuing a CPED-influenced education doctorate) through to the end and completion of the program. Mentoring assists students, who are typically full-time professionals, in successfully completing the rigorous and often compact timeline of an EdD program. Faculty, however, who enter the academy are rarely trained to mentor students (Nettles & Millet, 2006) and often may mentor students in the manner that they experienced, emulating practices that are more appropriate for a full-time tenure-track position (Blackburn, Chapman, & Cameron, 1981). In contrast with the PhD, where the emphasis is training students to become educational researchers who typically work in a university setting, the aims and scope of the CPED-influenced EdD intends to develop practitioners who not only generate

The EdD and the Scholarly Practitioner, pages 65–77
Copyright © 2016 by Information Age Publishing
All rights of reproduction in any form reserved.

new knowledge, but also integrate theory and research to address complex problems of practice. Therefore, mentoring practices for EdD students should be congruent with the aims and scope of the CPED-influenced EdD program.

Mentoring EdD students in a CPED-influenced program requires an understanding of the principles that underlie the EdD design. The CPED-influenced EdD

1. Is framed around questions of equity, ethics, and social justice to bring about solutions to complex problems of practice.
2. Prepares leaders who can construct and apply knowledge to make a positive difference in the lives of individuals, families, organizations, and communities.
3. Provides opportunities for candidates to develop and demonstrate collaboration and communication skills to work with diverse communities and to build partnerships.
4. Provides field-based opportunities to analyze problems of practice and use multiple frames to develop meaningful solutions.
5. Is grounded in and develops a professional knowledge base that integrates both practical and research knowledge, that links theory with systemic and systematic inquiry.
6. Emphasizes the generation, transformation, and use of professional knowledge and practice. (CPED, 2009)

The mentor should have a working knowledge and understanding of these principles. Of special importance is the ability of the mentor to guide his/her students in the successful application of research to complex problems of practice.

MENTORING VERSUS ADVISING

This chapter is concerned with mentoring students in CPED-influenced EdD programs, a process which includes a deep and complex relationship that supports the development of habits of mind necessary to become scholarly practitioners. This kind of mentoring is distinct from academic advising. An advisor role is somewhat bureaucratic. He/she is responsible for guiding the student through the academic program requirements and needs to be familiar with the academic rules and regulations of the student's program of study. These responsibilities support the student in progressing through the program and fulfilling their graduation requirements. A mentor, alternatively, invests in the personal development of his/her students, extending their interest beyond the concern for completion of degree requirements (Ramirez, 2012). Galbraith (2003) explains this notion: "Mentoring is a more intricate, long-term, one-on-one relationship that goes well beyond simply providing information. True mentoring is a complex process between professor and college adult learner that supports a mutual enhancement of critically reflective and independent thinking" (p. 16). The mentoring relationship can positively affect degree completion, making it essential for ensuring the success of the EdD student (Creighton, Creighton, & Parks, 2010; Nettles & Millet, 2006; Welton, Mansfield, & Lee, 2014). Such skills are not inherent or intuitive for all faculty members, however.

Mindset of a Mentor

To be seen as a successful protégé often implies that the protégé follow a career path that emulates their mentor's (Blackburn et al., 1981). However, given that CPED-influenced programs develop scholarly practitioners who return to their professional settings, a tenure/tenure-track academic cannot mentor their students to be successful protégés. Mentoring in an EdD program requires the mentor to possess a different mindset, one that supports the development of a scholarly practitioner. For many education faculty members, this may require a shift in thinking and in ways of doing. Such a shift can be grounded in understanding what it means to become a scholarly practitioner. In my experience as a faculty member trained in a traditional PhD program, I have found that the following reference points are helpful to keep in mind when mentoring EdD students:

- The student is a working professional, balancing life, career, and scholarly studies;
- The doctoral work is collaborative, often situated within a laboratory of practice;
- The dissertation process addresses a complex problem of practice;
- The goal of the EdD program is to develop a scholarly practitioner who can apply systemic and systematic inquiry to these complex problems of practice.

This frame of reference may assist the mentor in tailoring the mentoring relationship to those pursuing the EdD. The remainder of this chapter is organized in three chronological sections: mentoring before, during, and after the EdD.

BEFORE ENTERING THE EDD

Faculty members who are approached by potential doctoral students should help those individuals clarify that the EdD program matches their career goals and aspirations. A first step is helping a potential student understand the rigors required of doctoral study, particularly in a program with a compressed timeframe (typically 3 years). I have found it helpful to ask the potential student to reflect on the following questions:

- Am I ready to balance the demanding load of graduate study as well as work (and family)?
- Am I ready to work collaboratively, as well as independently, on projects that stretch me further than I've ever been stretched before?
- Am I ready to be a change agent in my local context, integrating the theory I learn in my doctoral program to my professional practice on a regular basis?

Next, the faculty member should keep the potential student's career goals in mind when counseling them toward a doctoral program. Painter (2015) outlines two possible options for students choosing to pursue a doctorate. These include advancement in professional practice and acquiring a teaching position within higher education. Faculty mentoring candidates toward the EdD should help them to think deeply about their career aspirations and align them with the appropriate terminal degree. Students entering an EdD program should do so because they aim to become change agents in practice, not university faculty, which results from PhD preparation.

DURING THE PROGRAM

Once a student is admitted into the EdD program, the most important aspect of mentoring is guiding the student in developing the habits of mind of a scholarly practitioner. According to CPED, a scholarly practitioner "is grounded in and develops a professional knowledge base that integrates both practical and research knowledge, that links theory with systemic and systematic inquiry" (CPED, 2009). The process of becoming a scholarly practitioner centers on an understanding of the relationship between knowledge, inquiry, and practice (Anderson & Herr, 1999; Riehl, Larson, Short, & Reitzug, 2000). Though the students will learn this in their program, mentoring reinforces how such skills are used and for what ends.

Initial Mentoring

At the beginning of a program, an initial mentor should be assigned to each student. This person is responsible for socializing the student into the program (Nyquist & Woodford, 2000; Terrell, Snyder, Dringus, & Maddrey, 2012). This initial mentor need not necessarily become the dissertation chair but is the person responsible for guiding the student through the first stages of the EdD program and building their understanding of what it means to be a scholarly practitioner and agent of change. The initial mentor also guides the student in developing relationships with program faculty in order to identify a permanent mentor.

As the student progresses through the program and develops specific interests, a permanent mentor will take over. To identify this permanent mentor, program faculty should make themselves available to all students, providing them with information about their research interests and ways in which they can support them in developing their own scholarly inquiries in practice. Program faculty can assist students in choosing a potential permanent mentor by keeping their faculty profile website up to date and publicly sharing their curricula vitae. Program directors might also consider inviting program faculty to speak in the introductory course or holding student-faculty socials.

Understanding a Student's Laboratory of Practice

A permanent mentor will want to best understand the student's professional context and how that context defines and shapes the problem of practice that the student wants to investigate. The mentor may want to visit the student's work setting, which is often called their laboratory of practice. The laboratory of practice, as defined by CPED (2014), is a

> setting…where theory and practice inform and enrich each other; where ideas—formed by the intersection of theory, inquiry, and practice—can be implemented, measured, and analyzed for the impact made; and where transformative and generative learning that is measured by the development of scholarly expertise and implementation of practice is facilitated.

Students will often use this laboratory to test out what they are learning in the EdD program, to reflect on their leadership practices, and as the place where data for the dissertation is gathered. By visiting the laboratory of practice, the doctoral mentor can more fully understand the context in which the student's problem of practice is situated and thus more effectively guide the student in his/her research. Alternatively, if mentoring is done at a distance (e.g., in online programs) and it is not possible to visit a student's laboratory of practice, then it may be helpful for the student to prepare a rich description for the mentor.

Developing a Committee and the Dissertation Phase

A key role of the permanent mentor is aiding the student in organizing a dissertation committee. Given that the dissertation (or dissertation in practice) is practice based with goals of creating solutions to complex problems of practice, the committee member makeup must serve and support this goal. The committee will need members that have expertise in the student's topic area. It will also want members who can support the student in developing solutions to such problems. Such members may be those practitioner experts who hold terminal degrees but work in practice. Therefore, the EdD program may consider allowing such individuals to serve on their dissertation committees. This benefits both the student and the mentor—the practitioner-scholar appointed to the dissertation committee can contribute an important voice that models what it is like to apply scholarly knowledge within a real-world setting.

Once the committee is set, the EdD student enters the dissertation phase of their program. Though many CPED-influenced EdD programs incorporate the dissertation in practice at the beginning of a program, there is an end period where the student is gathering and analyzing data. In traditional programs, Tinto (1993) notes that doctoral students often face challenges during the dissertation that are different from those faced while completing coursework. In the CPED-influenced EdD, the dissertation process is a collaborative one. The mentor, along with the committee, works with the student in very collaborative ways. The student brings practitioner knowledge and expertise, while the mentor brings scholarly and research expertise. Together they design a research study that will best address the problem that the student seeks to address in their professional context. Making this relationship reciprocal is key to the student developing a successful dissertation in practice.

Anticipating Potential Mentoring Challenges

As with all doctoral programs, mentors may experience challenges while working with their EdD student. Given the short, intense nature of the EdD programs, such challenges may prove to be more difficult to manage. Below I have outlined several typical challenges that I have experienced when mentoring EdD students, including mentoring at a distance, changing careers or positions, switching focus to a PhD program, writing difficulties, and withdrawing from the program. Anticipating and preparing for these challenges will help the mentor to effectively address and support their student, often improving the student's experience.

First, for the many EdD programs that are fully online, mentoring at a distance can be challenging. It is not, however, impossible, and resources are available. Schichtel (2010), for example, identified seven competency skills of e-mentoring to support faculty:

1. Developmental competency: Mentors provide a learner centered environment.
2. Social competency: Mentors project their full personality through the medium being used.
3. Cognitive competency: Mentors provide an environment that fosters higher-order thinking and critical discourse.
4. Teaching competency: Mentors facilitate reflection and integration of learning rather than using a didactic approach.
5. Communication competency: Mentors understand "netiquette," a set of communication skills appropriate to the online medium.
6. Managerial competency: Mentors foster effective online policies, procedures, and organization.
7. Online technical competency: Mentors effectively utilize technology for online learning and know how to troubleshoot glitches.

Successful mentoring of doctoral students online is in many ways markedly similar to face-to-face mentoring. Kumar, Johnson and Hardemon (2013) note, however, that the mentor must take care to provide structured experiences for the student, timeliness of feedback, and communicate clearly using multiple modes. Following this advice, a mentor can learn to easily enact the seven competencies above.

Second, because EdD students are also full-time working professionals, career and position changes may occur at some point during their program. Such changes often affect the problem of practice that the student had chosen to study and may change or shift how the student can utilize their work place as a laboratory of practice. The mentor will need to assist the student in navigating how these changes affect their doctoral trajectory while also honoring the professional change for the student. In my experience mentoring EdD students, a change in career or professional position is often accompanied by an increase in responsibility. While added professional work may slow the student in his or her academic progress, a mentor can show the student how to turn the change into an opportunity. As an agent of change, EdD graduates are expected to impact practice. A professional change may increase the sphere of influence that could facilitate addressing the problem of practice. The student may also have the opportunity to view their problem of practice with a new perspective. The mentor can play an important role by aiding the student in reconceptualizing how their new role can be incorporating into their program and support their work on improving their problem of practice in this new environment.

Third, from time to time it happens that after beginning an EdD program a student may decide that he/she would rather pursue a tenure-track career in academia. Often, EdD students are midcareer; they may have robust experience in K–12, higher education, or affiliated settings and may want to pursue the next chapter in their career as a tenure-track academic. When this happens, I have asked students to consider the following questions prior to making the transition:

- What is the rationale behind the switch?
- A tenure-track academic position typically requires research, teaching, and service. Do my long-term career goals align with this orientation?
- A career in academe may seem appealing because, on the surface, it may seem "easier" than a position of practice. However, academic pressures are often intense and all-consuming. Am I prepared for the challenges of a tenure-track position?
- PhD graduates are rarely hired as tenure-track faculty at their home institution. Am I prepared to move to another city or state to accept a tenure-track position?

By considering these questions, students can make an informed decision as to whether entering academia is the right step in their career progression. If a student feels he/she wants to ultimately teach and conduct research in higher education but remain in practice in the immediate future, he/she should not switch to a PhD program. Their doctoral studies should prepare them for their immediate professional goals. Ultimately, if he/she would like to teach as a clinical faculty member, then the EdD will be suitable in the longer term as well.

Fourth, scholarly writing is a genre that can pose a challenge for many practitioners. Faculty members often assume that students enter a doctoral program knowing how to write in a scholarly manner (Caffarella & Barnett, 2000). Professionals, on the other hand, may have a very different writing style and do not write nearly the amount that a doctoral program requires of them. Furthermore, many doctoral students find research writing difficult and complex (Kamler & Thompson, 2014) and not easy to learn. In the academy, writing assignments are often designed as assessments rather than as vehicles for learning (Aitchison, 2009), and there are very few "low stakes" writing opportunities (Elbow, 1997). For these reasons, faculty and mentors must pay greater attention to writing support for doctoral students

(Kamler & Thompson, 2014; Paltridge & Starfield, 2007) if we are to foster their success. The process of critique (both peer and faculty) should be iterative, timely, and low stakes. Faculty and mentors must understand that writing is an emotionally charged and sometimes frustrating endeavor (Caffarella & Barnett, 2000) for students. They require ample opportunities to practice their writing in a low-stakes environment prior to assessment, and supports should be put into place to help them develop as scholarly writers, including an overview of basic writing techniques and the establishment of peer writing groups.

Finally, faculty must work to increase the persistence rate in EdD programs. Factors that influence successful completion include the relationship between the student and mentor (Gardner, 2009; Kluever et al., 1997) and departmental orientation, financial support, and the integration of coursework and research skills (de Valero, 2001). Faculty mentors in an EdD program can positively influence student persistence by actively ensuring a welcoming climate in the department and program, cultivating a supportive relationship with the student and working to formalize structures for student support throughout the program.

AFTER GRADUATION

The mentor-student relationship does not end after the student graduates from the EdD program. The success of a CPED-influenced EdD program also lies in its ability to help students become successful leaders and scholarly practitioners in their local contexts. Mentoring after graduation can help to achieve that goal. In a positive mentoring relationship, the student and the mentor become lifelong colleagues (Lage-Otero, 2005) and mentoring continues to occur as an intentional relationship (Women in Higher Education, 2004). The doctoral mentor should facilitate an ongoing relationship that allows the newly minted EdD holder to continue to ask questions and look for guidance as he/she assumes a scholarly practitioner role in his/her current position. For example, the mentor can alert the EdD graduate to new research that can inform practice and also act as a sounding board as he/she addresses problems of practice. The mentor may also help the graduate to develop a professional network. Conversely, the mentor continues to learn from the graduate by continuously connecting him/her to the issues inherent in the practitioner realm, serving as a contact for future students and potentially providing opportunities for the mentor to foster their own research agenda in practice settings. This symbiotic and reciprocal relationship offers long-term benefits to both the student and the mentor.

Measuring Success

Measuring the success of the dissertation in practice is one way to maintain this relationship. Success is context-dependent; that is, success means different outcomes in different contexts. Because CPED-influenced EdD dissertations in practice intend to address and impact a complex problem of practice, the mentor can ask the graduate the following questions to determine whether success was or continues to be achieved.

- How did the dissertation project resolve or address the complex problem of practice?
- How have behaviors changed as a result of the dissertation project?
- What evidence suggests that the change is sustainable?

Through these questions, the graduate can explore whether the dissertation in practice had a lasting impact on the complex problem of practice that it intended to address.

Enhancing the graduate's professional network and opportunities is another way to continue mentoring. Many students, once matriculated, will continue on their career trajectory and choose to pursue positions with increased responsibility. The mentor can assist the student in becoming competitive for the job market perhaps by supporting the publication of their work in practitioner or scholarly journals or presentations at conferences. This is where professional networking becomes essential. Mentors can enhance the graduate's professional connections and opportunities that may assist in obtaining positions with increased responsibility.

A final way for mentors to continue the mentor-mentee relationship is to nominate their graduate's accomplishments for dissertation and career achievement awards. Award opportunities are often found through academic professional associations such as the CPED Dissertation in Practice of the Year award, the American Educational Research Association awards, or the Association for the Study of Higher Education awards. Awards may also be found through professional groups such as Phi Delta Kappa or NASPA: Student Affairs Administrators in Higher Education.

Mentors may also be recognized through awards programs. The University Council for Educational Administration offers the Jay D. Scribner Mentoring Award, for example. Local awards for both graduates and mentors, such as those offered by the higher education institution where the EdD program is located, may also be available. Nominating graduates and mentors for various awards is a way to gain legitimacy for the EdD program and can be beneficial for both graduate and mentor.

CONCLUSION

Mentoring is a reciprocal personal relationship that begins before and endures beyond the program. In this chapter, I have attempted to provide a roadmap for effectively mentoring EdD students prior to their admission to the EdD program to after they have graduated. The mentor should guide the student through the doctoral journey with a deep concern not only for the student's progress, but also for keeping the end goal in mind—that the student becomes a leader in his/her local context.

Additionally, mentoring in a CPED-influenced program requires that the faculty member possess knowledge and a deep understanding of the CPED working principles for program design. This framework provides guideposts that orient the mentor toward the student's transformation through their doctoral program into a scholarly practitioner. Ultimately, at the conclusion of the EdD program, the student should be prepared to construct knowledge and apply theory and research to practice, taking informed actions that positively impact schools, communities, and organizations. Through this framework, a successful mentor-student relationship can be cultivated that endures beyond the EdD program.

REFERENCES

Aitchison, C. (2009). Writing groups for doctoral education. *Studies in Higher Education, 34*(8), 905–916. doi:10.1080/03075070902785580

Anderson, G. L., & Herr, K. (1999). The new paradigm wars: Is there room for rigorous practitioner knowledge in schools and universities? *Educational Researcher, 28*(5), 12–21. doi:10.3102/0013189X028005012

Blackburn, R., Chapman, D., & Cameron, S. (1981). "Cloning" in academe: Mentorship and academic careers. *Research in Higher Education, 15*(4), 315–327. doi:10.1007/BF00973512

Caffarella, R., & Barnett, B. (2000). Teaching doctoral students to become scholarly writers: The importance of giving and receiving critiques. *Studies in Higher Education, 25*(1), 39–52. doi:10.1080/030750700116000

Carnegie Project on the Education Doctorate (CPED). (2009). *Education doctorate definitions and working principles.* Retrieved from http://cpedinitiative.org/working-principles-professional-practice-doctorate-education

Carnegie Project on the Education Doctorate (CPED). (2014). *Design concept definitions.* Retrieved from http://cpedinitiative.org/design-concept-definitions

Creighton, L., Creighton, T., & Parks, D. (2010). Mentoring to degree completion: Expanding the horizons of doctoral protégés. *Mentoring & Tutoring: Partnership in Learning, 18*, 39–52. doi:10.1080/13611260903448342

de Valero, F. Y. (2001). Departmental factors affecting time-to-degree and completion rates of doctoral students at one land-grant research institution. *The Journal of Higher Education, 72*(3), 341–367. doi:http://doi.org/10.2307/2649335

Elbow, P. (1997). High stakes and low stakes in assigning and responding to writing. *New Directions For Teaching And Learning, 69*, 5–13. doi:10.1002/tl.6901

Galbraith, M. W. (2003). The adult education professor as mentor: A means to enhance teaching and learning. *Perspectives: The New York Journal of Adult Learning, 1*(1), 9–20.

Gardner, S. (2009). The development of doctoral students: Phases of challenge and support. *ASHE Higher Education Report, 34*(6), 1–14.

Kamler, B., & Thompson, P. (2014). *Helping doctoral students write: Pedagogies for supervision.* (2nd ed.). New York, NY: Routledge.

Kluever, R. C. et al. (1997, March 24–28). *Dissertation completers and non-completers: An analysis of psycho-social variables.* Paper presented at the Annual Meeting of the American Educational Research Association, Chicago, IL.

Kumar, S., Johnson, M., & Hardemon, T. (2013). Dissertations at a distance: Students' perceptions of online mentoring in a doctoral program. *International Journal of E-Learning and Distance Education, 27*(1), 1–50. Retrieved from http://www.ijede.ca/index.php/jde/article/view/835

Lage-Otero, E. (2005). Doctoral dissertation: Looking forward, looking backward. *Tomorrow's Professor Mailing List.* Retrieved from http://cgi.stanford.edu/~dept-ctl/tomprof/posting.php?ID=720.

Nettles, M., & Millett, M. (2006). *Three magic letters: Getting to PhD.* Baltimore, MD: John Hopkins University Press.

Nyquist, J. D., & Woodford, B. J. (2000). *Re-envisioning the PhD: What are our concerns?* Seattle: Center for Instructional Development and Research, University of Washington.

Paltridge, B., & Starfield, S. (2007). *Thesis and dissertation writing in a second language: A handbook for supervisors.* London, England: Routledge.

Painter, S. (2015). Choosing a doctoral program. *School Administrator, 72*(3), 30–32. Retrieved from http://aasa.org/content.aspx?id=36799

Ramirez, J. (2012). The intentional mentor: Effective mentorship of undergraduate science students. *The Journal of Undergraduate Neuroscience Education, 11*(1), A55–A63. Retrieved from http://www.funjournal.org/wp-content/uploads/2015/09/ramirez_11_1_a55_a63.pdf

Riehl, C., Larson, C. L., Short, P. M., & Reitzug, U. C. (2000). Reconceptualizing research and scholarship in educational administration: Learning to know, knowing to do, doing to learn. *Educational Administration Quarterly, 36*(3), 391–427. doi:10.1177/00131610021969047

Schichtel, M. (2010). Core-competence skills in e-mentoring for medical educators: A conceptual exploration. *Medical Teacher, 32*(7), e248–e262. doi:10.3109/0142159X.2010.489126

Terrell, S. R., Snyder, M. M., Dringus, L. P., & Maddrey, E. (2012). A grounded theory of connectivity and persistence in a limited residency doctoral program. *The Qualitative Report, 17*(Art. 62), 1–14. Retrieved from http://www.nova.edu/ssss/QR/QR17/terrell.pdf

Tinto, V. (1993). *Leaving college: Rethinking the causes and cures of student attrition* (2nd ed.). Chicago, IL: University of Chicago Press.

Welton, A., Mansfield, C., & Lee, P. (2014). Mentoring matters: An exploratory survey of educational leadership doctoral students' perspectives. *Mentoring &*

Tutoring: Partnership in Learning, 22(5), 481–509. doi:10.1080/13611267.20
14.983330

Women in Higher Education. (2004). How can lifelong mentoring help to develop
leaders? *Women in Higher Education, 13*(12), 1–2.

CHAPTER 6

THE ROLE OF RESEARCH COURSES

Ed Bengtson, Kara Lasater, Maureen M. Murphy-Lee, and Stephanie J. Jones

At the apex of graduate work, the doctorate degree stands as the highest level of education in a given field of study. During a student's journey to completion of the doctorate degree, two prevalent overarching activities related to research are emphasized: developing a knowledge base using existing research and conducting research to reach a defined goal (e.g., answering an unanswered question, more deeply understanding a phenomenon, etc.). As a result, research courses generally are a major part of the student experience. This chapter examines the role that research courses fill in Education Doctorate (EdD) programs in the Carnegie Project on the Education Doctorate (CPED) Phase I institutions. In addition, this chapter explores the emerging philosophy and ideology that perhaps undergirds the emerging purpose of research courses belonging to EdD programs in CPED-affiliated institutions.

There are two types of doctoral degrees in the field of education: the doctor of philosophy (PhD) and the education doctorate (EdD). The EdD is considered to be a "professional doctorate" or "doctor of practice" by

The EdD and the Scholarly Practitioner, pages 79–101
Copyright © 2016 by Information Age Publishing
All rights of reproduction in any form reserved.

many, including CPED. Both are considered terminal degrees involving intense research experiences, and both are recognized by the field of education. Nonetheless, the doctor of philosophy and the professional doctorate have been identified as two distinct categories of degrees serving two contrasting purposes (Malfroy, 2005; Manathunga, Smith, & Bath, 2004; Neumann, 2005). The purpose of the doctor of philosophy is to develop and produce scholars who pursue the generation of new knowledge and/or test existing theories; whereas, the purpose of the professional doctorate is to prepare practitioners to be the top-educated leaders in their professional field. The Council of Graduate Schools (2007) underlined this difference:

> Professional doctoral degrees comprise an important and growing component of higher education. The programs offering these degrees can provide valuable benefits to society by preparing leaders who will transform professional practice, just as the doctor of philosophy degree prepares those who will transform their field of knowledge. (p. iv)

Given this fairly recent acknowledgement that there should be a difference between the professional doctorate and the doctor of philosophy, a history of the EdD reveals that there has not always been a significant difference between the two.

THE HISTORY OF THE EDUCATION DOCTORATE

In 1920, Harvard University created the EdD as a terminal degree for the practicing professional educator. According to Addams (2009), the Association of American Colleges and Universities defines the EdD as a terminal degree that prepares graduates for academic, administrative, or specialized positions in education and favorably places them in areas of promotion and leadership responsibilities or high-level professional positions of the education industry (as cited in Normore & Cook, 2011, p. 105). The EdD is designed for the working educator who hopes to climb the ladder of success in administration and master the skills needed for effective educational leadership; whereas the PhD in education is a more research-oriented degree that fits the traditional social science PhD model (Anderson, 1983; Deering, 1998; Dill & Morrison, 1985; Levine, 2005). At most academic institutions where doctorates in education are offered, the institution chooses to offer either an EdD, a PhD, or both (Osguthorpe & Wong, 1993), and both doctorates are recognized as appropriate preparation for academic positions in education (Murphy & Vriesenga, 2005; Schulman, Golde, Bueschel, & Garabedian, 2006).

Though the theoretical distinction between the doctor of philosophy and education doctorate is clear, the actual differences between the degrees in terms of program design and implementation are nebulous at best. The search for a distinction between the two has been driven by the notion that a specific criteria of knowledge should characterize the purpose of each degree (Costley & Armsby, 2007; Nowotny, Scott, & Gibbons, 2003). For example, in the professional doctorate, knowledge of real-time issues that include the contextual awareness of political and ideological factors that might influence professional practice might be considered most important (i.e., problem-solving skills). While in the research doctorate, knowledge that might lead to discovery or explanation of an existing gap in the understanding of our world might be most suitable (i.e., research skills). However, many people perceive that the EdD has become a watered-down research doctorate (or what is often referred to as a "PhD-lite"). Thus, for nearly a century, the purpose, legitimacy, and value of the EdD has been debated.

The EdD has been further criticized because historically there appears to have been no unified vision underpinning the experiences students are expected to complete when achieving the EdD (Normore & Cook, 2011). There have been reports indicating inconsistent and unclear expectations, uneven student access to important opportunities, poor communication between members of the program, and an inattention to patterns of student progress and outcomes (Carnegie Foundation, 2007; Evans, 2007; Normore, 2004; Shulman et al., 2006; Walker, Golde, Jones, Conklin-Bueschel, & Hutchings, 2009). Critics assert that EdD programs that mirror PhD programs do little to increase the school leader's capacity to positively influence local practice (Murphy & Vriesenga, 2005; Osguthorpe & Wong, 1993). Dadds and Hart (2001) claim that the "mainstream, traditional research approaches do not always suit the needs and available resources of practitioner-researchers" (p. 7). Further, it is believed that knowledge generated from a practical research approach associated with the professional doctorate may be more valuable to society than the knowledge generated through the more traditional research approach of the research doctorate (Usher, 2002). These criticisms have led many scholars to conclude that constructing a doctoral degree specifically designed for the professional education practitioner is necessary (Jean-Marie, Normore, & Brooks, 2009; Murphy & Vriesenga, 2005; Murphy & Zirkel, 2007; Schulman et al., 2006).

As a result, in 2007, CPED was launched to explore, redesign, and promote the EdD as a viable and impactful professional doctorate degree. The complex nature of doctoral work has been evident in the work of CPED as the signature pedagogies, laboratories of practice, and capstone experiences continue to be discussed, debated, and studied. One of the questions at the center of these conversations has been the role of research in the EdD and more specifically, the design of research courses that support inquiry in the professional doctorate.

A Different Type of Inquiry for the EdD

There is a somewhat different view of the role inquiry plays in the learning process required for the development of the scholarly practitioner. The Carnegie Project on the Education Doctorate (2015) identifies this view through the following definition of the design concept Inquiry as Practice:

> Inquiry as Practice is the process of posing significant questions that focus on complex problems of practice. By using various research, theories, and professional wisdom, scholarly practitioners design innovative solutions to address the problems of practice. At the center of Inquiry as Practice is the ability to use data to understand the effects of innovation. As such, Inquiry as Practice requires the ability to gather, organize, judge, aggregate, and analyze situations, literature, and data with a critical lens. (para. 4)

In traditional research pursuits at the doctoral level, the purpose of research is to fill the gaps of existing knowledge or challenge an established premise through investigation and inquiry. These research endeavors may or may not be related to problems that actually exist in the field of practice. On the other hand, the EdD focuses on actual problems of practice found in specific work settings in which the researchers (i.e., students) are immersed. The work setting then becomes what is referred to as a laboratory of practice (CPED, 2015).

The role of existing literature in the research process also shifts between the research and professional doctorates, from knowledge creation in the PhD to solving problems of practice in the EdD (Belzer & Ryan, 2013). In the research doctorate, existing research serves to create a conceptual framework which assists the researcher in finding gaps in the literature, generating further questions to either extend or challenge the existing knowledge around a particular topic, or actualizing a new theory. In the EdD, the existing knowledge serves to inform the problem of practice by providing a framework for identifying, analyzing, and creating solutions.

Defining the EdD Research Curriculum

Research methods courses have historically maintained a prominent and often exclusive position in doctoral curricula and have been well-defined for the PhD as courses that cover both quantitative and qualitative research paradigms. More recently, the development of mixed-methods research has evolved as the complexities of the social sciences have led to the belief that research can be more effective if the contrasting philosophies of positivists and constructivists were combined in meaningful ways to better understand the phenomenon or problem being studied (Creswell, 2015;

Johnson & Onwuegbuzie, 2004; Onwuebuzie, Johnson, & Collins, 2009). According to Onwuegbuzie and Leech (2005), graduate programs should pursue the development of pragmatic researchers who utilize their understanding of both qualitative and quantitative methods to answer identified research questions. Onwuegbuzie and Leech further believe that graduate programs can begin to accomplish this goal through the elimination of research courses that teach exclusively qualitative or quantitative methods.

Action research is one popular approach to research in the field of education that uses both qualitative and quantitative methods of inquiry when appropriate (Johnson, 2008). However, according to Dadds and Hart (2001),

> Much action research and practitioner research continues to draw upon the methods and methodologies of traditional social science research. While this "methodological borrowing" (Winter, 1989) can be appropriate to some degree... it is often not situationally appropriate for the professional contexts in which many practitioner researchers work, or for the kinds of research questions they choose to pursue. (pp. 7–8)

This disparity of beliefs surrounding the research approaches that are most appropriate for the EdD reflects the lack of clarity and shared understanding among those who have embarked on the transformation of the EdD as a professional doctorate. As a result, for many institutions, the realization of appropriate research courses has been one of the most difficult struggles in transforming the EdD (Marsh, Dembo, Gallagher, & Stowe, 2010).

Because of the challenge of transformation, an examination of how higher education institutions that have intentionally sought to transform the EdD into a professional doctorate has potential value. If indeed the EdD is to be different from the PhD, how might this difference be evidenced in the research courses that are delivered, if at all? A study of CPED Phase I institutions was undertaken through support from the US Department of Education Fund for the Improvement of Post Secondary Education (FIPSE) to gain a better understanding of how research courses might need to change to support the EdD as a professional degree.

EXAMINING RESEARCH COURSES IN CPED PHASE I INSTITUTIONS

The purpose of this study was to examine the perspectives of faculty, administrators, and students surrounding the research courses taught in EdD programs associated with the CPED consortium as Phase I institutions. The following research questions were used to frame the study:

- What changes in the content and focus of research courses have occurred as institutions have transformed the EdD?
- What are the perceptions of participants related to challenges in transforming research courses in the EdD?
- What are the perceptions of participants related to the impact of research courses taught in EdD programs?

In examining the perceptions of faculty, students, and program administrators, the goal of this study was to respond to the call made by Hochbein and Perry (2013) for an increased clarity in the role of research in the professional doctorate.

METHODS

Two phases of data collection and analysis were completed to answer the research questions (see Figure 6.1).

In the first phase, an open-ended survey was sent to each CPED Phase I institution. The survey was designed to obtain information directly related to the content and delivery of research courses within CPED Phase I EdD programs. Only six of the twenty-one Phase I CPED institutions responded for a 28.6% survey response rate.

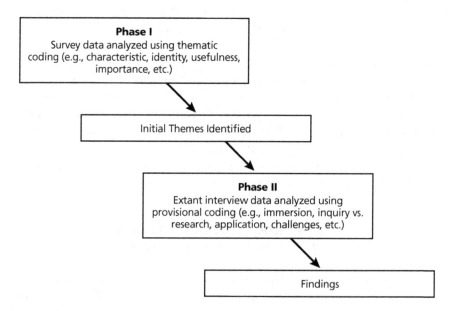

Figure 6.1 The analysis sequence initially using survey data to further analyze the extant interview data.

The data were used to identify emergent themes from the six survey responses. According to Saldaña (2013), "a theme is an extended phrase or sentence that identifies what a unit of data is about and/or what it means" (p. 267). The analytic goals of theming the data were "to develop an overarching theme from the data corpus, or an integrative theme that weaves various themes together into a coherent narrative" (p. 267). General themes from the survey data were identified as follows:

Research courses became more immersed throughout the program of study;

There was attention given to the application of research courses to the world of practice;

Reports of impact were client oriented (related to the student's workplace) as opposed to the research field;

There was a tendency for CPED Phase I institutions to refer to research courses as inquiry courses; however, there was not a clear distinction of the actual difference in course content in all cases; and,

There remained challenges in defining and establishing research courses that were a departure from typical research courses found in PhD-like programs.

The second phase of this study involved the analysis of qualitative data from a previous 2012 study of CPED Phase I institutions. Transcripts from 182 individual and focus group interviews were analyzed using a modification of provisional coding. Provisional coding "begins with a 'start list' of researcher-generated codes based on what preparatory investigation suggests might appear in the data before they are collected and analyzed" (Saldaña, 2013, p. 266). In this study, the provisional codes were developed after data collection but prior to data analysis. The preestablished codes utilized for analysis were the themes identified in the phase-one survey data. Data generated from the 2012 study of CPED institutions were related to overall program changes and not specifically to research courses; thus, the use of provisional coding allowed the researchers to focus analysis on participant responses that directly related to the purpose of this study. Frequency counts were used to determine the prevalence of themes within each subgroup. Finally, thematic analysis was used to construct and summarize the meaning of each theme.

Data Sources

The sources for data were 21 Phase I CPED institutions. These institutions initially joined the CPED consortium in 2007 and represented three private not-for-profit institutions and 18 public institutions. Phase I institutions were targeted because they have had the longest tenure in working with

TABLE 6.1 Participants by Subgroup	
Subgroup	Number of participants
Faculty	122
University/college administrators	31
Students	128

CPED to define and transform the EdD. Two of the Phase I institutions had implemented or were in the process of implementing the CPED principles through collegewide efforts, while the remaining institutions focused on the transformation on specific programs. Subgroups participating as data sources were program faculty, university/college administrators, and EdD students. Table 6.1 illustrates the number of participants within each subgroup.

Limitations

The survey distributed to CPED Phase I institutions yielded only six responses. These six responses were used to generate the themes upon which further data analysis was dependent. This is problematic as only 6 of the 21 CPED Phase I institutions were represented. Because of the limited survey data available, findings from this study relied heavily on data generated from the 2012 CPED study. However, the 2012 study was designed to examine perceptions of the changes in professional doctoral programs specifically related to the CPED principles. The 2012 study was not designed to elicit information directly related to research courses within these programs. Thus, participant responses often reflected perceptions of the doctoral program as a whole and only indirectly addressed the content and delivery of research courses.

Consequently, the use of provisional coding could also be considered a limitation. A risk of provisional coding is "trying to fit qualitative data into a set of codes and categories that may not apply" (Saldaña, 2013, p. 146). This risk was particularly prevalent in the present study because the 2012 CPED data used for analysis was not directly aligned with the purpose of this research. To minimize this risk, the researchers remained flexible and honest in the coding of data, which allowed for further exploration of ambiguities or contradictions in the data. This is consistent with the recommendations of Saldaña (2013) for analysis using provisional coding.

FINDINGS

Using the initial themes identified from the survey data to analyze the larger body of extant data, similar overarching themes were found. These themes included

- Making research more practical: While there were mixed messages from participants, there appears to be some reference to "inquiry" courses rather than "research" courses. This may indicate a desired shift away from the approaches of the traditional research methods courses of the PhD to a more practical approach which uses both qualitative and quantitative methods to emphasize an "action research" or "program evaluation" approach.
- Immersion of research thinking in practice and coursework: Many Phase I CPED institutions have immersed their research content to encapsulate the entire doctoral experience, starting with awareness of research or inquiry as a focus of the degree from the beginning of the program and continuing throughout.
- Many students identified that their experience with their CPED Phase I EdD Program had a positive impact on their practice.
- While there seemed to be more support from faculty for the shifting or re-creation of research courses, there were still some reports of bureaucratic challenges in meeting the requirements of graduate schools' capstone requirements (i.e., five-chapter research dissertation).

Making Research More Practical—Mixed Messages?

There was evidence to suggest that many of the CPED Phase I programs were still approaching research courses through the traditional topics of quantitative and qualitative methods; however, there were also indications that faculty were trying to make these approaches more practical. This was often manifested in the use of terms such as "action research" and "mixed methods" or titles of courses such as "Qualitative Inquiry for Practitioners" or "Applied Quantitative Research Methods."

Additionally, participants appeared to prefer the term *inquiry* rather than *research*, which might indicate a shift away from the approaches of the traditional research methods courses of the PhD. As one faculty member explained, "The theme that embeds everything is inquiry, and I think that's where we're trying to capture this action research emphasis on problems of practice and getting people to become inquirers." This change in terminology stems from the recognition that the professional doctorate's emphasis on practice requires a different use of existing research than the traditional research doctorate's use of existing research to fill knowledge gaps or disprove existing theories. For example, as one faculty member explained, "What I see as a very basic difference is that [in] the research degree, the literature drives the question. In the practice degree, the problem area defined in the local context defines the question." One student further explained the use of existing literature in practice-based research:

In the PhD, you look at all the literature, and you say, "Okay, what's the gap in literature? What do we need to know next?" And that's what you research, and that's what you try to figure out. Whereas in the field, you look at the research, you look at the literature, and you say, "Okay, this is what works. Let's try this, and modify it for our local setting."

When comparing the program from past programs at the same institution, one student gave this account:

So the difference I'm seeing between what we've done and what others before us have done is we've got something that is immediately applicable but still grounded in studies and others' research, and it's just a constant work—research is—we also find that we don't say "research says" anymore. We say "A study by Tom says," and it's a whole different way of looking and appreciating. I think we appreciate theory more than some of the others [students who have gone through the program before].

This account, as well as others, demonstrates the laboratory of practice that draws a distinction between traditional research courses and more applicable inquiry courses. The evidence suggests that, to some degree, the research courses are being embedded in problems that are derived from the workplace, not the literature. While there were not clearly defined laboratories of practice in the data, there were elements that suggested moving the work of applying research into the field of practice.

On the other hand, it is important to recognize that, given the wide range of data from the different institutions, there was some concern from students that the research courses in some programs were still traditional in nature. As one student reflected,

We were given course work that was very specific to statistical analysis and research. There was a stretch there where a few of the statistic courses—we needed a little more experiential learning. We needed less, "Read the text book and then there's the PowerPoint of the thing that we just read, and walk us through it." How about giving us a data set and make us struggle through it a little bit and practice it? . . . I would say the statistics people [referring to professors] were pretty traditional.

Another student commented, "We had more—we had statistics and we had statistics and we had statistics, and now that I'm doing social network analysis, I'm thinking, 'Why—wouldn't that be nice if I could have had a course in social network analysis in lieu of statistics?'" For clarification, social network analysis as defined here is the premise that social life is created primarily through relations and the patterns formed by these relations. A social network therefore is a set of network members that are connected by one or more relations (Marin & Wellman, 2011). In other words, a network analysis examines the context of individuals and their relations with others within a social structure framework. Thus, due to the highly contextual nature of the settings in which the students in the study were enrolled, there were apparent differences in the perceptions of the nature of research courses in relation to the approach taken by faculty and how this approach might be interpreted as being more or less functional to the practitioner.

Interestingly, there were also differences in faculty perceptions regarding the shift of emphasis or content in their research courses. While some faculty referred to "inquiry" courses when asked about research courses, others openly stated that their research courses had not changed. In one case, there was no differentiation between EdD and PhD research courses:

> As we do not distinguish between EdD and PhD research courses, I don't think perceptions have changed too much. The faculty has had more conversations about what students will use research methodologies for and this may affect the examples provided in class.

In contrast, another faculty member from a different institution offered, "We have developed a new inquiry sequence that is styled after the CPED themes and principals—data-based decision making, program evaluation, and action research." It is apparent in the data that CPED Phase I institutions are at different places concerning the development of research courses that might be unique to the professional doctorate.

Immersion of Research Thinking in Practice and Coursework

A distinction made by many participants in the study was when research or inquiry courses took place during the program of study. While it has been observed that there is very little difference in program structure between professional doctorates and PhDs (Deering, 1998), we found that in the professional educational doctorates supported by CPED, there seemed to be some movement away from the traditional programs of study found in most PhDs and PhD-modeled educational doctorates. For example, one student offered, "The staff has been helping me [during] every class to build on the proposal that I want to give to my district." Faculty felt that in their program, "students are beginning to gain in knowledge and skills associated with working within a leadership context—using research, doing research within a leadership context [or] practice-based context."

In other cases, there appeared to be a practice of developing course content as students progressed through the program. As one faculty member explained, "The students can work on a problem, and then it tells you the kinds of things to look for or whether it's research or theories or whatever." Another faculty member explained,

> I like the fact that different ones of us have different strengths and when we come together to develop the syllabi, the syllabi change every time the course is taught. Now at first you might think well gosh there's no stability to the program. No, that's not the case. The basic tenets and our goals, our course goals and student objectives are all pretty much the same, but how we get to the end might be different.

In this sense, the faculty members were suggesting a developmental progression in which the problems examined and students' current understanding of their inquiry dictated course content decisions regarding theory and research.

Combining research-oriented content with course content that addressed leadership concepts and principles was found in the planning stages of one institution. According to one faculty member,

> The plan is right now that on some of the days you won't really be able to tell if you're in research methods or leadership studies because they are going to be using the problems that come from leadership studies and then learn how to use the research methods to study those problems.

When asked about their research course offerings, a faculty member at a different institution explained,

> Inquiry became a big focus, but it was inquiry of practice and how the system was working, being able to look at regularities and understand what those regularities mean and how they're formed; and that became a part of our curricular sequence which we decided to kind of put in the middle of the program of study.

The above account blends the first two themes that emerged in this study with an acknowledged shift in focus to inquiry throughout the program of study. We interpret the immersion of research courses throughout the program of studies to the establishment of a laboratory of practice. In this laboratory of practice, students work in the field on coursework as they simultaneously learn theory and research skills to solve real-world problems of practice.

Impact of Research Courses

The impact of the research courses was varied in terms of the defined end product (e.g., capstone); however, there was more agreement related to the impact of the research courses on students' practice in the field (e.g., client-based). The capstone experience for CPED institutions is referred to as the dissertation in practice and was still in the design process among the 21 Phase I institutions at the time of this study.

While not defining a prescribed format, CPED maintains the goal of a dissertation in practice as being a scholarly work that impacts professional practice. There was evidence that the goal of enhancing practice was achieved as respondents in this study identified research courses leading to capstones that were at times "client-based" which "get very positive feedback that the discoveries and recommendations are extremely helpful. Students indicate that they learn a lot through the process." At the same time, while there were data that suggested research courses had changed in some instances to align with CPED, some faculty really had not been able to change the capstone from the traditional five-chapter research dissertation. This has been a point of contention for some Phase I institutions as described by one respondent: "Action research is not a good fit for the five-chapter [dissertation] and we continue to grapple with redesign and development of a capstone project. The five-chapter product remains an expectation of the college. This remains a hard sell." Tradition often trumps innovation from an institutional view. In addition, student expectations may demand a more traditional dissertation if a different format is perceived to be less rigorous or prestigious.

Discrepancy regarding the impact of research courses on capstone products or capstone experiences might be related to the fact that in the traditional research doctorate, or PhD, the research courses are designed toward a well-defined capstone—the five-chapter dissertation.

In research doctoral programs, quantitative and qualitative methods courses are designed to prepare students to conduct a study and write about it in such an academic fashion that they reflect preparedness to "do research" at the highest level. The capstone (five-chapter research dissertation) then becomes the "calling card" for the graduate as they pursue a job in academia. Until the EdD can define its "calling card," it stands to reason that there are discrepancies between Phase I institutions regarding the impact of EdD research courses on the capstone.

In contrast, there seems to be more consistency among Phase I institutions when reporting the impact of EdD research courses on practice, or at least the impact of the CPED EdD in general. For example, one faculty member reported,

> The work done in program evaluation has been received exceptionally well given the tight connection between the process and practice. Our first class graduated in May, and for many [of the graduates] the work they did has been recognized in their divisions and a few are looking toward publishing.

Although not necessarily empirical in nature, this statement boldly reflects a foundational goal of CPED—the positive impact on the field of practice. Another Phase I institution offered, "Informal feedback suggests that some of our students look at problem-solving and innovation implementation/ evaluation differently than they did before." Another CPED program made a similar repor: "We regularly hear our students say that they are able to successfully write grants, develop small evaluation projects to support innovations in their work, and write reports based on empirical data as a result of their training."

Students reported that the ability to apply what they learned in their coursework allowed them to be more productive and have greater impact in their work settings. One central office leader stated,

> So we began to apply those things along the way, think differently about the work, but in the end with two years into the program when we had to determine our capstone, we really wanted to study the most aggressive thing we were doing in turnaround and it really helped us. It motivated us to not only do the work, but see the theory behind it. It, for me, has changed what happens in our principals' meetings.

Overlapping with the second identified theme of immersion of research thinking into practice, there were many student accounts of the job-embedded nature of the coursework and how that had a significant impact on their practice. For example, one student reflected,

> Every time we were asked to do something, practice any kind of statistics, we were using our own data as opposed to we worked through the book and used the database that the book provides and those kind of questions. I feel like there's been a bigger effort, a more concerted effort, to infuse our work and the collaboration between [public school system] in general and [the university], and infuse the resource that we have in our own backyard into what we do in the K–12 system.

In addition, there were accounts of how individuals felt their personal leadership was enhanced through their experience with the research courses:

> It fundamentally changed me as a leader in that I viewed leadership through a different lens when I was done with this program. Of course, my study lent itself to that going through a study on developing and stretching leadership within the school. As far as the research aspect, again I will just say that I view research through a different lens now than I did say two or three years ago. . . . it helped me and it helped my staff because my staff now views research in a different lens, and my staff views leadership in a different lens and our students will benefit from that. I really believe that.

Caution must be used with such data as represented above as these statements are anecdotal in nature and at best illuminate the perspectives of the participants. Nonetheless, the various student narratives, in general, give a positive account of how their experience in the CPED EdD program impacted their practice as educational leaders and their respective organizations.

Existing Challenges

Moving from traditional research courses found in research doctoral programs to a new type of research course for the professional doctorate, there were reported challenges that remained for the CPED Phase I institutions. As with the previous two findings, there were differences in accounts among the faculty of CPED Phase I institutions. This is interpreted as a contextual issue that largely depended on the environment of each Phase I member institution. The challenges seemed to fall into three broad categories: (a) bureaucratic barriers, (b) faculty and student buy-in, and (c) developing faculty to handle the new research course design (see Figure 6.2).

Bureaucracy was evident in the accounts that spoke to scheduling of research courses and gaining the flexibility required from graduate schools. As one faculty member alluded, "The bureaucracy of the university (e.g., silos protecting turf) has been the biggest challenge to effective delivery and scheduling, particularly the research blocks." As an example of protecting turf and speaking more broadly to the changes in the EdD program, one university administrator commented, "Initially we had some resistance to coming back with an EdD program because senior faculty felt that it would impact our PhD numbers." As CPED institutions continue to transform their research course offerings, it is possible that those teaching traditional

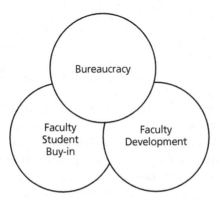

Figure 6.2 Overlapping challenges to creating and implementing nontraditional research courses in the EdD as reported by CPED Phase I institutions.

research courses will feel threatened either by the creation of different courses that will diminish the enrollment numbers in the traditional courses or faculty requirements to learn new approaches to research. This phenomenon also speaks to the lack of faculty buy-in.

Survey data reported a perceived improvement in faculty and student buy-in compared to the transcript data analyzed from the previous study; however, faculty and student buy-in was still an issue for some CPED Phase I institutions. For example, one respondent described the challenge as

> the tension between helping faculty and students understand why the courses should be designed this way. There are faculty and students on both ends of the spectrum in terms of wanting more "traditional" and in terms of questioning why they need this much on research methods at all.

The lack of buy-in was also related to some faculty wanting the "EdD research courses to be more rigorous." Nonetheless, there was evidence that for some CPED Phase I institutions, there were "Minimal challenges [as] the faculty has [sic] been very positive and encouraging of this adventure." Another respondent reported, "The faculty has [sic] embraced them [research courses] and they are now elective options within the PhD programs."

Related to faculty buy-in and the tension mentioned above is the third category of faculty development. Even when there is an endorsement from faculty for "different" approaches to research courses for the EdD, some CPED Phase I institutions found the ability of faculty to actually facilitate the new courses to be a challenge. As one respondent indicated, "There is a need to be more intentional with delivering instruction on research methods and design and appropriate statistical analyses." This call for intentionality may suggest that faculty are not sure how to go about teaching courses that are different from traditional research courses which address quantitative and qualitative approaches. Perhaps this stems from the fact that many faculty were taught and learned to use the traditional approaches; therefore, they are much more comfortable in teaching these approaches.

Overcoming tradition in the sense of what faculty, themselves, have experienced as well as tradition in the sense of the purpose of the doctorate seems to remain a challenge in some programs. For example, one report indicated, "The main challenges continue to be working through faculty hesitation when introducing changes, helping some faculty understand the differences in preparing educational leaders versus preparing research faculty." In addition, as one principal investigator observed, "If faculty are not well versed in a particular method, it is problematic."

SIGNIFICANCE

The results of this study are significant for three major reasons. First, CPED Phase I institutions are, for the most part, offering different descriptions of the research courses delivered in their respective programs. Second, there seems to be a change in the role and rationale for research courses in the EdD—breaking away from the tradition of the PhD. Finally, there is a relationship between the findings of impact, immersion, and practicality, and that symbiosis aligns with the laboratory of practice concept promoted by CPED.

Different Ideas Surrounding Research

Many of the respondents claimed to be conceptualizing research courses based on what is involved in the examination and resolutions of problems of practice. This suggests that many institutions who have been working at redesigning the EdD have come to the realization that the type of research that practitioners should understand and conduct is different than the research that researchers know and conduct; however, unlike the traditional PhD research doctorate, the EdD does not have a uniform understanding of what research courses should look like. This is not a criticism of the CPED initiative, but more of an observation that much of the ongoing process of CPED is developing an understanding of the work entailed in the creation and sustainment of a true professional doctorate in the field of education. Furthermore, there could be an argument made that supports diversity in the types of programs of study offered by EdD programs.

To some extent, the challenge of defining what research courses should look like in the EdD is driven by the contextual nature of a particular program and the constituents that it serves. For example, one program might have considerably more or less faculty positions, which might relate to whether research courses are actually taught by program faculty or by faculty in other programs that might offer traditional PhD research method courses. As mentioned in the findings section, one of the challenges is to develop program faculty who are capable of designing and teaching research courses that meet the niche of the EdD as a professional doctorate.

The context of the broader community might influence programs of study and the nature of research courses offered in a particular program. While some programs might be embedded in societies where there is much sociological work to be done to gain a better understanding of the communities that are being led by EdD candidates, there might be other contexts that present a need for program evaluations of existing programs in a particular educational setting. These examples illuminate the question of whether EdD programs should have the same universality that PhD programs seem to have in terms of their approach to research courses and the research process.

Changing Purpose of Research Courses

The second point of significance is that, in the institutions surveyed, there appears to be emphasis placed on research courses that assist in developing professional practitioners versus the production of a capstone project. CPED Phase I institutions seem to focus on research courses that promote the professional skills necessary for their students to solve problems of practice in their workplace. To a great extent, this indicates a shift from the measure of success being the production of a capstone to the production of an impactful professional practitioner. The only mention of capstone projects in the survey data was the challenge of convincing graduate schools of the necessity to have an end product that might be something different than a five-chapter dissertation.

While the value of the capstone project in the EdD has been critically examined (Murphy, 2014), most of the CPED Phase I institutions agree that a capstone is necessary; however, it needs to look and function differently from a PhD capstone. While the traditional research dissertation has been seen as a significant rite of passage into the elite population of doctorate degree holders, the capstone in the EdD symbolizes the maturation or development of the elite practitioner who is ready to make a positive impact on the field of practice (Belzer & Ryan, 2013).

Unlike the ambiguous definition of the research course mentioned as the first significant point of the findings, the purpose of the research courses has been clearly defined by CPED as inquiry as practice. Indeed, what most CPED Phase I institutions seem to agree on is that the research courses they offer are aimed at problems of practice. Therefore, this could be interpreted to mean that there is some universality in the concept of purpose and that would be to pursue the idea of inquiry as practice as defined by CPED; however, beyond this general regularity there seems to be a lack of a common research course design that has been identified among CPED institutions. Again, this could be the result of the contextual nature of how different institutions decide to apply research knowledge to the concept of inquiry as practice.

Impact, Practicality, Immersion, and the Laboratory of Practice

Professional doctorates hold in common the idea that improving or transforming professional practice is a main goal that is pursued through the experiences given to students who are engaged in one of the various types of professional doctorate (Council of Graduate Schools, 2007). The EdD shares this goal; however, it is unique among the professional doctorates. Students who pursue an EdD are most likely already practitioners in the field of education. Many, if not most, EdD students are involved as a professional on some level, and generally are working full-time as a professional educator. Students in other professional doctorate programs (e.g., MD, DNP, JD, etc.) most often pursue those degrees as full-time students and then become a practicing professional.

While there might be concern over the lack of ability for EdD students to commit all of their time to their doctoral studies, this nonpareil characteristic of full-time professionals working on degrees while pursuing their career does allow for both EdD faculty and students to see the workplace as the laboratory of practice where students work deeply with a problem that exists within their own organization or in the field of practice. In this sense, it can be argued that, indeed, students who are busy working in their professional positions on legitimate problems of practice while learning (through coursework) how to identify, define, present, and solve real problems are actually full-time students.

The first three findings—making research more practical, immersion of research courses, and impact of research courses—are related to each other, and each can be linked reciprocally to the concept of laboratories of practice (see Figure 6.3).

Making Research More Practical

Many of the student narratives from the CPED Phase I institutions indicated that there was a connection between the coursework they experienced and their actual practice in the field. For example, using actual data from their home school district to investigate a problem and learning how to use

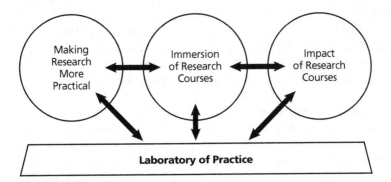

Figure 6.3 The relationship between the first three findings and the concept of laboratories of practice.

various research approaches to deepen their understanding of the problem. Making research more practical does not imply making coursework less rigorous. As Hochbein and Perry (2013) suggest, working on problems that educational leaders face is often much more complex than working through isolated problems designed to help students understand how to "do" research. How students visualize real problems of practice through a researcher's lens is perhaps the most significant step toward making research courses more practical to the field of practice and to those who aspire to lead organizational improvement through scholarly and critical examination of the real-world problems that they face as leaders in their profession.

Allowing for the examination of authentic problems of practice through research courses underscores the importance of the establishment of a laboratory of practice. It is the connection between the coursework and the laboratory that assists in eradicating the perception that programs of study in the EdD are often disconnected from the real world of practice—a complaint that is often expressed by many students experiencing various levels of preparation for professional practice in the field of education.

Immersion of Research Courses

Related to the finding of making research more practical to the field of practice is the concept of immersing the coursework directly into the context (or as close as possible) where the practitioner-scholar is working. Requiring students to directly apply the course content to their workplace reinforces the concept of a living laboratory of practice that serves as an environment that ties theory to practice in a meaningful way for the student. Furthermore, faculty must be willing to stretch and bend course content to accommodate the highly contextual nature of problems of practice.

Embedding research course content into laboratories of practice allows for the realization of how research can inform practice. The content of coursework intertwined with a real problem of practice can assist in the development of scholarly problem-solving skills that leaders in the education profession need to be successful. This intentional and deliberate building of problem-solving skills through inquiry could result in having more of an impact on the performance of the individual as an educational leader than perhaps more traditional, stand-alone research courses.

Impact of Research Courses

The impact of research courses in the EdD is elusive at best; however, there is a relationship between the ability to determine impact and establishing a live and vibrant laboratory of practice. If the practitioner-scholar is successful in identifying, presenting, and solving/informing their problem of practice through systematic inquiry that is ongoing throughout the coursework, then impact might be considered at least to some degree. Students in the study discussed in this chapter implied that the research courses, when focused on their own problem of practice, were highly effective as they developed a better understanding of their context and led them to viable solutions. Students who experienced more traditional forms of research methods courses questioned the significance or effectiveness of their experiences with their programs of study. As this study suggests, perhaps there is a strong relationship between the quality of the laboratory of practice, the nature of the research courses, and the impact of those courses.

CONCLUSION

While understanding and acknowledging the diverse contexts of higher education institutions, one unique characteristic of research courses that might be considered for CPED institutions is the link between research courses (whatever they might be) and a laboratory which is in a real professional context that has real professional problems of practice. Because of the nature of the professional doctorate, skills used in traditional research methods may not be enough for students to successfully impact their practice. Therefore, we suggest that CPED pursues a framework of understanding that will guide EdD programs in the development of research courses that address the unique skills and abilities to conduct meaningful and impactful inquiry in the laboratories of practice (e.g., action research, etc.). In this sense, research courses would be required to have a degree of flexibility to address the different needs of each singular problem of practice; however, the research approach to identifying, defining, and presenting the problem might be consistent as a suggested signature pedagogy of all EdD programs in CPED institutions. This might include attending to distinct issues surrounding ethics of researching in the workplace, managing the fluidity of the research process, and navigating the political context.

The CPED Phase I institutions, while in widely different contexts, offer some insight to how research courses might be evolving as interest in making the EdD a true professional doctorate continues to be generated. The polemic of making the EdD a unique professional doctorate degree that serves the purpose of transforming practice and serving the practitioner needs for scholarship continues to gain momentum as CPED continues to delve into the process of dissecting and examining the EdD. It is necessary for CPED institutions to go beyond the philosophic underpinnings of the CPED initiative and move into a more direct examination of the actual ingredients of the EdD. It is here that attention must be paid to the components (and the application of these components) of research courses and how each support the CPED principles and promote the transformation of the scholar-practitioner as a dynamic and impactful educational leader.

REFERENCES

Anderson, D. G. (1983). Differentiation of the EdD and PhD in education. *Journal of Teacher Education, 34*(3), 55–58.

Belzer, A., & Ryan, S. (2013). Defining the problem of practice dissertation: Where's the practice, what's the problem? *Planning and Changing, 44*(3/4), 195–207.

Carnegie Foundation for the Advancement of Teaching. (2007). Collections. *Gallery of Teaching & Learning.* Retrieved from www.gallery.carnegiefoundation.org/gallery_of_tl/collections.html

Carnegie Project on the Education Doctorate (CPED). (2015). *Design concept definitions.* Retrieved from http://cpedinitiative.org/design-concept-definitions

Costley, C., & Armsby, P. (2007). Research influences on a professional doctorate. *Research in Post-Compulsory Education, 12*(3), 343–355.

Council of Graduate Schools. (2007). *Task force report on the professional doctorate.* Washington, DC: Author.

Creswell, J. W. (2015). *A concise introduction to mixed methods research.* Thousand Oaks, CA: Sage.

Dadds, M., & Hart, S. (2001). *Doing practitioner research differently.* London, England: RoutledgeFalmer.

Deering, T. E. (1998). Eliminating the doctor of education degree: It's the right thing to do. *Educational Forum, 62*(3), 243–248.

Dill, D. D., & Morrison, J. L. (1985). EdD and PhD research training in the field of higher education: A survey and a proposal. *Review of Higher Education, 8*(2), 169–186.

Evans, R. (2007). Existing practice is not the template. *Educational Researcher, 36*(9), 553–559.

Hochbein, C., & Perry, J. A. (2013). The role of research in the professional doctorate. *Planning and Changing, 44*(3/4), 181–194.

Jean-Marie, G., Normore, A. H., & Brooks, J. (2009). Leadership for social justice: Preparing 21st century school leaders for a new social order. *Journal of Research on Leadership Education, 4*(1), 1–31.

Johnson, A. P. (2008). *A short guide to action research* (3rd ed.). Boston. MA: Allyn & Bacon.

Johnson, R. B., & Onwuegbuzie, A. J. (2004). Mixed-methods research: A research paradigm whose time has come. *Educational Researcher, 33*(7), 14–26.

Levine, A. (2005). *Educating school leaders.* New York, NY: Education Schools Project.

Malfroy, J. (2005). Doctoral supervision, workplace research and changing pedagogic practices. *Higher Education Research and Development, 24*(2), 165–178.

Manathunga, C., Smith, C., & Bath, D. (2004). Developing and evaluating authentic integration between research and coursework in professional doctorate programs. *Teaching in Higher Education, 9*(2), 235–246.

Marin, A., & Wellman, B. (2011). Social network analysis: An introduction. In J. Scott & P. J. Carrington (Eds.), *The SAGE handbook of social network analysis* (pp. 11–25). London, England: Sage.

Marsh, D. D., Dembo, M. H., Gallagher, K. S., & Stowe, H. (2010). Examining the capstone experience in a cutting-edge EdD program. In G. Jean-Marie & A. H. Normore (Eds.), *Educational leadership preparation: Innovation and interdisciplinary approaches to the EdD and graduate education* (pp. 203–235). New York, NY: Palgrave MacMillan.

Murphy, J. (2014, June). *Productive professional doctorate programs.* Keynote address presented at the June 2014 Carnegie Project on the Education Doctorate Convening, Denver, CO.

Murphy, J., & Vriesenga, M. (2005). Developing professionally anchored dissertations: Lessons from innovative programs. *School Leadership Review, 1*(1), 33–57.

Murphy, J., & Zirkel, P. (2007). Questioning the core of university-based programs for preparing school leaders. *Phi delta Kappan, 88*(8), 582–585.

Neumann, R. (2005). Doctoral differences: Professional doctorates and PhDs compared. *Journal of Higher Education Policy and Management, 27*(2), 173–188.

Normore, A. H. (2004). Socializing school administrators to meet leadership challenges that doom all but the most heroic and talented leaders to failure. *International Journal of Leadership in Education, Theory and Practice, 7*(2), 107–125.

Normore, A. H., & Cook, L. H. (2011). The new "proposed" doctoral degree in educational leadership (Ed. D.) at a comprehensive university in southern California. In D. M. Callejo Pérez, S. M. Fain, & J. J. Slater (Eds.), *Higher education and human capital* (pp. 103–127). Rotterdam, The Netherlands: Sense.

Nowotny, H., Scott, P., & Gibbons, M. (2003). Introduction: 'Mode 2' revisited: The new production of knowledge. *Minerva, 41*(3), 179–194.

Osguthorpe, R. T., & Wong, M. J. (1993). The PhD versus the EdD: Time for a decision. *Innovative Higher Education, 18*(1), 47–63.

Onwuegbuzie, A. J., Johnson, R. B., & Collins, K. M. (2009). Call for mixed analysis: A philosophical framework for combining qualitative and quantitative approaches. *International Journal of Multiple Research Approaches, 3*(2), 114–139.

Onwuegbuzie, A. J., & Leech, N. L. (2005). Taking the "Q" out of research: Teaching research methodology courses without the divide between quantitative and qualitative paradigms. *Quality & Quantity, 39*(3), 267–296.

Saldaña, J. (2013). *The coding manual for qualitative researchers* (2nd ed.). Thousand Oaks, CA: Sage.

Shulman, L. S., Golde, C. M., Bueschel, A. C., & Garabedian, K. J. (2006). Reclaiming education's doctorates: A critique and a proposal. *Educational Researcher, 35*(3), 25–32.

Usher, R. (2002). A diversity of doctorates: Fitness for the knowledge economy? *Higher Education Research and Development, 21*(2), 143–153.

Walker, G. M., Golde, C. M., Jones, L., Conklin-Bueschel, A., & Hutchings, P. (2009). *The formation of scholars: Rethinking doctoral education for the twenty-first century* (Vol. 11). San Francisco, CA: Jossey-Bass.

SECTION II

HIGHLIGHTS FROM CPED-INFLUENCED EdD PROGRAMS

CHAPTER 7

THE PRACTITIONER-SCHOLAR DOCTORATE

Not a PhD Lite

Jim Allen, Michael Chirichello, and Mark Wasicsko

Hyphen: A punctuation mark that joins two ordinarily separate words to derive a new meaning that is a compound of the two.

In this chapter, the authors reason that the practitioner-scholar doctorate in leadership is a degree that differs radically from the PhD/EdD traditions of the past. It is distinctive because it integrates three equally important elements that, the authors contend, are the essential ingredients for effective practitioner-scholar leaders: knowledge of theory and research, application of best practices and skills, and the dispositions to lead, or human elements that inspire and magnify the first two.

Defining, let alone bringing into existence, a terminal "degree of practice" is a herculean task made even more difficult because it has to be conceived in an environment dominated by century-old, PhD-type thinking. However, for over a decade, conversations among an expanding number of higher education institutions in the United States and Europe have begun under the umbrellas of the Carnegie Project for the Education Doctorate (2015) and the UK Council for Graduate Education (2015), with the intent

The EdD and the Scholarly Practitioner, pages 105–130
Copyright © 2016 by Information Age Publishing
All rights of reproduction in any form reserved.

of creating a framework for such a degree. Agreement regarding every-thing from the theoretical and philosophical basis for a practitioner-scholar degree to the elements and requirements that make up such a degree is fraught with near-intractable hindrances. These issues stem from both sides of the hyphen—practitioners and scholars—with long histories and emo-tional contexts making it even more complicated. Examples include the conflicts that have come from "town-gown" relations to the old arguments about "ivory towers" verses the "real world" learning and application. From the practitioner viewpoint, purely academic degrees may be held suspect as being just "academic" having little utility in the daily lived experiences of leaders. One does not need an extensive literature review to learn that many people succeed in careers without college degrees (e.g., Steve Jobs, Bill Gates, Mark Zuckerberg, etc.) or, on the flipside, that a college degree necessarily brings with it a higher level of accomplishment or increased ethical practice. "Doers," practitioners might say, don't have time to argue if a cited volume in a reference should be italicized to meet APA guidelines. Those who can, they argue, do, and those who cannot, teach (like many in higher education).

On the scholar side of the hyphen, many pedigreed academicians see such a practitioner-scholar degree as reeking of "trade-schoolism," which is compounded further by of the choice of nomenclature for the degree—the Education Doctorate, or EdD. In many institutions over the past decades, the EdD encompassed most, if not all, of the same components of a PhD program (in the case of the authors, the differences between the degrees were language proficiency and an additional statistics course or two). Now, it is feared (and with some justification) that this new type of degree, the practitioner-scholar EdD will devalue the more research intensive PhD look-alike EdD degrees of the past.

THE NEW EDD DEGREE—THE PROFESSIONAL PRACTICE DOCTORATE

Envisioning what a practitioner-scholar degree should look like is a chal-lenging task that must start with agreement on the underlying philosophi-cal tenets. We believe that a terminal, practitioner-scholar degree is con-structed of three equally important and proportionally weighted foci: (a) knowledge of theory and research, (b) application of best practices or skills, and (c) the dispositions to lead—the human elements that inspire and magnify the first two. What would the degree look like? What might be the signature pedagogies? And, probably most importantly, would it have appeal and utility in creating a new breed of scholarly informed and more effective practitioners?

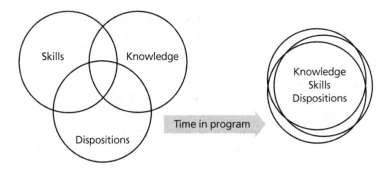

Figure 7.1 Conceptual framework: Perceptual dispositions model—Effective leader as effective person.

Candidates bring to their doctoral study plentiful background knowledge (the scholarly literature), skills (best practices informed by research and experience), and dispositions (the human factors associated with good leadership). Figure 7.1 illustrates the conceptual framework used in the *Perceptual Dispositions Model—Effective Leader as Effective Person* (Wasicsko, 2007). From this perspective, the primary goal of a leader preparation program is to facilitate the growth and amalgamation of candidates' dispositions, knowledge, and skills, thus increasing the area of overlap. Or, said more simply, the goal is to develop a more effective and integrated person who can use her or himself as an instrument to foster positive change in people and organizations. The leaders engaged in such a program would expand their knowledge, skills, and dispositions (larger circles) and exhibit increased integration (indicating a more thorough amalgamation) as she/ he moves toward completion of the program. Note that this conceptualization keeps the three components (knowledge, skills, and dispositions) somewhat distinct thus allowing for the use of preexisting components for knowledge and skills but still recognizing that the "effective leader" is an amalgamation of all three. We propose that the ultimate outcome of the practitioner-scholar degree is to foster this union and by doing so increase the potential for transformational leadership to occur.

The Practitioner Doctorate: What Does It Look Like?

Universities throughout the United States are intentionally collaborating through the Carnegie Project on the Education Doctorate (CPED) to "refashion the EdD and transform it into a degree that truly serves professional practitioners" (Perry, 2012, p. 41). In 2009, CPED published its definition of the EdD: "The professional doctorate in education prepares educators for the application of appropriate and specific practices, the generation of new knowledge, and for the stewardship of the profession" (Perry, 2012, p. 43). Presented elsewhere in this edition are the working principles and design concepts developed through CPED collaboration that provide a framework for developing programs that support this definition of the EdD. Northern Kentucky University is a proud member of the Carnegie Project for the Education Doctorate (CPED) and has embraced this framework.

With the intent of creating a practitioner-scholar degree, the faculty in educational leadership at Northern Kentucky University (NKU) initiated in 2008 an innovative EdD as a practitioner-scholar degree for experienced educational leaders and, in 2011, expanded the program to include an executive doctoral cohort specifically for practicing school superintendents in the Commonwealth of Kentucky. The initial NKU Doctor of Education (EdD) in Educational Leadership Program, now entering its 8th year and 11th cohort, aims to enhance leadership skills for instructional and administrative leaders in P–16 settings and other human services areas. As of this date, two cohorts of Kentucky superintendents have completed the NKU executive model of the EdD program. In both programs, graduates meet a set of "best practice" competencies/outcomes integrated with individual career and personal goals for leaders with 5 or more years of successful professional leadership experience. The practices described herein will include design examples from these practitioner-scholar programs.

Eight Signature Practices

Eight signature practices are the cornerstone of the EdD program at Northern Kentucky University that, to a significant degree, align with CPED thinking and could be applied to any practitioner-scholar doctorate. The practices include: (a) designating EdD candidates "learning associates," not students; (b) creating leader-scholar communities; (c) developing leadership dispositions; (d) operationalizing a competency-based curriculum; (e) engaging in international experiences; (f) implementing action research; (g) pursuing regional stewardship; and (h) the capstone outcome, the dissertation in practice. In the remainder of this chapter, we will discuss these eight signature practices and detail how they are applied within the executive-model EdD program for superintendents at Northern Kentucky University.

Learning Associates, Not Students

In the NKU program teaching and learning is, by intention and design, a bidirectional process. Our model asserts several innovative design features, including the democratic context in which the superintendent participants and program faculty become learning associates—mutually teaching and learning together (Olson & Clark, 2009). Historically, teaching has been viewed as a unidirectional activity in which the teacher, who possesses the knowledge, imparts it to the mostly passive students. While most higher educators believe this to be an archaic conception of teaching, one would not need to venture too far down the college hallways to see it to be alive and well today. In more recent years, the spotlight has moved away from teaching and has been focused on learning, essentially questioning the impact or outcomes of teaching on the students. The next evolution, we believe, is to recognize that leaders and future leaders enrolled in practitioner-scholar doctorates bring with them a wealth of practical knowledge and experience that can, when intentionally integrated, bring increased fidelity to the learning experiences of students and teachers alike. This begat the concept of a "community of scholars" in which all participants in our program—professors and students—are both teachers and learners. Hence, the nomenclature of "learning associates" for all participants in the learning endeavor.

Learning associates (LAs)—superintendents and program faculty—co-develop content and delivery for each session. In this sense, the superintendents and faculty are both leaders and learners who contributed to the learning outcomes of the cohort. These LAs have access to the content on Wikispaces, the online platform use for setting our session agendas, activities, and outcomes. All LAs are responsible for adding content, discussion board conversations, and resources to the agenda for each learning session. The superintendent learning associates frequently work in smaller teams to plan for and facilitate topical discussions during many sessions. Though the faculty members maintain responsibility for most measures of accountability, including competency assessments and assigning grades, student learning associates contribute. The use of learning associates results in the traditional roles of faculty as teachers and students as learners being replaced by a model where everyone mutually teaches, learns, and assesses.

Leader-Scholar Community

The Leader-Scholar Community (LSC) concept was developed at Arizona State University (ASU) (Olson & Clark, 2009). The LSC process assumes that both faculty and learning associates possess expertise and are shareholders in the learning process. At ASU, LSCs are composed of five to seven students, two faculty members, and a qualified topical expert external to the university. This unique approach views students *and* faculty as experts: "Faculty members are experts at applied research, writing, and scholarly literature, and the students are experts and responsible leaders in the particular practices and context in which they conduct research and effect change" (Olson & Clark, 2009, p. 217). The NKU model employs a similar design.

In the NKU model, two faculty members and the superintendents (six in one cohort and eight in another) worked as an LSC. In this model, both the learning associates and the faculty are experts and share in the learning process. All attended each session throughout the program as they supported, guided, and collaborated on all program outcomes. These meetings strengthen and build a learning community and give opportunities to discuss the ongoing dissertation process and its challenges. Learning associates receive feedback on their writing and help each other to stay current in knowledge and outside learning opportunities. Faculty may also meet individually with the learning associates throughout this process. The LSC became the foundation for the committee where the two faculty members with the addition of an external faculty member served as the committee for the superintendents' collaborative dissertation in practice.

As a result of employing the LSC, we believe that it is a program component that (a) provides our learning associates with support and guidance, and strengthens the collaboration of each cohort; (b) results in a consistent community of peers and faculty with whom our learning associates will lead and learn; (c) promotes the concept of critical friends that results in a mutually supportive collaborative; and (d) results in a higher completion rate (Olson & Clark, 2009). Additionally, the LSC "socializes educational leaders to examine their practice thoughtfully and systematically together in a research community focused on making a difference in schools" (Olson & Clark, 2009, p. 220). The accomplishments of our superintendent EdD cohorts support this assumption. These included early childhood initiatives, transforming a human relations department around the concept of dispositions for hiring and staffing, innovative school programs, redesigning professional learning for the life cycle of the career teacher, a multidistrict retreat for school administrators, and new community partnerships, to name a few. It was clear from the work they did that, as a leader scholar community, their outcomes were stronger than would have been the case with individual efforts.

Focus on the Effective Leader as Effective Person

In most programs that prepare leaders, the major programmatic focus is on content rather than on enhancing the personhood of the leaders; that is, growing their dispositions, providing authentic feedback, and implementing personal leadership growth plans. Without the intentional inclusion of discussions, activities, and reflections on matters of dispositions, a key element to leader effectiveness is missed (Allen, Wasicsko, & Chirichello, 2014). Too often leadership programs shy away from dealing with such issues because of their potential social, political, and/or moral connotations, the perceived nebulous nature of their definition and measurement, or they are assumed to be too personal and individual and therefore inappropriate for inclusion. To the contrary, a significant focus of the NKU program is selecting for and developing the learning associates' dispositions— the human elements that impact peoples and organizations' ability to grow and change. Our program's mantra—the person you are determines the leader you become—is reinforced throughout the program starting with the admissions process and including both a 360° Individual Leadership Self-Assessment (ILSA) (see Appendix A) and a growth plan. The ILSA is designed to provide authentic "critical friends" feedback to our learning associates, while the Leadership/Dispositional Growth Plan (LDGP) (see Appendix B) provides a mechanism for using the insights gained from the ILSA to enhance learning associates' leader dispositions. Since the development of dispositions is one of the most unique elements of the NKU program, the authors have taken liberties to supply more detailed information than on the other seven practices.

The Perceptual Dispositions Model, the framework used for dispositions, relies on the theory and research pioneered by Arthur W. Combs (Combs, 1974), psychologist/educator (1935–1999). Combs spent his professional career investigating the dispositions of effective "helping" professionals, people who were able to significantly and positively affect others' lives (Richards, 2010). The Perceptual Dispositions Model

> drills down into the essence of the person to the attitudes, values, beliefs, or perceptions level of the personality. This allows for a more manageable number of variables to define and measure, and more predictive value, but with the trade-off of requiring the use of more qualitative assessment measures. (Wasicsko, Wirtz, & Resor, 2009, p. 20)

As a result of the research by Combs and colleagues (Combs & Snygg, 1949; Combs et al., 1969), Wasicsko (2007) categorized dispositions into four general areas that differentiate effective from ineffective leaders:

(1) *Perception of Self*, as the name implies, focuses on the personhood of the leader. Leaders who have positive perceptions of self are confident without being overbearing, identify more readily with others, they can see diverse points of view, and they display a positive attitude toward life and work. Because of a positive sense of self, they tend to be more self-trusting and thus, less threatened by others. They have less difficulty accepting constructive criticism and can provide others with feedback that is more likely to be nonthreatening and thus heard.

(2) Leaders who have positive *Perception of Others* see people with whom they work as having the capacity to face up to challenges and be successful when given the opportunity, resources, and support. They demonstrate a belief in others' ability to find adequate solutions to events in their own lives; display a general belief that all people are valuable, able, and worthy of respect; share responsibilities with others; and share or give away credit for accomplishments.

(3) Leaders who have high *Perception of Purpose* have goals that extend beyond the immediate to broad implications and contexts. They tend to

see the big picture and yet have an uncanny ability to be present in the moment. They are committed to life-long learning and mentoring; treat everyone equitably and fairly; avoid being sidetracked by trivia or petty issues; and see work in the larger context of life. They realize that what they do as leaders is more than a mere job but less than a life.

(4) Finally, leaders who are people oriented have a *Frame of Reference* that recognizes that people, with all their human strengths and frailties, are the valuable human resources through which goals get met rather than cogs in a complex mechanical machine. They understand that, while order, management, mechanics, and details of things and events are necessary, long-term success must be concerned with the human aspects of affairs— the attitudes, feelings, beliefs, and welfare of persons. They understand the importance of maintaining positive relationships with colleagues, and they focus on the human dimensions rather than (or at least in addition to) the "things" associated with the work.

These dispositions are integrated into key program elements in the NKU program: (a) the candidate admissions process, (b) a 360° evaluation using the Individual Leadership Self-Assessment Instrument (ILSA) (Appendix A) and (c) a Leadership/Dispositional Growth Plan (LDGP) (Appendix B).

First, the admissions application includes a required Leadership Situation Essay that is evaluated for evidence of the desired dispositions.

> Describe an event that is meaningful to you in which you served in a formal or informal leadership role. Include as much detail as possible when answering the following questions:
>
> 1. Describe the situation as it occurred at the time.
> 2. What did you do in that particular situation?
> 3. How did you feel about the situation at the time you were experiencing it?
> 4. How do you feel about the situation now?
> 5. What would you change, if anything?
>
> (see: coehs.nku.edu/gradprograms/edd/admission.html)

All candidates for whom evidence of the dispositions is found are scheduled to take part in a group interview that delves further into the candidates' leadership capabilities. Candidates who have the background, skills, and abilities normally associated with doctoral level study as well as the prerequisite dispositions are ranked and offered admission until all seats are filled.

Second, the ILSA is a tool designed to give candidates insights into how their leadership skills and dispositions are viewed by others. Candidates assess themselves on 50 characteristics using a Likert scale and then ten or more "critical friends" (colleagues, peers, employees, etc.) assess the candidates on the same scales. Their results are aggregated and provided in graphic form to the learning associate. Learning associates use these results to better understand themselves as leaders and as a basis for creating a growth plan. Leadership/Dispositional Growth Plans (LDGP) are the final place where dispositions play a role in the NKU program. The plans are developed during the first year of the program and assessed and revised annually. Learning associates are expected to formulate the plan to include (a) two or more goals related to improving their effectiveness as a leaders, (b) a specific plan for working toward each goal during the current academic year, and (c) the evidence that they believe will demonstrate progress toward each goal.

Competency-Based Outcomes

There is considerable agreement among theoreticians and practitioners alike that outcomes, rather than inputs, are the measure of the success of any endeavor. Successful program completers should have demonstrable knowledge, skills, and dispositions rather than only marks or grades that may have little correlation with performance.

Instructional strategies that incorporate job-embedded "puzzles of practice" that have meaningful and useful benefits to the organizations in which LAs work are supplanting more abstract or contrived activities that are common (albeit pragmatically necessary) in nonpractitioner programs. In many cases solutions to these authentic and potentially impactful "puzzles" offer benefit to the LA's organization and provide a unique measure of the LA's abilities and competencies.

The NKU executive EdD program for superintendents is grounded on 36 competency-based outcomes that replace traditional grading and credit-earning practices. The outcomes are job-embedded applications with measurable impact on the learning associates' school districts. These competencies are individually assessed for each LA at the beginning of the program—first by the LA him/herself and then by the faculty and are continually revisited until evidence of their successful completion is provided. Superintendents provided evidence that each competency was successfully achieved by linking each one to substantive, job-embedded artifacts in an electronic portfolio, competency chart. The faculty reviews the portfolio entries for each competency and decide when the evidence is sufficient to meet each one. The competency chart became part of the approval process for the degree (Appendix C). In order to meet university and accreditation requirements, traditional grades are assigned when clusters of related competencies were met. Grades are part of a self-assessment process, and each superintendent provided evidence to support their grade to the faculty who either agreed or developed a conversation focused around the "disagreement." In several cases, the grade was either lowered or increased as a result of this process.

Several interesting benefits—some anticipated and some not—were the by-products of this approach. The use of competencies provided for more "real world," less hypothetical learning experiences and adapted to the needs of the superintendent cohort, built leadership capacity, and engaged learners actively in their own transformation. The major unanticipated benefit was that the LAs came to see the mastery of the competency as the important element, and the grades became inconsequential. When submitting their self-assessments for the grades that would appear on their transcripts, some LAs requested grades less than an "A" when they struggled with particular competencies.

International Experience

In an ever-shrinking world it is imperative that leaders be able to think globally. To develop this skill, an integral part of the superintendent EdD program includes an international study experience in which all learning associates are required to participate. The international experience takes place in a mutually selected, high educationally performing country where LAs explore how governmental, political, cultural, and social systems impact education and better understand the broad concepts of leadership in an international context. The first superintendent cohort chose to investigate the education system of Finland by visiting Helsinki and surrounding cities. The second cohort chose the province of Ontario, Canada.

The Finish experience provided a firsthand account of how Finland has built a world-class educational system during the last 30 years. The complexity of educational change was explored and, at the same time, presented the learning associates with an opportunity to develop solutions for the challenges their own schools, districts, and states face in the complex, rapidly changing educational landscape in the United States. As a result, the experience led to improvements in each superintendent's district. One example was the incorporation of second-language learning at the elementary level in one of the districts.

The Ontario experience had similar outcomes. Subsequent to the experience, our learning associates affirmed that this study-abroad program enabled them to observe a systems approach that was laser-focused and well-connected to all parts of the educational community. Our learning associates uncovered that Ontario's Leadership Framework (Ontario Institute for Educational Leadership, 2013) and four overarching educational goals led to multiple pathways for achieving Ontario's success for graduates in apprenticeships, colleges, universities, and the world of work. The Ontario Leadership Framework is the causal factor for a single-minded approach for over 12 years, which has made a significant contribution to the successful educational outcomes for Ontario's students.

As a result of these international experiences, the impact on the superintendents and their districts resulted in (a) an awareness of the need to move from an Ameri-centric to a more global curriculum, (b) the implementation of new curricular initiatives such as early second language acquisition,

(c) a renewed awareness to center on the whole child, and (d) a laser-like focus on the few, most important educational outcomes rather than the latest educational fad.

Quantitative/Qualitative Action Research Project

Action research is used in many EdD programs to help school leaders create effective change, and is, for example, a signature pedagogy at Arizona State University and Northern Kentucky University. Within Arizona's EdD program, students conduct mixed methods, action research cycles each semester at their worksites. Action research aims "to create stewards of practice, that is, school leaders who have the knowledge, skills, and dispositions to pinpoint educational problems, design solutions, and create effective change" (Zambo, 2011, p. 261).

Northern Kentucky University's EdD program uses a similar action research process. This quantitative/qualitative action research project fulfills core "competencies" in the NKU program: "Each LA develops a quantitative and qualitative line of inquiry that resulted in meaningful analysis, conclusions, and recommendations for a district-specific problem of practice" (see Appendix C).

Using a mixed-methods design, each superintendent identified an educational program or practice within his or her district to evaluate in order to inform the decision-making process. Action research is taught in the core courses, the research courses, and supported by Leader Scholar Communities (LSCs). Each learning associate selects a problem to solve, "explain[s] why it is a challenge of importance to them, investigate the literature for viable solutions, take action, collect and analyze data to determine the effectiveness of their action, reflect on what they learned and consider next steps" (Zambo, 2011, p. 263). Each action research project was presented to the LSC and to the superintendents' boards of education at a public meeting.

One superintendent completed a comparative analysis of a full-day and half-day kindergarten program in her district. Another explored the relationship between an extended school day program and its effects on students who had an achievement gap of 2 or more years in reading and/or mathematics. As a result of these mixed-methods action research studies, specific recommendations were implemented to improve program effectiveness. A third LA investigated the impact of a computer-based mathematics program on third-grade student-learning outcomes. The results indicated that the use of the program showed a statistically positive impact on student learning outcomes; teacher satisfaction with the program was high, and students enjoyed learning with this program.

Regional Stewardship

Superintendents are civic and organizational leaders whose purview extends beyond the district walls and into the communities of the schools they serve (Wasicsko, Chirichello, & Allen, 2014). LAs in the NKU program develop a heightened understanding of regional stewardship and their role in advancing regional progress. They do this by exploring ways in which organizational leaders can exercise leadership in the larger external community as a means to achieve community progress and ultimately improve organizational performance. Working together in consulting teams, LAs review and analyze literature that describes the key competencies associated with successful community change strategies; evaluate specific community needs using the elements of successful change strategies; and design and implement a change strategy for a community problem or opportunity using the 13 community change competencies from the Community Tool Box developed at the University of Kansas (2015). The life of this project extends beyond the awarding of the degree.

Additionally, this outcome develops a deeper personal insight into each LA's capacity to accomplish significant community change, which is a required competency of the program. For example, one superintendent focused on the heroin crisis in his community by joining with county and state officials in an outreach program to educate citizens on the effects of heroin and prescription opioid painkillers. In another example, several superintendents collaboratively focused on workforce readiness to accelerate the region's industrial growth and secure certification as a Work Ready Community.

The Capstone Outcome: The Dissertation in Practice

Many disciplines have considered alternative formats for the dissertation. It is time for education to do the same (Archbald, 2010; Duke & Beck, 1999; Imig, 2011; Wergin, 2011). Although many universities are engaged in creative endeavors regarding the (re)design and development of the final culminating experience of the DiP, many campuses are faced with the ongoing challenge of determining and agreeing on what that final experience should look like. Jon Wergin (2011) reminds us that "a professional doctorate in education should not have as its capstone experience a watered-down dissertation, but should instead require a demonstration of expertise that showcases the candidate's mastery of inquiry into practice" and that "the design of an appropriate capstone experience is ripe for creative thinking" (p. 130). In this final section, we highlight the final culminating experience at NKU.

At Northern Kentucky University, among the most "edupreneurial" elements of the executive program is shifting the culminating experience from a traditional, one-dimensional, individual, five-chapter dissertation to a collaborative, multifaceted/multimedia DiP. In line with program outcomes and CPED principles, the NKU culminating experience is intended to be scholarly, relevant to one's professional leadership, publically available, and impactful on schools and students. To this end, the DiP is structured to encourage creativity and innovation and to empower learning associates to explore a variety of 21st century media options, including electronic formats and the use of social media. By expanding beyond the boundaries of the traditional five-chapter dissertation, program participants have the opportunity to reach a broader audience and still meet the scholarly standards expected of those earning the doctorate.

The DiP in the executive EdD program is designed to (a) bring about solutions to complex puzzles of practice, (b) make a difference for the shareholders both internal and external to the organizations in which our learning associates work, (c) emphasize collaboration between and among the learning associates rather than work in isolation, (d) link theory to practice, (e) be transferable to other school districts, and (f) add new knowledge to district level leadership best practices. In order to bring about solutions to complex puzzles of practice, our LAs approach the DiP in the context of action research which we describe as

> a participatory process concerned with developing practical knowing in the pursuit of worthwhile human purposes. It seeks to bring together action and reflection, theory and practice, in participation with others, in the pursuit of practical solutions to issues of pressing concern to people, and more generally the flourishing of individual persons and their communities. (Reason & Bradbury, 2008, p. 4)

Perhaps the most revolutionary element of the action research DiP is the shift of the capstone experience from a one-dimensional, five-chapter individual dissertation to a companion capstone that pushes learning associates to explore a variety of 21st century media. It was our desire to create a learning community through which our primary audience—school superintendents—can learn from us and from one another and have access to relevant, just-in-time resources that will inform their practice in pertinent and responsible ways. To that end, our first cohort of superintendents' DiP features an interactive series of Superintendent Effectiveness Modules made available to new, experienced, and aspiring superintendents who choose to participate as members of an exclusive, online professional learning community. All six learning associates collaborated on the overall design and implementation of the website, working individually and collectively to develop the thematic modules. Each module contains a variety of topical resources, including a repository of electronic resources, exemplar video clips, and a comprehensive annotated bibliography.[1]

Our second executive superintendent cohort included eight learning associates who decided to work in two teams on two different dissertations in practice. At the start of the DiP process, each person created a written scholarly "blueprint" consisting of an introduction, an "environmental scan" (review of literature), the methodology, and their anticipated results, conclusions, and implications. This blueprint becomes the framework for the development of the signature outcome for the program. One of the teams, consisting of six Kentucky school superintendents, came together through a collaborative dissertation in practice to collect and share best strategies to nurture a vibrant culture of collaborative leadership, shared decision making, and transparent self-assessment practices. The website they have created to help leaders leave a legacy provides six strategies with numerous resources designed to help new and experienced superintendents and school leaders to lead from the heart and to matter (http://www.aspirationalschool.com/). The website provides strategies for planning for succession, implementing 21st century planning, integrating communication, improving professional learning, innovating instruction, and individualizing success.

A second team focused on an action research outcome to assess elements of the Kentucky Association of School Administrator's (KASA) new superintendent onboarding program as it related to the Individualized Learning Plan (ILP) team and its effectiveness. The ILP team was charged with the responsibility to support the first-year transition of the new superintendent and included the new superintendent, an executive coach, an experienced superintendent mentor, and the school board member liaison. The DiP involved collecting and analyzing data from the members of the ILP teams that previously participated in the initial program. The results of the interviews and surveys were analyzed and resulted in making recommendations for improvement in the onboarding program. These recommendations were vetted with the current year ILP teams and integrated into a manual of best practices (eBook) for new superintendents who entered the program in July of 2015. This study was vital to ensure new superintendents successfully completed the onboarding program.

CONCLUSION

Doctoral education for practitioners is ripe for redesign. The types of degrees and skills needed by today's educational practitioners must meet the demands of our time. Yet in many cases, the content, delivery, and context of the doctorate, even in those designed for practitioners, are reflections of the bygone era of mortarboards, gowns, and hoods.

The work currently taking place to rethink the professional doctorate for educational leaders provides some of the most exciting and challenging opportunities to shift the educational paradigm and bridge the "hyphen" separating practitioners and scholars. If successful, the benefits to the educational endeavor will be great and the impact made by our graduates will be magnified. We at NKU have been fortunate to see our executive program completers have a significant impact on their districts and within the Commonwealth (Chirichello & Wasicsko, 2015). The school leaders completing NKU's executive cohorts have already advanced to positions of greater responsibility and made substantive change in the Commonwealth's educational system. As our graduates take on new responsibilities in their careers, we are optimistic about the future and see tangible evidence that the combination of "practitioner" and "scholar" can be and is a reality.

NOTE

1. Our first executive cohort's DiP may be accessed at http://connect.kasa. org/leadershipresources/nkuexec. This electronic-based DiP is also available from UMI as a one-dimensional written document. The webpage is housed at the Kentucky Association of School Administrators site (www.KASA.org) to give all superintendents in the Commonwealth of Kentucky and beyond an opportunity to take advantage of these modules to inform their practice.

REFERENCES

Allen, J. G., Wasicsko, M. M., & Chirichello, M. (2014). The missing link: Teaching the dispositions to lead. *International Journal of Educational Leadership Preparation, 9*(1), 135–147.

Archbald, D. (2010). "Breaking the mold" in the dissertation: Implementing a problem-based, decision-oriented thesis project. *Journal of Continuing Higher Education, 58*(2), 99–107. doi:10.1080/07377361003617368

Carnegie Project on the Education Doctorate (CPED). (2015). *The Carnegie project on the education doctorate: A knowledge forum on the EdD.* Retrieved from http://cpedinitiative.org/

Chirichello, M., & Wasicsko, M. (2015). From 'PhD Lite' to a Practitioners' EdD. *School Administrator, 3*(72), 24–25.

Combs, A. (1974). Why the humanistic movement needs a perceptual psychology. *Journal of the Association for the Study of Perception, 9,* 1–3.

Combs, A. W., & Snygg, G. (1949). *Individual behavior: A perceptual approach to behavior.* New York, NY: Harper & Row.

Combs, A. W., Soper, D. W., Gooding, C. T., Benton, J. A., Dickman, J. F., & Usher, R. H. (1969). *Florida studies in the helping professions* (Social Science Monograph #37). Gainesville: University of Florida Press. Retrieved from http://www.fieldpsychtrust.org/florida_studies.pdf

Duke, N. K., & Beck, S. W. (1999). Education should consider alternative formats for the dissertation. *Educational Researcher, 28*(3), 31–36.

Imig, D. G. (2011). Dissertations or capstones: The conundrum facing EdD programs. *UCEA Review, 52*(3), 12–13.

Olson, K., & Clark, C. M. (2009). A signature pedagogy in doctoral education: The leader-scholar community. *Educational Researcher, 38*(3), 216-221. doi:10.3102/0013189X09334207

Ontario Institute for Educational Leadership. (2013, September). *The Ontario leadership framework: A school and system leader's guide to putting Ontario's leadership framework into action.* Retrieved from http://www.education-leadership-ontario.ca/en/resource/ontario-leadership-framework-olf/

Perry, J. A. (2012). To EdD or not to EdD? *Phi Delta Kappan, 94*(1), 41–44.

Reason, P., & Bradbury, H. (2008). *The Sage handbook of action research: Participative inquiry and practice* (2nd ed.). Thousand Oaks, CA: Sage.

Richards, A. C. (Ed.) (2010). *Matters of consequence: Selected writings of Arthur W. Combs, PhD.* Carrollton, GA: A Field Psych Trust Publication.

UK Council for Graduate Education. (2015). [Home page]. Retrieved from http://www.ukcge.ac.uk/

University of Kansas. (2015). *Community tool box.* Retrieved from http://ctb.ku.edu/en

Wasicsko, M. (2007). The perceptual approach to teacher dispositions. In M. E. Diez & J. Raths (Eds.), *Dispositions in teacher education* (pp. 53–89). Charlotte, NC: Information Age.

Wasicsko, M. M., Chirichello, M., & Allen, J. G. (2014). Signature practices for redesigning the practitioner's EdD for school superintendents. *Journal of School Public Relations, 35*(3), 348–362

Wasicsko, M., Wirtz, P. & Resor, C. (2009, Summer). Using dispositions in the teacher admissions process. *SRATE Journal 18*(2), 19–26.

Wergin, J. F. (2011). Rebooting the EdD. *Harvard Educational Review, 81*(1), 119–140.

Zambo, D. (2011). Action research as signature pedagogy in an education doctorate program: The reality and hope. *Innovative Higher Education, 36*(4), 261–271. doi:10.1007/s10755-010-9171-7

Zambo, D., & Isai, S. (2012). Lessons learned by a faculty member working in an education doctorate program with students performing action research. *Educational Action Research, 20*(3), 473–479. doi:10.1080/09650792.2012.697668

APPENDIX A
Individual Leadership Self-Assessment (Sample Version)
(ILSA)
Northern Kentucky University
EdD Program

Capacity to Lead

Instructions: On the scale below, choose the number that best matches your current perception of the trait/behavior indicated on this survey.

1. I do not exhibit this trait/behavior
2. I infrequently exhibit this trait/behavior
3. I occasionally exhibit this trait/behavior
4. I exhibit an average amount of this trait/behavior
5. I exhibit an above average amount of this trait/behavior
6. Many other people believe that I exhibit this trait/behavior
7. Most other people believe that I exhibit this trait/behavior

I am...							
Self-confident	1	2	3	4	5	6	7
Trustworthy	1	2	3	4	5	6	7
I am skilled at...							
Communicating my vision	1	2	3	4	5	6	7
Planning/organizing/Strategic thinking	1	2	3	4	5	6	7
I can (am)...							
Inspire others	1	2	3	4	5	6	7
Tell stories	1	2	3	4	5	6	7

Note: This version contains several questions from each section of the ILSA©. A full version is available by contacting the authors.

Dispositions

Instructions: On the scale below, choose the number that best matches your current perception of the disposition indicated on this survey.

1. I do not exhibit this disposition
2. I infrequently exhibit this disposition
3. I occasionally exhibit this disposition
4. I exhibit an average amount of this disposition
5. I exhibit an above average amount of this disposition
6. Many other people believe that I exhibit this disposition
7. Most other people believe that I exhibit this disposition

Perception of Self						
1. I identify positively with others even those who are different than I am						
1	2	3	4	5	6	7
2. I always try to see the other person's point of view						
1	2	3	4	5	6	7
Perceptions of Others						
1. I display a general belief that all people are valuable, able, and worthy						
1	2	3	4	5	6	7
2. I collaborate positively with others						
1	2	3	4	5	6	7
Perceptions of Purpose						
1. I see the "big picture" in most situations						
1	2	3	4	5	6	7
2. I treat everyone equitably and fairly						
1	2	3	4	5	6	7
Frame of Reference						
1. My primary focus is on the success of the people with whom I interact						
1	2	3	4	5	6	7
2. I balance work and life						
1	2	3	4	5	6	7

Note: Adapted from Wasicsko (2007).

APPENDIX B

District
Superintendent
Standard 8—Dispositions: the human elements of leadership
Goal 1—Strength:

Reflection: Why did I choose this goal?

Action Steps/Strategies	Timeline and Milestones	Evidence Indicators for meeting Goal	Impact on Self and Others	ExpectedOutcome

Goal 2—Growth:

Reflection: Why did I choose this goal?

Action Steps/Strategies	Timeline and Milestones	Evidence Indicators for meeting Goal	Impact on Self and Others	ExpectedOutcome

APPENDIX C

Competencies Self-Assessment (CSA)

Name:

Date:

Description:

The Competencies Self-Assessment (CSA) is an instrument to help us better understand your knowledge, understandings, and experiences as leader in order to help us design an optimal learning experience within the cohort. It is a self-assessment instrument listing competencies that are aligned with our course goals and objectives for which you will provide experiential evidence. This instrument is the cornerstone of our competency-based, accelerated Executive EdD program.

If multiple courses are listed, the bold course indicates seminal outcome for that course.

Module	#	Competency	Course(s)/Semester	Evidence of Competency
	1	Recognize qualities of great leaders based upon theoretical constructs, biographies, autobiographies, and professional/personal experiences; and apply them to my effectiveness as leader.	EDD 801 Spring 2013	
	2	Enhanced my decision-making skills by analyzing authentic case studies.	EDD 801 Spring 2013	
	3.	Demonstrated creative problem solving within my district.	EDD 801 Spring 2013	
	4.	Demonstrated innovative leadership development and/or work with a high performance team.	EDD 821 Spring 2013	
	5.	Effectively engaged with the community to impact needs within that community.	EDD 802 Fall 2013 EDD 829 Summer 2014	

Module	#	Competency	Course(s)/Semester	Evidence of Competency
	6.	Positively influenced change within community organizations.	EDD 802 Fall 2013 EDD 829 Summer 2014	
	7.	Influenced greater connections between schools/districts and community agencies.	EDD 802 Fall 2013 EDD 829 Summer 2014	
	8.	Promoted growth of personnel at the individual level.	EDD 803 Summer 2013 EDD 825 Spring 2014	
	9.	Positively influenced change at the system level.	EDD 821 Fall 2013 EDD 825 Spring 2014 EDD 894 Fall 2014	
	10.	Positively influenced change at the community/state/federal level.	EDD 821 Fall 2013 EDD 894 Fall 2014	

Module	#	Competency	Course(s)/Semester	Evidence of Competency
	11.	Critically analyzed a body of research related to a specific problem of practice.	EDD 810 Spring 2013 EDD 825 Spring 2014 EDD 849 Spring, Summer 2014 EDD 812 Summer 2014	
	12.	Developed a quantitative line of inquiry that resulted in meaningful analysis, conclusions, and recommendations for a district-specific problem of practice.	EDD 810 Spring 2013 EDD 825 Spring 2014 EDD 849 Spring, Summer 2014 EDD 812 Summer 2014	
	13.	Developed a qualitative line of inquiry that resulted in meaningful analysis, conclusions, and recommendations for a specific district-specific problem of practice.	EDD 811 Summer 2013 EDD 825 Spring 204 EDD 849 Spring, Summer 2014 EDD 812 Summer 2014	

Module	#	Competency	Course(s)/Semester	Evidence of Competency
	14.	Applied organizational theory to address a need within my district.	EDD 821 Fall 2013	
	15.	Applied theories of change to address a need within my district.	EDD 821 Fall 2013 / EDD 825 Spring 2014	
	16.	Influenced the development and implementation of a vision and mission for a district.	EDD 821 Fall 2013	
	17.	Participated in the development/ implementation/application of a professional code of ethics.	EDD 822 Fall 2014	
	18.	Resolved legal conflicts in a complex educational environment among parents, community and/or school personnel.	EDD 822 Fall 2014	
	19.	Effectively and ethically responded to expressions, acts, or policies that devalue other persons from a multicultural perspective.	EDD 833 Spring 2014	
	20.	Investigated and/or responded to constitutional and legal issues related to the status of women and various racial, ethnic, and cultural groups.	EDD 833 Spring 2014	
	21.	Taken measures to evaluate the impact of the forces of discrimination (especially racism and sexism) on any of the following: language, instructional materials, learning activities, learning styles, interaction between staff and students, tests and measurements, educational environments, and/or assessments.	EDD 833 Spring 2014	
	22.	Applied theory and research related to human resource management, human potential, and adult learning to positively impact student, organizational and personnel growth within my system.	EDD 825 Spring 2014	

Module	#	Competency	Course(s)/Semester	Evidence of Competency
	23.	Used a variety of data collection techniques to identify the strengths and needs of my system personnel.	EDD 810 Spring 2013 EDD 811 Summer 2013 EDD 825 Spring 2014 EDD 849 Spring, Summer 2014 EDD 812 Summer 2014	
	24.	Applied curriculum theory to critically analyze curriculum designs, content, and processes.	EDD 830 Summer 2013	
	25.	Made curricular decisions based upon a unified theoretical perspective.	EDD 830 Summer 2013	
	26.	Engaged stakeholders within the schools and community to make systemic curricular decisions.	EDD 830 Summer 2013	
	27.	Led a team of stakeholders to develop and implement a comprehensive curriculum evaluation process.	EDD 830 Summer 2013	
	28.	Influenced a coherent vision and implementation of that vision regarding the role of technology in a school/district/state curriculum	EDD 832 Fall 2013	
	29.	Designed and successfully implemented a professional development program at the system or state level.	EDD 830 Fall 2013 EDD 829 Summer 2014	

Module	#	Competency	Course(s)/Semester	Evidence of Competency
	30.	Influenced district or state policies regarding the digital divide.	EDD 832 Fall 2013	
	31.	Taken a leadership role in responding to state/national initiatives.	EDD 894 Fall 2014	
	32.	Identified appropriate action research topics as a result of data analysis for state/district/school improvement.	EDD 810 Spring 2013 EDD 811 Summer 2013 EDD 812 Summer 2014 EDD 849 Spring, Summer 2014 EDD 898 2015	
	33.	Instructed personnel in developing an understanding of the collaborative action research process that resulted in initiating (sustaining) the process at the school or district level.	EDD 810 Spring 2013 EDD 811 Summer 2013 EDD 849 Spring, Summer 2014 EDD 812 Summer 2013	
	34.	Developed a better understanding about the human, dispositional qualities associated with facilitating transformative change in individuals, classrooms, schools, and organizations.	EDD 803 Summer 2013	

Module	#	Competency	Course(s)/Semester	Evidence of Competency
	35.	Expanded self-awareness and self-knowledge necessary for developing and implementing the Individual Leadership Development Plan (ILDP) from the Individual Leadership Self-Assessment (ILSA).	EDD 803 Summer 2013	
	36.	Increased personal effectiveness in their relationships with others as they expanded their understandings about transformational leadership.	EDD 803 Summer 2013	

Notes:

CHAPTER 8

THE SINGLE-DISTRICT DISSERTATION

Craig Hochbein

MAXIMIZING THE REWARDS AND REDUCING RISKS WHEN PURSUING DOCTORAL RESEARCH IN EDUCATIONAL LEADERSHIP

After 11 persistently low-performing high schools in Jefferson County, Kentucky posted impressive gains on the state-administered tests in math, various leaders and groups near and far clamored to claim responsibility for the improvements. These stakeholders cited public accountability measures, supplemental school funding, replacement of educators, and sundry other reasons for the test score improvements. One district administrator even suggested the gains occurred because the district's teachers "finally got fire in their bellies." Three of my doctoral students felt otherwise and confirmed their beliefs.

For months, they and their colleagues had diligently collaborated to develop and implement Project Proficiency, a districtwide reform intended to raise student achievement in schools with stubbornly low performance by emphasizing standards-based grading. From my graduate students' daily interactions, experiences, and observations as administrators in Jefferson

The EdD and the Scholarly Practitioner, pages 131–136
Copyright © 2016 by Information Age Publishing
All rights of reproduction in any form reserved.

County, they believed Project Proficiency was responsible for the rising performance. Seizing the opportunity presented by their doctoral dissertations, we developed a rigorous research design that used school district data to examine the influence of Project Proficiency (http://bit.ly/tandf-project-proficiency). The students' research not only confirmed their professional opinions, but also earned them doctoral degrees.

Historically, in the process of developing a dissertation, doctoral chairs have advised students to design a study that fills a gap in the literature. Doctoral students who intended to return to educational practice have considered the dissertation an artificial exercise that lacked relevance to educational leadership. Today, many professional doctoral programs attempt to close this research/practice gap by fostering dissertations focused on problems of practice within a single district. This style of dissertation promises rewarding experiences and informative products for all participants, including the superintendent whose district permits the embedded research. However, to reap these benefits, districts and doctoral students need to avoid common pitfalls.

Relevant Studies

Even in large school systems, the limited number of schools, especially high schools, hinders the statistical analysis of school reforms. Glenn Baete, in pursuit of his doctoral degree, tackled this complex problem by focusing on the performance of classrooms. Using data not readily available to outsiders, Baete, an educator for 23 years in Jefferson County, employed multilevel modeling to examine the relationship between students' achievement and their classrooms. His well-designed study yielded results that demonstrated the influence of Project Proficiency to raise student achievement and reduce the influence of the student composition of classrooms.

In another doctoral study, Joe Burks, assistant superintendent for high schools in Jefferson County, wanted to understand if Project Proficiency helped students who now were in high schools. From his literature review and own experience, Burks understood that many high school reforms occurred too late, offered too little or required too much time for current high school students. Burks also capitalized on underused school district data to study cohorts of students at risk of dropping out. His unique approach to comparing cohorts revealed that vulnerable students who experienced Project Proficiency achieved statistically significant and meaningful gains on the state-administered mathematics assessment.

To better understand how Project Proficiency achieved these results, Marty Pollio, in his dissertation research, examined one of the primary instructional mechanisms of the reform—standards-based grading. From his position as a high school principal, Pollio understood the monumental shift required for teachers to abandon their traditional practices and adopt standards-based grading. Therefore, he wanted to document whether the educational benefits justified the politics, time commitment, and cultural cost. Again, analyzing data collected and stored by the Jefferson County district, Pollio compared students' characteristics, grades, and test scores. He demonstrated that standards-based grades better predicted student achievement on standardized testing than grades assigned via traditional practices. Pollio continues to cite his results to justify why his school uses standards-based grading.

Rewards and Risks

These doctoral studies, which focused on a single school district, rewarded all involved parties. The district received high-quality and actionable research findings that confirmed the effectiveness of Project Proficiency. Each of the doctoral students worked on a dissertation that directly related to their professional endeavors. Additionally, their work has resulted in three scholarly journal articles (Baete & Hochbein, 2014; Burks & Hochbein, 2015; Pollio & Hochbein, 2015).

Yet these rewards did not result simply from focusing dissertation studies on a single district. Each participant managed numerous academic and professional risks. Dissertations that focus on a single district must satisfy the conditions of three entities—the school district, the dissertation-granting institution, and the doctoral student. The ideal single-district dissertation combines a meaningful problem of practice with a high-quality research design while also capturing the professional and academic interests of the graduate student. To produce successful single-district dissertations, school districts and doctoral students ought to consider these four questions:

How Are Research Questions Developed?

As an alternative to doctoral students developing research questions independent of district input, some graduate programs in educational administration rely on districts soliciting research questions from students. These collaborations facilitate students' access to research sites and data collection while providing districts with free evaluation services and extended contact with potential candidates for leadership positions.

However, with solicitations, participants must guard against political influence. Potentially contentious topics or preferred outcomes could narrow students' access to data, limit research designs, and yield biased results. Any single-district dissertation is susceptible to political considerations, but working on solicited research questions raises the level from possible to plausible. The most successful single-district dissertations exhibit collaboration between partners to identify meaningful questions that involve sufficient rigor and data to meet the doctoral committee's requirements and align with students' interests, resources, and skills.

What Logistics Are Required to Complete the Dissertation?

A lack of specificity about the research plan will frustrate both student and district participants. Vague agreements between participants tend to overlook critical logistics, which can lead to disastrous results for all participants. Students and districts need to stipulate and abide by the parameters of the research plan. To facilitate with specificity, simply start by answering the questions of who, what, when, where, why, and how.

For instance, specify when data collection will occur. Does the proposed timeline interfere or compete with other district initiatives? Will the timeline satisfy doctoral requirements, or will students miss graduation deadlines? Similarly, be specific about data and site access. Do not rely on assurances. Students need to confirm that data exist in the needed format or that access will be granted. Districts need to approve collection and analytical techniques to ensure that regulations, policies, and contracts are not violated.

Can the Questions Be Adequately Answered?

Every research study includes limitations and weaknesses. To produce a successful single-district dissertation, districts and students need to understand how well a question can be answered. Even a well-executed qualitative research study cannot adequately explain if a switch to block scheduling increased student achievement. To ensure receipt of valid and actionable results, district administrators need to probe the students about their research skills and the techniques involved in the study. Similarly, students need to be clear about exactly what answers their study will provide.

What if the Results Are Not Positive?

One of the greatest risks of pursuing a single-district dissertation involves the results. In the case of Burks, Baete, and Pollio, their doctoral studies in educational leadership and organizational development at the University of Louisville (where I was an assistant professor at the time) involved rigorous research that returned positive results. However, what if the findings indicated that Project Proficiency had no influence, or worse yet, had a negative influence? Furthermore, if a dissertation employs weak or questionable methods, even positive results can be questioned.

Unlike an internal evaluation, a dissertation's results and conclusions must become public as part of the defense process. Moreover, the scrutiny of the dissertation committee likely minimizes the amount of "spin" that can be applied to disappointing results. To minimize this risk, school district administrators and doctoral students need to discuss the meaning of potential findings. Results perceived as negative still can be constructive. Negative results returned from high-quality research can be used as a strong foundation upon which to design and measure future improvements.

No Rigor, No Reward

National organizations don't track the number of single-district dissertations in educational leadership, but Jill Perry of the Carnegie Project on the Education Doctorate sees a definite trend toward doctoral research focusing on problems of practice. "Historically, practitioners who have gone through doctoral programs, whether an EdD or PhD, have been more focused on their own context and that has raised questions of rigor in doctoral study," she says.

Doubts about the rigor of single-district dissertations typically arise from the usage of weak methodology, not their context, questions, or data. Practicing leaders routinely derive insightful questions from their daily experiences and have access to troves of high-quality data. Yet single-district settings pose substantial challenges to research. As doctoral students, educators need to receive preparation and advising that affords them the capabilities to employ research methods that address these challenges to return valid and actionable results.

The single-district dissertation can yield valuable experiences and information for all involved parties—the students seeking doctorates in educational leadership, the school districts being studied, and the degree-granting universities. Unfortunately, the benefits associated with authentic settings and problems of practice carry numerous risks for the participants. No amount of planning, deliberation, and understanding can totally eliminate the risks. Yet thoughtful preparation and collaboration can minimize exposure to these risks, while maximizing the rewards by aligning doctoral research interests with the needs of districts.

ACKNOWLEDGMENT

Originally published in *School Administrator* (2015, March), pp. 26–29.

REFERENCES

Baete, G. S., & Hochbein, C. (2014). Project Proficiency: A quasi-experimental assessment of high school reform in an urban district. *Journal of Educational Research, 107*(6), 493–511.

Burks, J. C., & Hochbein, C. (2015). The students in front of us: Reform for the current generation of high school urban high school students. *Urban Education, 50*(3), 346–376.

Pollio, M., & Hochbein, C. (2015). The association between standards-based grading and standardized test scores in a high school reform model. *Teachers College Record, 117*(11), 1–28.

CHAPTER 9

USING ACTION RESEARCH TO DEVELOP EDUCATIONAL LEADERS AND RESEARCHERS

Ray R. Buss and Debby Zambo

In this chapter, we focus our discussion on action research and the Action Research Dissertation in Practice (AR DiP) as signature pedagogy (Shulman, 2005) in EdD programs as a means to appropriately prepare scholar practitioners. We begin with essential elements that characterize institutions affiliated with the Carnegie Project on the Education Doctorate (CPED) that are working to reform and reimagine the Education Doctorate (EdD). We then offer an overview of the personal and professional motivations EdD students bring to their programs. Following that discussion, we provide an explanation of the tenets/traditions of action research and how these align with CPED's principles and design concepts and also meet the needs and motivations of working professionals. Next, we examine action research from a pragmatic perspective and suggest nine reasons it is particularly beneficial to students who wish to become leaders of change. We then discuss the transformative nature of AR and how it influences students and graduates of doctoral programs. Finally, we complete the chapter by offering some conclusions about action research dissertations and EdD programs.

The EdD and the Scholarly Practitioner, pages 137–152
Copyright © 2016 by Information Age Publishing

The Influence of the Carnegie Project on the Education Doctorate

In their influential work advocating redesign of EdD programs, Shulman, Golde, Bueschel, and Garabedian (2006) suggested EdD programs function more like the professional practice doctorates (PPD) of other professions such as law, medicine, and the clergy rather than as programs that mimicked PhD preparation. Moreover, Shulman and his colleagues advocated that those redesigning/developing EdD programs (a) employ signature pedagogies, (b) require practice-related research skills, (c) expect program participants to be engaged in prior and ongoing practice experiences, and (d) envisage that individuals participating in such programs "would be skilled in carrying out local research and evaluations to guide practice" (p. 29).

Consistent with these recommendations, the Carnegie Project on the Education Doctorate was established in 2007 to better differentiate and transform the EdD into a professional practice degree (Perry, 2012, 2015; Perry & Imig, 2008). Before the emergence of CPED, this was a formidable challenge because many EdD programs lacked focus and prepared graduates for a variety of positions including training researchers for positions in tenure-track positions where they would conduct research, teach, and serve their profession as well as preparing school leaders as administrators, principals, and for other leadership roles (Levine, 2005; Shulman et al., 2006). Because these EdD programs prepared students for such a broad array of positions, there was a great deal of criticism. Programs were seen as lacking focus, preparing leaders in superficial ways, leading to poor research skills, and so on (Levine, 2005). As noted above, Shulman and his colleagues (2006) challenged these criticisms and articulated a vision for new, redesigned EdD programs that overcame these shortcomings and provided for the development of effective educational leaders in rigorous, focused, professional practice programs, like the ones CPED-affiliated programs have developed (Perry, 2012, 2015; Perry & Imig, 2008).

Institutions that have embraced CPED principles and design concepts have crafted substantive program changes that established a focus on developing scholar practitioners, individuals capable of

- blending their practical wisdom with their professional skills and knowledge to identify, frame, and solve problems of practice;
- using practical research and applied theories as tools to understand the impact of their actions; and
- collaborating with key stakeholders and disseminating solutions in multiple ways (CPED, 2010).

CPED offered a framework rather than a prescriptive program model. As its foundation, this framework presented a set of guiding principles, which emphasized the importance of preparing practitioners to be educational leaders. Additionally, CPED recommended a set of design concepts that highlighted the importance of practicing the skills of a scholar practitioner. The details of the CPED principles and design concepts were explained more fully elsewhere in this book. Use of these principles and design concepts has encouraged faculty members at CPED-affiliated institutions to reflect on and revise/design their curricula to create programs that met the needs of their particular contexts and were consistent with the hallmarks advocated by Shulman et al. (2006). Institutions affiliated with CPED have employed CPED's principles and design concepts to change their mission, goals, admission criteria, coursework, support structures, and dissertations so that the needs and motivations of students in their programs can be met (Perry, Zambo, & Wunder, in press).

MOTIVATIONS TO SEEK AN EdD

Scott, Brown, Lunt, and Thorne (2004) investigated why individuals sought Professional Practice Doctorates (PPD) in business, engineering, and education. Results showed students enrolled in PPD programs for a variety of reasons, and these reasons differed depending on "where they were in their careers." Those new to careers sought a doctoral degree for extrinsic, professional reasons. They wanted to gain the knowledge they needed to do a good job and move up the career ladder. By comparison, individuals in the middle of their careers sought a PPD for extrinsic *and* intrinsic reasons. Midcareer individuals wanted to become better at their jobs, develop their leadership capabilities, and contribute to their profession in varying ways. In contrast, those most established in their careers sought a PPD for more intrinsic reasons such as its intellectual challenge and because of their own values and goals. Established professionals wanted to engage in research focused on making a difference in their contextual settings, their professions, and themselves. Additionally, established individuals sought fulfillment, self-discovery, and change.

Similarly, Wellington and Sikes (2006) investigated the motivations, aspirations, and identities of 29 students seeking PPDs and like Scott et al. (2004) found variation in their responses. Individuals in Wellington and Sikes' (2006) study sought a PPD for (a) job promotion and/or retention, (b) the challenge of doctoral work, and (c) the insight they would gain into theories and research methodologies. They wanted a doctorate to change the status quo in their work settings because they were frustrated with the way things were and wanted to foster change by collaborating with individuals from different backgrounds and disciplines.

The authors of this chapter have collaborated on a study on this same topic. Zambo, Zambo, Buss, Perry, and Williams (2014) surveyed students from the CPED Consortium to understand why individuals were pursuing or had pursued an EdD from a CPED-affiliated program. Using an online survey, we collected data from 296 participants at fourteen institutions across the United States and found their responses included career-related goals stemming from external motivations, personal goals deriving from internal motivations, and aspirations attributed to satisfaction derived from the degree itself or working toward the degree.

Those with career-related goals sought an EdD because they wanted to move up the career ladder, have more options, be marketable, and feel secure. These individuals were satisfied working in education and wanted to continue working in the field. Others noted they sought an EdD for long-held, personal reasons. These individuals wanted to fulfill childhood dreams, give back to their communities, and, because some were first-generation college students, be role models for their children and students. For these individuals, getting an EdD was the next logical step in their personal journey toward personal and professional fulfillment. To them, learning about theory, policy, and research would make them better problem solvers and agents of change.

Additionally, participants also sought an EdD because of the degree itself. They thought the programs in which they were enrolled, or from which they had graduated, valued their practical and professional knowledge, allowed them to work on problems of practice that mattered to them, were offered support, corresponded with their schedules (e.g., evening classes, classes on weekends, heavy summer load), and allowed them to complete their programs in 3–4 years. In sum, CPED-affiliated programs have been designed or redesigned to meet the needs of working professionals.

HOW ACTION RESEARCH ALIGNS
WITH THESE MOTIVATIONS

Action research is a...process concerned with developing practical knowing in the pursuit of worthwhile human purposes, grounded in a participatory worldview which we believe is emerging at this historical moment. It seeks to bring together action and reflection, theory and practice, in participation with others, in the pursuit of practical solutions to issues of pressing concern to people, and more generally the flourishing of individual persons and their communities. (Reason & Bradbury, 2001, p. 1)

There have been many definitions of action research and most, like the one above, have captured its active, reflective, and problem-solving nature. Action research has best been characterized as a strategic process or approach for an investigation; not a method or research design (Ivankova, 2015; Levin & Martin, 2007). Action research has required an action, or intervention, and the systematic study of that action through collection of quantitative data, qualitative data, or mixed-methods data. Rather than discovering universals, action researchers sought to understand the multiple co-realities that existed in a specific context, or fostered deep understanding of specific situations among various stakeholders (Hinchey, 2008). Action research has been shown to be both practical and emancipatory, building craft and professional knowledge and collaborative leadership skills (Furman, 2011, 2012). Action researchers have generated knowledge that has been useful to both academic and practitioner communities.

Ideas like these were aligned with the motivations of students enrolled in CPED-influenced EdD programs because these individuals tended to be action oriented, struggling with problems of practice, wanting to make changes that mattered, and wanting to be intellectually challenged. Carr and Kemmis (1986) suggested four reasons action research was aligned with the professional and personal motivations of students in EdD programs. First, doctoral students were able to investigate theory as it was applied to practice by employing various frameworks in their attempts to resolve their problems of practice. Second, students were offered opportunities to explore the moral/ethical dimensions of practice by conducting action research in their work settings. Third, students were presented with occasions to build theory from practice by engaging in work resembling grounded theory work. Finally, doctoral students were afforded opportunities to examine practice using a professional and critical lens, which allowed then to become more expert practitioners. Similarly, Reason and Bradbury (2001) as well as Herr and Anderson (2015) have noted those conducting action research built new knowledge, fostered learning in the profession, transformed individuals and work places, democratized the educational or work setting, and changed the status quo in their local contexts.

Nevertheless, despite these powerful reasons to perform action research, there have been tensions for researchers conducting insider work. When a researcher has been immersed in an organization and has experiential knowledge about it, challenges arise. Being an insider researcher applied to students in EdD programs because they often bridge the world of practice and the world of scholarship (Herr & Anderson, 2015). Students in EdD programs understood the jargon, routines, and norms of their contexts and examined these with the theoretical and research skills learned at the university. Adopting dual roles built leadership capabilities, but it also redefined relationships and power. Action research has been shown to be intensely political and can be uncomfortable when norms are questioned and inequalities are challenged.

Students in EdD programs who want to enact their values and blend their problem solving capabilities (contextual knowledge) with their professional knowledge, leadership, and the coursework (theory and research) will want to perform action research and write an Action Research Dissertation in Practice (AR DiP) because it can be a meaningful, sustainable, and transformative experience for their organizations and them.

HOW THE ACTION RESEARCH DISSERTATION IN PRACTICE (AR DiP) ALIGNS WITH THESE MOTIVATIONS

Action research developed out of critical theory, and went beyond. Critical theory asked: "How can this situation be understood in order to change it?" but aimed only on understanding, not for action. Action research went into action and asked: "How can it be changed?" (McNiff & Whitehead, 2006, p. 41)

According to the Oxford English Dictionary a dissertation is a formal, comprehensive discourse on a topic, either written or spoken. To distinguish the EdD from the PhD, members of CPED have developed their own description of a practitioner-oriented dissertation, or what they call a Dissertation in Practice (see definition above). We pose the action research dissertation in practice (AR DiP) as a combination of these ideas. An AR DiP is a scholarly written discourse focused on a problem of practice set in one's own laboratory of practice, in which a student has intimate knowledge, responsibility, and interest. These ideas are reflected in the chapters of an AR DiP because they typically contain

Chapter 1: Leadership Context and Purpose of the Action
Chapter 2: Review of Supporting Scholarship
Chapter 3: Action and Method
Chapter 4: Analysis and Results/Findings
Chapter 5: Discussion and Implications for Future Studies

At first glance, this may look like the traditional five-chapter dissertation, but it is not. Importantly, the content of the DiP clearly distinguishes it from the more traditional five-chapter dissertation. Details about the structure of an action research DiP and especially its content are available in a document developed to assist students in writing an action research dissertation (Buss & Zambo, 2014). The authors have prepared a comprehensive, easy to follow guide entitled, "A Practical Guide for Students and Faculty in CPED-Influenced Programs Working on an Action Research Dissertation in Practice." The document provides information about the each chapter as well as examples from dissertations to assist in the development of an action research DiP.

Writing an AR DiP can be beneficial for working professionals seeking a doctorate because it affords various opportunities. Doctoral students can ask pragmatic questions about teaching, learning, policy and institutional environments, and the research and tools being used to make critical decisions. Thus, they can bring together workplace-situated problems of practice and engage in applied research on the matter. Moreover, students can focus on a small but substantial problem linked to one's full-time work, which is highly motivating and which supports professional growth. Additionally, students can employ their research skills to advocate for equity, social justice, and opportunity as they enrich and expand their professional knowledge and skills.

Students doing action research can examine literature in a targeted, selective, and comprehensive manner and use it to ground and enrich their work. They can engage in collaborative efforts by working with others to make changes/improvements. As they do action research, students can gather and use meaningful data because they collect data from those closest to the problem. Importantly, they can build their research capabilities through successive approximations in an iterative cyclical manner. Action research offers an intellectual challenge to doctoral students. Additionally, action research provides opportunities to meet personal goals and be transformed into a better leader. Finally, students engage in work and write a thesis/dissertation that breaks the traditional research-oriented mold.

The AR DiP aligns with CPED's working principles because it is collaborative, is often focused on issues of equity and justice, uses multiple frames to develop meaningful solutions, is grounded in, and developed by professional knowledge, and communicates findings to those who need them. However, there can be tensions if programs do not support these ideals. To successfully write and defend an AR DiP students need to

- have a high leverage problem of practice that matters to their stakeholders and to them;
- have a sphere of influence (a setting in which they have responsibility, authority and intimate contextual/professional knowledge);
- be exposed to literature and prior research that can inform and enrich their work or, in CPED's terms, use various research, theories, and professional wisdom to design innovative solutions to problems within one's own context;
- be willing to conduct research as a participant observer;
- take risks to systematically and methodically inquire into their own practice;

- believe in the philosophy and goals of action research (be interested in building local theory and knowledge and as opposed to filling gaps in a discipline);
- be supported in all aspects of their work;
- share their findings with varied and multiple stakeholders; and
- have a committee who understands action research and dissertations based on it.

A PRAGMATIC VIEW OF ACTION RESARCH: NINE REASONS WHY ACTION RESEARCH CAN BE USED EFFECTIVELY IN DOCTORAL PROGRAMS

Our own work with students over time has indicated students initially find action research to be somewhat troubling because of being steeped in more traditional postpositivist perspectives or because of a lack of preparation in the fundamentals of research in any fashion (Buss, Vasquez-Robles, & Paredes, 2013; Buss, Zambo, Zambo, & Williams, 2014). Nevertheless, program students rapidly recognize the utility of the action research process and its applicability to their situations. In the section that follows, we articulate the utility of action research, why doctoral students realize it is so beneficial (useful), and why other doctoral students might find it beneficial as well.

Action research has served as a framework that guided our program efforts from the beginning because of its flexibility and functionality. We have highlighted action research in our doctoral program because it has nine characteristics that made it useful for students in our program. These characteristics are presented in Table 9.1.

TABLE 9.1   Nine Useful Characteristics of Action Research (AR) for Doctoral Students
Action research has been shown to be
adaptable to various problems of practice doctoral students wanted to confront.
compatible with limited resources.
functional in allowing students to ease into research efforts over time.
compatible with smaller- or larger-scale improvement/change efforts.
serviceable in terms of seeing immediate results and collecting data to inform the next step.
flexible with regard to trying out and changing the intervention as necessary.
suitable with regard to developing systematic inquiry over time.
functional in terms of collaboration with colleagues.
sustainable within the program and after it because of its cyclical nature.

As the first criterion suggested, we have found the use of action research to be extraordinarily adaptable to a variety of problems of practice, which our students wished to confront. These types of problems ranged from classroom to school and/or organizations. For example, students in our program have attacked such classroom issues as literacy, STEM issues, mathematics, and such at the K–12 level. Others have implemented practices that influenced whole school sites and dealt with district issues. For example, some doctoral students have focused on improving a failing school, assessing teacher effectiveness more effectively, and developing leadership skills in high school students. Finally, at the higher education level, other doctoral students have conducted interventions aiding students in making the transition from community college to the university, influencing faculty members to employ flipped learning during college instruction, and developing new programs or advising processes to foster retention of undergraduates.

Second, action research has been compatible with limited resources. Our doctoral students must have been able to implement their research efforts using the resources readily available to them. Action research was ideal in this circumstance because it has been readily adapted to the resources at their disposal. Moreover, because we wanted our graduates to continue to implement their work beyond their efforts during the program and dissertation in practice, we have found action research to be consistent with this desired outcome.

Third, action research allowed students to ease into research efforts over time. Because action research has been conducted in cycles across time, it gave students an opportunity to begin their research work with small, more tractable efforts. For example, in one cycle students may have tried out an instrument or two or conducted a preliminary implementation of their innovation or intervention. By continuing with such cycles of action research across time, students have developed an extraordinary and deep understanding of their problems of practice, innovation, and the instruments they used to assess the effectiveness of their intervention. Additionally, as research skills developed over time, students were encouraged and motivated to build upon their action research efforts. Thus, when they attempted their dissertation in practice work, they have gathered data and attained skills and confidence necessary to carry out the dissertation work and continued research beyond the program.

These perspectives were supported in a study conducted by Buss and Avery (2015). The researchers examined how end-of-first-year students in a CPED-affiliated EdD program were developing professional identities as educational leaders and educational researchers. Quantitative and qualitative data revealed perceptions changed substantially with respect to development of leadership skills, but there was even greater growth in perceptions of their research skills. Qualitative data showed end-of-first-year students were changed by their program professionally with emerging, research skills, research reflective capacities, and confidence in their abilities as educational researchers. Qualitative data also indicated students "tried out" leadership and research skills in their workplaces and worked to develop these skills. These provisional efforts in leadership and research areas were consistent with the notion of possible selves or provisional selves in which individuals try on identities, which they practice on a trial basis and reformulate over time as they become more accomplished (Ibarra, 1999; Markus & Nurius, 1986).

Fourth, action research has been compatible with efforts of various scales. Action research in our program has been conducted at the classroom, school, and district levels with equal levels of effectiveness. For instance, in one smaller-scale study, Otstot (2015) examined the effectiveness of a collaborative apprenticeship model of professional development (PD) in which she loosely "paired" 11 "more expert" classroom users of bring your own technology (BYOT) with 11 "novice" teacher users of BYOT at a school where she served as principal. Novices received training from their more expert peers on how to employ BYOT for classroom instructional purposes. Only data for the novice teachers were analyzed. Quantitative and qualitative outcomes showed the effectiveness of this narrowly focused, highly relevant PD process. Results suggested novice teachers made substantial gains in using student-owned devices during instruction; reduced instructional and management concerns with regard to using mobile devices; and transformed their perspectives of using mobile devices for classroom instruction. Moreover, perceived barriers to using mobile devices were mitigated by using the collaborative apprenticeship model.

By comparison, Lindsey (2015) conducted a larger scale study in which she explored the value of using a technology infusion support system to help college of education methods course instructors effectively teach digital citizenship (DC) using four DC modules she developed. The DC modules included copyright/fair use, digital footprint/social media, acceptable use policies, and responsible student behavior and were presented using a flipped learning process. She provided training and support to instructors who incorporated the modules into their methods classes, which were part of the teacher preparation program at her institution. She gathered data from three technology infusion specialists who provided training and support to the instructors, interview data from five instructors, quantitative data from 113 of the instructors' students, interview data from approximately 36 students in six focus groups, and classroom observations of the discussions of the DC materials from the modules. Results from the quantitative and qualitative data indicated the technology infusion support system was effective in aiding instructors to deliver the material. Further, their students, prospective teachers, showed significant increases in their intentions to promote and model DC in their future classrooms.

Fifth, action research has been serviceable in terms of doctoral students' seeing immediate results and collecting data to inform the next step. Because action research was conducted in cycles, which may break the problem of practice into more manageable parts, doctoral students gained the advantage of obtaining results very quickly. Ongoing data collection and analyses have informed doctoral action researchers about the effectiveness of the step that has just been taken and what needs to be done next. Action research has acted as a data-informed process, which required that doctoral action researchers never move far from the data and the actions that delivered those data, which kept them in the middle of the process at all times.

Sixth, the action research process has been flexible with regard to trying out and changing the intervention as necessary. Perhaps, one of the greatest strengths of the action research process has been its adaptability. If data suggested the intervention has not been working as effectively as it was hoped to be, the action research approach has allowed doctoral students to modify the intervention to enhance its effectiveness. Unlike more traditional research approaches, action research has allowed researchers to make midcourse corrections based on the researchers' knowledge of the desired outcome and what the current data have suggested. This has been a particularly powerful aspect of action research given that doctoral students were new to the research process and frequently were seeking the ideal intervention and might otherwise have hesitated in initiating their research efforts.

Seventh, action research has been suitable with regard to developing systematic inquiry over time. In particular, action research has lent itself to a four-step process that has roughly translated to (a) studying and planning, (b) taking action, (c) collecting and analyzing data, and (d) reflecting of the data (Mertler, 2014; Mills, 2014). Because these steps were small and natural, doctoral students have taken ownership of them over time. As a result, doctoral students readily have shown they attained one of the primary objectives of doctoral programs—instilling research skills in their graduates that will be used long after completion of the program. Importantly, Buss, Zambo, and Zambo (2015) have found graduates of an EdD program have continued to apply action research to their original problem of practice or transferred it to "new" problems of practice in their workplace settings. Thus, action research has fostered a systematic approach to dealing with problems of practice that has been applicable across time and settings.

Eighth, action research has been functional in terms of doctoral students' collaboration with colleagues. Usually, doctoral students have not conducted their work alone. In general, doctoral students' problems of practice have required them to work in collaboration with workplace colleagues. For example, teachers and principals have typically worked with other teachers, whereas doctoral students from higher education settings have often worked with staff member colleagues to conduct their action research efforts. At noted above, doctoral students have eased into AR and importantly, they have also eased colleagues into the action research process. Further, colleagues have normally collaborated because they have shared the problem of practice identified by their doctoral student colleague.

Ninth, action research has been shown to be sustainable as students pursue their degree and afterward. Students have engaged readily in the action research process and viewed it as sustainable because one cycle built on the next and often revealed the hidden complexities of the problem, fundamental tenets of action research. Moreover, because each cycle built incrementally on the previous one, students' motivations to employ action research and continue its use were substantial. For example, Buss and Avery (2015) found end-of-first-year students perceived themselves as much more accomplished researchers than when they had begun the program. Further, they indicated their efforts at trying out the AR process, the provisional selves construct noted above, were essential in developing these heightened perceptions. Additionally, in other recent research work, Buss et al. (2015) examined what graduates of a CPED-affiliated EdD program were doing in their professional practices following program completion. The researchers explored the sustainability of graduates' action research dissertation work and whether and how they continued to conduct action research among other matters. Results from interviews showed graduates had influenced and continued to influence their workplaces. They were stronger leaders, innovators, and researching professionals. Moreover, although some graduates of the program continued to carry out research work in the area related to their dissertation in practice work, many others had employed action research to examine other, "new" problems of practice that had arisen in their workplace settings.

The extraordinarily functional and flexible nature of action research has been amply demonstrated in evidence related to these nine criteria. Students readily embraced action research after they have seen how useful it can be. Its adaptability to a range of problems, ease of implementation, cyclical nature, and practical value in their workplace setting have been particularly compelling in terms of why doctoral students readily employed action research during their program, as they conducted their DiP, and subsequently in their professional practices.

THE TRANSFORMATIVE NATURE OF ACTION RESEARCH

Up to this point, we have considered a variety of matters, but we have not discussed the transformative nature of action research on students participating in EdD programs. We now turn our attention to this critical outcome. Upon completion of a doctoral program, it is presumed that program graduates will be different in some important ways as compared to when they entered the program. Generally, these differences have been reflected in program goals/objectives or outcomes; for example, program outcomes such as enhancing students' life-long learning mindset; increasing their leadership abilities; fostering additional collaboration skills; and developing research competences have been typical goals for EdD programs. Importantly, faculty members who developed programs typically desired that EdD students not only enhance and/or develop skills in these areas, but that students were transformed in substantive ways. For example, faculty members have desired that students view problems through new lenses by exposing students to new and differing theoretical perspectives than they had known previously. As another example, faculty members desired that students more often view their world using a research perspective. In the next section, we focus on the transformative nature of action research and how it affected students and graduates' identities as action researchers and their practice during and after the program.

With respect to students' identities as researchers, Buss and Avery (2015) gathered quantitative and qualitative data to investigate end-of-first-year students' identities as researchers. Results showed these students had very low perceptions of themselves as researchers at the beginning of the program and were developing modest views of themselves as researcher by end of the first year of the program. Thus, the transformation with respect to being a researcher was beginning during the first year.

In another study, Buss et al. (2014) compared the research identities of students new to the program with graduates of the program. Quantitative results showed dramatic differences in scores about the perceptions of themselves as action researchers when students new to the program and graduates of the program were compared. The qualitative data demonstrated complementarity (Greene, 2007) and indicated students just entering the program suggested they were not action researchers. By comparison, those who just graduated indicated they had been transformed and viewed themselves as action researchers as demonstrated in the following quotes: "I'm . . . more strategic in how I approach a problem;" and "I'm constantly experimenting and finding solutions to different problems" (Buss et al., 2014, p. 153). Similarly, Zambo, Buss, and Zambo, (2015) asked students beginning the program and graduates whether they considered themselves to be action researchers. Students at the beginning of the program were hesitant to claim the identity of action researcher; "did not yet own the process of action research;" (p. 244) and considered themselves to be problem solvers, but not action researchers in their workplace settings. On the other hand, graduates who just had completed the program considered themselves to be action researchers as illustrated in the following quote: "To them this identity meant acting to make things better, viewing problems through new lenses, thinking in systematic and sophisticated ways, and seeing possibilities" (Zambo et al., 2015, p. 242).

The transformation was more evident among those students who had graduated from the program between 2 to 5 years ago (Buss et al., 2015). These "older" graduates indicated they had developed practice-related research and inquiry skills that transformed them as action researchers. Specifically, they suggested they conducted action research regularly, were more analytical/reflective in their work; engaged in systemic/systematic research approaches; and had developed and honed practice-related action research skills (Buss et al., 2015).

Taken together these results suggested students and graduates had benefited greatly from using action research as a method of inquiry. The progression from students new to program who claimed they had no action research skills to end-of-first-year students who were developing action research skills was clear (Buss & Avery, 2015). Moreover, the differences between students new to the program compared to recent and older graduates was compelling and indicated action research skills continued to develop among graduates even years after graduation (Buss et al., 2014, 2015; Zambo et al., 2015).

CONCLUSION

In sum, we have reviewed how elements that characterize CPED-influenced programs are being used in reforming and revitalizing the EdD, why students come to these programs, and how action research and dissertations influenced by these processes are aligned with students' motivations and needs to transform themselves into better leaders and agents of change. When students focus on a problem that matters to them they remain motivated throughout their doctoral work and matriculate to graduation. Further, their work is transformative because their program: (a) allows them to blend their practical wisdom with their professional skills and knowledge to name, frame, and solve problems of practice; (b) fosters a practical research approach, which allows them to apply theories as tools to understand the impact of their actions; and (c) encourages them to collaborate with key stakeholders and disseminate solutions in multiple ways (CPED, 2010). These transformative qualities help to meet the needs and motivations of good leaders and change them into scholarly practitioners who can deal with the complex problems of practice that arise routinely in educational settings.

REFERENCES

Buss, R. R., & Avery, A. (2015). *Research becomes you: Cultivating EdD students' identities as educational researchers in a Carnegie-Project-on-the-Education-Doctorate-affiliated program and learning research by doing research (A study within a study).* Manuscript submitted for review.

Buss, R. R., Vasquez-Robles, V., & Paredes, M. C. (2013). Becoming scholarly and influential practitioners: The journeys of two professionals in a new, innovative doctoral program. In J. A. Perry & D. L. Carlson (Eds.), *In their own words: A journey to the stewardship of the practice in education* (pp. 107–127). Charlotte, NC: Information Age.

Buss, R. R., & Zambo, D. (2014). *A practical guide for students and faculty in CPED-influenced programs working on an action research dissertation in practice.* Carnegie Project on the Education Doctorate.

Buss, R. R., Zambo, R., & Zambo, D. (2015). *Realizing Shulman's vision: Carnegie-Project-on-the-Education-Doctorate-affiliated program graduates' influence on professional practice.* Manuscript submitted for review.

Buss, R. R., Zambo, R., Zambo, D., & Williams, T. R. (2014). Developing researching professionals in an EdD program: From learners and leaders to scholarly and influential practitioners. *Higher Education, Skills and Work-based Learning, 4*, 137–160. doi:10.1108/HESWBL-11-2013-0022

Carnegie Project on the Education Doctorate (CPED). (2010). *Carnegie Project on the Education Doctorate design concept definitions.* Retrieved from http://cpedinitiative.org/design-concept-definitions

Carr, W., & Kemmis, S. (1986). *Becoming critical: Education knowledge and action research.* London, England: Falmer Press.

Furman, G. (2011, November). *School leadership, social justice, and action research.* Paper presented at the annual meeting of the University Council for Educational Administration, Pittsburgh, PA.

Furman, G. (2012). Social justice leadership as praxis: Developing capacities through preparation programs. *Educational Administration Quarterly, 48*(2), 191–229.

Greene, J. C. (2007). *Mixed methods in social inquiry.* San Francisco, CA: Jossey-Bass.

Herr, K., & Anderson, G. L. (2015). *The action research dissertation: A guide for students and faculty* (2nd ed.). Thousand Oaks, CA: Sage.

Hinchey, P. H. (2008). *Action research.* New York, NY: Lang.

Ibarra, H. (1999). Provisional selves: Experimenting with image and identity in professional adaptation. *Administrative Science Quarterly, 44*, 764–791.

Ivankova, N. V. (2015). *Mixed methods applications in action research: From methods to community action.* Thousand Oaks, CA: Sage.

Levin A., & Martin, A. W. (2007) The praxis of educating action researchers: The possibilities and obstacles in higher education. *Action Research, 5*(3). 219–229. doi:10.1177/1476750307081014

Levine, A. (2005). *Educating school leaders.* Princeton, NJ: Woodrow Wilson National Fellowship Foundation.

Lindsey, L. (2015). *Preparing teacher candidates for 21st century classrooms: A study of digital citizenship*. (Doctoral dissertation). Retrieved from http://repository. asu.edu/attachments/150461/content/Lindsey_asu_0010E_14677.pdf

Markus, H., & Nurius, P. (1986). Possible selves. *American Psychologist, 41,* 954–969.

McNiff, J., & Whitehead, J. (2006). *All you need to know about action research.* Thousand Oaks, CA: Sage.

Mertler, C. A. (2014). *Action research: Improving schools and empowering educators* (4th ed.). Thousand Oaks, CA: Sage.

Mills, G. E. (2014). *Action research: A guide for the teacher researcher* (5th ed.). Boston, MA: Pearson.

Otstot, M. L. (2015). *iEngage, iEducate, and iEmpower: A collaborative apprenticeship project in a "bring your own technology" school.* (Doctoral dissertation). Retrieved from http://search.proquest.com/docview/1677008921

Perry, J. A. (2012). To Ed.D. or not to Ed.D. *Phi Delta Kappan, 94*(1), 41–44.

Perry, J. A. (2015). The EdD and the scholarly practitioner. *School Administrator, 20*(3), 20–25.

Perry, J. A., & Imig, D. G. (2008). A stewardship of practice in education. *Change: The Magazine of Higher Learning, 40*(6), 42–49.

Perry, J. A., Zambo, D., & Wunder, S. (in press). Understanding how schools of education have redesigned the doctorate of education. *Journal of School Public Relations, 36,* 58–85.

Reason, P., & Bradbury, H. (2001). Inquiry and participation in search of a world worthy of human aspiration. In P. Reason & H. Bradbury (Eds.), *Handbook of participatory action research: Participatory inquiry and practice* (pp. 1–14). Thousand Oaks, CA: Sage.

Scott, D., Brown, A., Lunt, I., & Thorne, L. (2004). *Professional doctorates: Integrating professional and academic knowledge.* Maidenhead, England: Open University Press.

Shulman, L.S. (2005). Signature pedagogies in the professions. *Daedalus, 134*(3), 52–59.

Shulman, L. S., Golde, C. M., Bueschel, A. C., & Garabedian, K. J. (2006). Reclaiming education's doctorates: A critique and a proposal. *Educational Researcher, 35*(3), 25–32.

Wellington, J., & Sikes, P. (2006). 'A doctorate in a tight compartment': Why do students choose a professional practice doctorate and what impact does it have on their personal and professional lives? *Studies in Higher Education, 31,* 723–734.

Zambo, D., Buss, R. R., & Zambo, R. (2015). Uncovering the identities of students and graduates in a CPED-influenced EdD program. *Studies in Higher Education, 40,* 233–252. doi:10.1080/03075079.2013.823932

Zambo, R., Zambo, D., Buss, R. R., Perry, J. A., & Williams, T. R. (2014). Seven years after the call: Students' and graduates' perceptions of the re-envisioned EdD. *Innovative Higher Education, 39*(2), 123–137. doi:10.1007/s10755-013-9262-3

CHAPTER 10

THE PROBLEM OF PRACTICE DISSERTATION

Matching Program Goals, Practices, and Outcomes

Alisa Belzer, Tali Axelrod, Cathleen Benedict, Tara Jakubik, Michelle Rosen, and Olcay Yavuz

In its early history, the Education Doctorate (EdD) at Rutgers University was the only doctorate that the Graduate School of Education (GSE) could award; it did not have a PhD program (Ryan, De Lisi, & Heuschkel, 2012). The school was allowed to grant PhDs starting in 1997, but the addition of four new PhD programs did not spur discussion about differences between the two doctoral programs. The main adjustment to the EdD program made after the PhD program was initiated was to bring down the number of credits required for graduation so that it matched the PhD. After that, the EdD program sputtered along more or less untouched for years. The GSE ran multiple EdD programs which coexisted, and sometimes overlapped, with the PhD programs, all functioning as relatively separate programs and with no articulated or substantial operational

The EdD and the Scholarly Practitioner, pages 153–175
Copyright © 2016 by Information Age Publishing
All rights of reproduction in any form reserved.

differences in mission, content, format, or learning goals (Ryan et al., 2012). Whether a particular area of study had an EdD, Phd or both programs affiliated with it was more an artifact of school history and politics than rational decision-making. All programs required the same number of credits, a set number of research courses, and a dissertation, but they had little else in common and there was no significant, schoolwide oversight to insure consistency across programs. Each EdD and PhD program had its own coordinator and set its own rules for course requirements and qualifying exams. Not only was there no thought given to the relationship of programs within the PhD or the EdD, there was very little talk about what distinguished the EdD from the PhD. Among the many areas that could have been adjusted to differentiate the two programs was the dissertation. However, no one thought it necessary to define the EdD dissertation as distinctive from a PhD dissertation, and everyone took it for granted that they would know a defendable one in either program when they saw it (Lovitts, 2005). At that time, EdD dissertations could run the gamut from philosophical to historical, phenomenological to empirical; and while they might be practice based, they were just as likely not to be. The same could be said of PhD dissertations at the time.

In a desire to make doctoral programs at Rutgers more driven by a set of appropriate and distinctive learning goals, and responding with interest and enthusiasm to the developing efforts spearheaded by Lee Shulman at the Carnegie Foundation to reenvision the education doctorate as a distinct and valued degree, in 2006 then-Dean Richard De Lisi jumped at the opportunity to join the national consortium of universities engaging in and collaborating on this design process. Rutgers became a Phase I member of the Carnegie Project on the Education Doctorate (CPED). When Dean De Lisi charged faculty with redesigning our Education Doctoral (EdD) program in 2008 as part of this process, it was clear that a key component of the change would need to be the reconceptualization the EdD dissertation.

In this chapter, we report on the outcome of this process. By using the dissertation work of five Rutgers graduates as our "data," we focus on the ways in which the EdD program's "problem of practice" dissertations that our graduates complete enact the program goal of improving learning opportunities and outcomes for learners across the lifespan in formal, informal, and nonformal educational contexts (Rutgers University, 2015). We also describe the impact of their dissertation work on their professional roles and responsibilities. This is important because students do not participate in programs simply out of an altruistic hope of improving learning opportunities; they also want to use the degree to advance their careers. After a brief description of the program, the sources of their problems of practice and research designs, the remainder of this chapter is organized around the types of impact their work had, what elements of the EdD program they report contributed to these, and the barriers they felt occasionally put the breaks on what they were able to accomplish. We conclude by reflecting on the importance of purposefully rethinking and redesigning the dissertation process as programs reenvision their EdD programs so that it truly aligns with the purpose of the EdD as an impactful and valued degree that can successfully train scholarly practitioners to be change agents who have the skills and dispositions to improve educational outcomes for learners.

The co-authors of this chapter are five program graduates, Tara, Tali, Cathy, Michelle, and Olcay, as well as Alisa, the former EdD Program Director. The five graduate co-authors were the ones who responded to Alisa's call for writing partners that went out to all graduates. While their willingness to volunteer for this project suggests their satisfaction with and enthusiasm for their experience in the program, they were neither selected as "best case" nor representative examples. Although we met twice to brainstorm and discuss the contents of the chapter, the writing was done individually. Each graduate wrote a case description of his or her dissertation and its impact. After we all read these cases, we met to look across them to identify key themes and program elements which emerged as supporting their process. Alisa then synthesized and summarized the case descriptions around the identified themes and added in her own description of the program. The other authors provided feedback on the draft before it was completed. Although the case descriptions were written in the first person, in an effort to simplify and clarify, the graduates are referred to in the third person or as a collective "they," except when quoted directly from their own case descriptions. Text from their case descriptions is generally paraphrased and synthesized; direct quotes are used only occasionally.

THE RUTGERS EdD AND THE PATH TO A PROBLEM OF PRACTICE DISSERTATION

In 2010 the Graduate School of Education accepted its first cohort of students for the newly redesigned EdD program. The new, revised EdD program was distinguished from the PhD program in terms of mission, format, course requirements, organizational structure, and dissertation requirements. Its goals focus on training change leaders who have the skills and dispositions to use research to guide and improve the learning opportunities of students across the lifespan in a wide variety of contexts. This interdisciplinary, schoolwide, cohort-based, 72-credit program has four concentrations: Design of Learning Environments; Education, Culture, and Society; Educational Leadership; and Teacher Leadership. Within the cohort, students take eight three-credit "core" courses together. These courses are intended to give students a range of theoretical lenses and inquiry approaches that can help them name, frame, and analyze problems of practice. Students also take eight required and elective courses in their concentrations intended to deepen their content knowledge in a specific area, and 24 dissertation credits. The program is designed for completion in a little over 3 years, although a small handful of students elect to slow down during coursework traversing more than one cohort, and some students spread out their dissertation work over an additional semester or two.

The program's cohort model has three layers. Each year the program accepts approximately 30 students who all start the program together and take all of their core courses together; this is the first layer of the cohort. Not only are they connected by their shared academic experiences in the program, the cohorts have come together around birthdays, births, weddings, deaths, and other life events as well as for sporting events, drinking events (e.g., end of semester celebrations), and other social occasions. In other words, they tend to form a significant connection with each other. The second layer of cohorts is within the concentrations. Students from each concentration take required concentration courses together and often form a very tight bond as these smaller groups enable everyone to get to know each other very well. The third layer of the cohort develops when dissertation groups are formed. Students, not necessarily from the same concentration, are placed in groups of approximately five around a common theme, all with the same dissertation chair. Although they each do their own study, the intent is that the group structure facilitates the opportunity to do peer review on drafts, share resources as appropriate, and collaboratively engage in data analysis sessions. The group meets regularly with their chair throughout the dissertation process. Because they all receive the same direction from their faculty leader, they can help each other reinforce their learning outside of meetings. This group works intensively together for 15–18 months from dissertation proposal writing to dissertation defense.

The emphasis of the program is on solving problems of practice; research is construed as a way to understand problems in systematic, complex, and meaningful ways such that substantive implications for practice emerge or as a way to evaluate the impact of innovations designed to address those problems. In order to align program goals with program practices, this improvement and change focus suggested that new definitions of and formats for the dissertation were needed. Our first step was to develop a set of guiding principles for the dissertation which explain that the dissertation

> should focus on a problem of practice that is relevant to the student and his/her professional context (when possible), have direct implications for policy and practice, uphold common standards of high quality (well written, rigorous, and coherent approach to methodology, thorough grounding and bounding, etc.), [and] have a final chapter that outlines how this study helps/ informs everyday work of practitioners and a section that makes specific sug-

gestions for improved practices based on the findings of the study. (Rutgers University, 2015, p. 13)

However, our path to alignment between program goals and ideals and actual implementation was not a straight one. For example, we used the term *problem of practice* often with students, with each other, and in promotional materials. Yet midway through the second year of the program, as faculty members worked together to increase interrater reliability when assessing qualifying papers that require students to articulate and frame the problem of practice they will address for their dissertation studies, it became clear that there was not agreement on what the term means and that definition of the term relative to the dissertation was necessary. Faculty raised questions and often disagreed about what constituted an acceptable problem of practice and therefore a passing paper. To address this need, core course faculty and the program's Curriculum Committee worked together to develop a definition of the *problem of practice dissertation*, which is now published in the Rutgers University Graduate School of Education EdD Student Handbook. The Handbook states that a problem of practice dissertation

> Describes a challenge in educational practice, seeks empirically to investigate the challenge and/or test solution(s) to address the challenge, generates actionable implications, and appropriately communicates these implications to relevant stakeholders. Dissertations that investigate or test solutions to a challenge in educational practice typically formulate research questions that in some way ask "What's going on here?" or "What happens when I, we, or they do...?" "Appropriately communicates" could mean policy briefs, journal articles, curriculum designs, evaluation reports, etc. Communication should be matched to audience. "Stakeholders" (in addition to the dissertation committee) could include colleagues, supervisors, administrators, parents, community members, policy makers, etc. (Rutgers University, 2015, p. 13)

Students have the option of completing their dissertations using one of three formats: a traditional five-chapter type document, a semitraditional format, and an alternative/portfolio format. The semitraditional and alternative formats were designed to reflect our definition of a problem of practice dissertation because both have elements that break away from the notion of academic audience as the main consumers of the work and instead focus on products that are appropriate for relevant stakeholders in the problem of practice context. Dissertations that are addressed to relevant audiences seem more likely to have an impact in the research setting.

The semitraditional format is composed of the same first four chapters as a traditional dissertation (Introduction, literature review, research methods, and findings), but ends with a product rather than a concluding chapter. This product is meant to be designed and constructed to reflect the student's findings in a format appropriate for and usable by likely consumers in practice contexts. Examples of acceptable products include a presentation (and supporting materials) for relevant stakeholders such as teachers, school board members, conference attendees, or community members which report on findings and implications of the study; an evaluation plan; a curriculum design or curriculum materials; a professional development design; a policy brief; a practitioner or academic journal article; a funding proposal; or a video documentary. For example, a student who implemented a research-based new teacher-induction program in her school developed a handbook for novices and mentors as a result of data collected during her study. Although she stuck to the traditional format and attached the handbook as an appendix, it could have been a stand in for her final chapter.

The alternative format dissertation is made up of three such products, one of which must include a description of the research design and relevant research literature as well as demonstrating clear linkages between data collected, analysis, and findings (typically in the form of a journal article). Each product must focus on unique aspects of the study and be designed for distinct audiences and purposes. The products must be bracketed by an introduction which describes the problem of practice, previews the products, and describes the design or intervention, if one was implemented specifically for the purpose of the study, and a conclusion, which focuses on impact, next steps, and overall learnings. One example of an alternative format dissertation consisted of a journal article, a conference presentation, and a 15-hour professional development program design, all of which the student used in his practice. His journal article was accepted in a peer reviewed, academic journal; he presented his work at a professional conference; and he implemented the professional development design several times for teachers in his school. Although the alternative format has been slow to catch on, an increasing number of students are implementing it each year.

THE STORY OF THE QUESTION: WHERE PROBLEMS OF PRACTICE COME FROM

At the time the program graduate authors of this chapter designed their studies, faculty members had not yet articulated what the program meant by the term *problem of practice* dissertation. Yet the guidance they received during coursework and from their dissertation advisors helped them move organically in the direction that program planners had intended. Belzer and Ryan (2013) analyzed 21 dissertation abstracts from the program's first cohort and found that the site where students conducted their research could be proximal, such as their own classrooms, or more distal but still touching on the context in which they to do their work, but they always focused specifically on improving learning opportunities and outcomes. The abstracts showed that students asked one of three types of questions:

> questions that evaluate an initiative or policy that is already in place, questions that ask what happens when the student implements an initiative to solve a problem and improve outcomes, and questions that seek to describe current conditions as a way to generate appropriate and contextualized solutions to problems. (p. 203)

The dissertation studies of the five co-author graduates that are described here are well aligned with this description.

Tara

Tara, who was a student in the Design of Learning Environments Concentration, is a high school English teacher. Her dissertation study was conducted in her own classroom as a design-based, teacher research project aimed at improving her students' reading comprehension of graphic novels. Her study was grounded on her observation that even her high school seniors struggle to gain deep meaning from texts, especially those that are multimodal (including graphic novels). Knowing that successfully constructing meaning from such texts requires different skills than when reading traditional texts, and that they are increasingly common in day-to-day life (e.g., web pages), she implemented a new instructional format in her classroom—literature circles—and compared the reading strategies utilized when interacting with graphic novels in the group context to the strategies students employed when they read individually.

Cathy and Tali

Cathy and Tali both focused on improving the quality and outcomes of teacher collaboration in Professional Learning Communities (PLCs). Tali, a student in the Educational Leadership Concentration and a new principal at the time she began the EdD program, noted that teachers in her school had been asked to implement a reading workshop approach without adequate buy-in or training. Although she knew that PLCs might be an excellent venue for professional growth in this area, she felt she needed to know more about how teachers in her school worked together in this context to support each other's learning. She believed that this understanding could help her better support teacher work in existing PLCs. In other words, before she intervened, she wanted to know more about how teachers worked together in this setting. Therefore she framed her study around the generic question "What's going on here?" with regard to teacher collaboration in the context of a new instructional initiative they were expected to implement. In particular, she was interested in the structures and routines they used, the artifacts and tools they brought in to their meetings, the discussion and collaboration patterns that emerged, and the value that teachers attach to these interactions. To address her research questions regarding teacher collaboration, she observed team meetings, collected field notes, and conducted interviews.

Cathy, a student in the Teacher Leadership Concentration and a 4th-grade teacher, already knew from firsthand experience that PLCs in her school were dysfunctional. Unlike Tali, she was ready to study an intervention designed to improve the function of her grade-level PLC. While there had been initial enthusiasm for PLCs at her school, teachers received virtually no training or sustained support for implementing them. By the time Cathy undertook her study, the grade-level PLCs that all teachers were required to participate in were PLCs in name only. Meetings were used largely for carrying out organizational tasks, completing classroom prep work, or venting negative feelings. After learning about effective, teacher-led, collaborative professional development strategies during coursework in the EdD program, Cathy understood that specific structures and routines were needed to make PLCs effective. She then decided to study what would happen when a research-based PLC procedural structure is used to do instructional problem solving related to a particular learning challenge that students in her grade level demonstrated through their standardized test results. After providing professional development to prepare her grade-level team for the new approach, she facilitated and observed PLC meetings and gathered data with before and after surveys and interviews.

Michelle

As co-director of the University Professional Development Center (UPDC), which provides professional development (PD) to teachers in surrounding districts, Michelle knew that teacher leaders who participated enjoyed the experience. What she did not know was how these teachers were using what they were learning from PD offerings at the Center as they in turn facilitated PD in their home schools. She was also curious to learn what else might be influencing their work as professional development leaders. Michelle decided to use her dissertation work to learn more about how their learning shapes their role as PD providers and what the UPDC could do to enhance their capacity and support improved practice. In her study, Michelle followed three teacher leaders who participated in UPDC activities designed to increase teacher content knowledge. She observed and logged their PD activities in their home schools and interviewed them in conjunction with the activities they led to understand what influenced their work as PD leaders and what role the Center played in shaping their role enactment.

Olcay

Olcay, a student in the Teacher Leadership Concentration and a high school guidance counselor during his enrollment in the EdD program, had observed an extremely low rate of college attendance among the graduates from the urban school serving low-income students where he worked. To address this, he had already designed a comprehensive school counseling program, the College Readiness Access and Success Program (CRASP), when he began his dissertation work. Although he knew that the model had significantly increased the number of students applying and being accepted to college, he did not know as much about what happened to them after graduation or what program elements contributed to the positive outcomes he had observed. He used his dissertation to study the impact of CRASP and sought to understand how it influences students' college readiness, pursuit, access, and persistence. Employing a multiple regression strategy, he was able to compare the impact of CRASP participation among students who participated in it along a continuum from not at all to up to 4 years of high school.

Commonalities Across Experiences

All five of these studies are not only grounded in personal experiences and interests, but also centered around issues that reflect broad trends and topics that are current, significant, and aimed at making practical and concrete improvements in the educational outcomes of learners. They are both personally meaningful and publicly significant. As a benefit of studying existing problems and practices in authentic contexts, Cathy and Tara became more systematic and drew more intentionally on research-based best practices. Tali, Olcay, and Michelle's work served to shine a light on a "black box" aspect of their practice, or, to draw on a similar metaphor, Tali explained, "This work provided a window." Both Olcay and Michelle knew their work was having a positive impact to some extent, but they wanted to know more than they could without doing systematic inquiry. Tali assumed she needed to provide scaffolding to improve the impact of teacher interaction as an appropriate way to improve practice, but understood that she could be most effective if she had a deep understanding of current conditions before she started making changes. In gaining an understanding of what was happening in a space that had not previously been visible to them but was relevant to their increasing effectiveness, they were able to derive meaningful implications for practice.

DISSERTATIONS THAT MATTER: THE IMPACT OF PROBLEM OF PRACTICE DISSERTATIONS

The dissertation studies that Tara, Cathy, Tali, Michelle, and Olcay carried out were aimed at deepening understanding to solve authentic and meaningful problems of practice and improve educational opportunities for practitioners and learners. In turn, each had a significant impact by changing the way the graduates did their work or in how they understood that implementation of innovations should be carried out, how they related to their colleagues or promoted collegial relationships, and on their career trajectories. In general, the work that these five graduates did for their dissertation had an impact on professional relationships within a range of learning contexts that enhanced collaboration and centered on learning. Finally, they demonstrated that their dissertations functioned as their "opening night" as scholarly practitioners, demonstrating their capacity to "perform" research studies that improve practice, but also that they would engage in many repeat performances in which research would drive decision making and change efforts well beyond their time as doctoral students (L. Shulman, personal communication, June 2012).

Impact on Practice

Tara

Tara's dissertation work focused on a specific instructional challenge—helping students gain more meaning from multimodal texts and graphic novels specifically, but what she learned has had an impact on her teaching overall. In particular, her observations of students' work in literature circles when working together to make meaning from a graphic novel has influenced her reading instruction more generally. In her effort to improve her students' reading comprehension when grappling with the challenge of reading graphic novels that require the integration of multimodal media, Tara implemented a more student-centered, collaborative approach to making meaning from texts. As a result of analyzing the reading strategies her students used to make meaning from graphic novels and the success they experienced when doing so collaboratively, she now creates far more instructional activities that draw on group work in other aspects of reading instruction. Students are more often encouraged to communicate with their small-group colleagues and with the entire class about texts instead of reading independently and then learning about the text through her interpretations. Tara has observed that the use of shared reading strategies has provided students with the opportunity to find more meaning from a variety of texts. In addition, she now steers away from "some old methods of teaching" (e.g., giving students study guide questions to complete independently) and focuses more on encouraging students to share their thoughts relating to the text they are reading. As a result of improving learning opportunities related to just one aspect of instruction as a result of her dissertation study, "I gained confidence as a classroom teacher [in general] because I found a way to ensure all students were participating and improve interaction with and comprehension of texts."

Cathy

Cathy's research not only had an impact on her practice and her grade-level team members who participated in the PLC but also more broadly on the professional culture of her school. She and her colleagues utilized data to identify a shared challenge their students faced related to vocabulary development. Using a structured work cycle, the participants in Cathy's PLC collaboratively developed, implemented, and studied the impact of an instructional intervention designed to more effectively help students learn, retain, and use higher-order vocabulary. Cathy, along with her grade level team, implemented this intervention in their classrooms. Their efforts seemed successful; their Grade 4 NJ ASK (state standardized assessment used for accountability purposes) language arts literacy scores that year showed significant improvement. Without conducting an experimental design study, it is impossible to attribute this success to the work of the PLC, but this outcome led to positive talk among the participants and other faculty members about what had been accomplished.

Additionally, the focus on more effective implementation of PLCs had a systemic impact within Cathy's school. The participants actively analyzed student data to determine a need, identified the related Common Core State Standards, researched instructional practices to increase student learning in that area, implemented new, collaboratively designed strategies, and reflected on the outcomes. This approach to improving classroom practice has had some lasting effects on the participants. Cathy reports that even though the grade-level team that participated in her study has broken up, they are still using techniques they learned and utilized to make the PLC teacher and student centered. For example, they make sure that agenda topics at team meetings are driven by the needs of teachers and are based on the results of data collected from assessments. Additionally, they still recognize and value the teacher learning that can occur when teams of teachers collaborate within a community driven to improve student learning. The norms the PLC developed during the study year are also still invoked. For example, one important norm still in place was the result of problem solving the group engaged in to address the need to take care of administrative business in spite of their ongoing commitment to professional learning and improved practice. As a result, they agreed to set aside the last 5 minutes of every meeting to discuss everyday administrative decisions, such as budgetary items, that needed to be made. Additionally, she sees that her colleagues' focus in PLC meetings are more often determined as a result of looking at student data and that they are making decisions about changing teaching strategies based on best practices research rather than an attitude of "that's how I've always done it."

Tali

Tali's study also led to systemic changes. She did not implement a new practice as part of her study, but the findings that emerged as a result of looking closely at teacher interactions in a PLC had clear implications that have shaped her subsequent practice as a building principal. Her observations of the focal PLC led her to be more proactive as an instructional leader in supporting the development of teacher leaders and to put structures in place that could encourage more collaborative interactions. These leadership actions offer potential to improve teaching practice from the bottom up. For example, she prioritized teacher-led professional learning in the budget and built the school schedule to allow for common planning time. She hired literacy coaches from within the staff's teacher leaders and has an active school leadership committee composed of teachers who are committed to discussing instructional issues, helping guide the building's professional development needs, and taking charge of teacher learning, sometimes by joining her as she makes presentations at faculty meetings. Additionally, an important result of her research has been initiating cross-classroom visitations among teachers, and teachers have become much more open to sharing their practice with each other as a strategy for learning. These efforts have also helped the staff see their colleagues as both learners and experts. As a result, teacher leadership has spread throughout the school community.

Michelle

Michelle has changed jobs since she completed her dissertation, moving from co-director of a university-based professional development resource center to a faculty position in higher education. However, she has had the opportunity to build a similar professional development resource center in her new job and this has given her an opportunity to start from scratch using the knowledge she gained as a result of conducting her dissertation study. In general, she designed this center to draw on research-based principles of professional development best practices, concepts that had not explicitly informed the conceptual underpinning of the Center where she had been previously employed. For example, in the new Center, PD activities are offered over the course of a year in a series of related topics aligned with district needs rather than as a series of unrelated topics. Each session includes presentations on new instructional strategies accompanied by PD aimed at helping teacher leaders develop their capacity to help their colleagues learn and change. The series also includes a mandatory weeklong summer follow-up course, and onsite coaching supports teacher leaders as they seek to implement what they have learned. Overall, these efforts are designed to sustain learning and make it much more likely that teacher leaders can be effective professional developers within their own schools by providing ongoing and coherent support that focuses not just on developing content knowledge but also professional development leadership skills. This is in contrast to what Michelle had observed during her dissertation work when the PD offerings were one-shots and without focus on developing skills teacher leaders need to be effective professional developers.

Olcay

Olcay's study yielded significant, substantive, and concrete implications for practice, many of which could be implemented in his school, others which may have an impact on the field more generally. In particular, he observed the ways in which the CRASP model fell short in helping the hardest-to-reach students—those with the lowest GPAs, those least likely to take the SAT, or those with the lowest SAT scores including ESL and special-education students. The school-level changes that Olcay recommended as a result of his study include training teachers to do effective SAT preparation instead of using an outside provider, taking advantage of test preparation applications on the iPads that each student receives, and working to improve the effectiveness of existing tutoring services. By presenting concrete evidence of the program's strengths and weaknesses, Olcay used his study to advocate for small-scale yet ambitious program improvements that are within reach for his school. These recommendations also have implications for other schools as his peer guidance counselors have asked to use the CRASP model. This type of dissemination of innovative ideas and scaling up in small increments demonstrates another way that practitioners can meaningfully impact practice.

Impact on Roles, Relationships, and Professional Positions

Not only did the problem of practice dissertation projects have an impact on educational opportunities for students and colleagues, they also had a personal impact on graduates by reshaping their roles, responsibilities, and professional positions. Completing their dissertation studies helped launch Cathy, Olcay, and Michelle into new positions, and their dissertation work provided them with skills and products to support them in these endeavors. Although Tara and Tali did not change jobs after completing the program, they found that they were interacting in new ways with colleagues and supervisees in their work contexts. Olcay and Michelle moved into higher education. In both cases their dissertation research was a demonstration, attractive to the prospective employers, of the ways in which they could connect to the field in practical and useful ways that would be likely to support mutually beneficial school-university relationships. As noted earlier, Michelle's experience as the co-director of a university-based professional development center and her perspective on best practices that she gained from her research were just the fit her department was looking for as they sought to build meaningful connections with surrounding districts. Olcay not only brought to his job search a fully developed model to increase college-going among urban youth which he could share with local districts and graduate students who would work in them, but also he brought data about how to improve the model and many connections with districts who were interested in implementing the model. In both cases, these EdD graduates continued to have an impact in their fields through service from within the context of higher education practitioner training.

Moving from practitioner to professor after receiving a doctorate may be a relatively normal career trajectory for many with a doctorate, but Cathy wanted to stay in "the field," working to improve learning opportunities, as a teacher leader in her school and district. Her transition was a bit rockier than what Michelle and Olcay have experienced because the trajectory was less clear. Cathy reports feeling she had the skills to be a scholarly practitioner and yearned to use these skills beyond the confines of her own 4th-grade classroom. Yet she also had a feeling that administrators recognized this but did nothing to take advantage of what she had to offer. The district where she works is small and the addition of a teacher leader position, she was told, was not in the budget. After she first graduated, she was asked to take on leadership roles related to carrying out state-mandated requirements such as the District Evaluation Advisory Committee (DEAC) and the School Improvement Panel (ScIP), and also to be a grade-level team leader. However, none of these positions got her out of the classroom, and she felt that her capacity to have an impact as a scholarly practitioner and teacher leader beyond her grade-level team was minimal. In spite of feeling somewhat stuck, Cathy offered professional development workshops on vocabulary instruction and the use of protocols for analyzing NJ ASK results for her colleagues. After significant effort to help district leaders understand what she could offer and approximately one year after graduating, she was offered two new positions, one managing new teacher induction and the other working to transition the district's Basic Skills program to a Response to Intervention approach for helping struggling students. The latter position involves seeking, developing, and implementing research-based practices to help struggling students. She will also have opportunities to work in partnership with teachers to analyze student data and implement new or refine current instructional strategies.

Tali and Tara have stayed in their positions, but both find themselves in altered relationships with teachers in their buildings. At the time she earned her EdD, Tara was one of the youngest teachers working in her district. Yet despite her age, her colleagues were impressed by her accomplishments. They have begun to ask her about their own further academic study and seek her help when writing professional memos, course proposals, and coursework. In addition, she has been invited to work with school administrators on district-level committees. Tali is working more collaboratively to distribute leadership and support the leadership development of teachers in her building. Both Tara and Tali have been recruited to teach as adjunct faculty at Rutgers. Tara reports that when she interviewed for the faculty position, she was able to demonstrate relevant content and pedagogical knowledge. Tali was hired to teach a required course in the EdD program. Not only is this an accomplishment for her made possible by her doctoral work, but her experience as a scholarly practitioner makes a significant contribution to the learning opportunities of current EdD students.

Impact on Stance as a Scholarly Practitioner

The Rutgers EdD program places an emphasis on problem of practice dissertations that have the potential to strengthen educational outcomes and improve practice in areas that are problematic for learners, teachers, administrators, and program managers. No matter how impactful this work is, if it is a once-and-done effort, the value added for the field of the EdD is limited. Scholarly practitioners who lead change efforts just once for the purpose of completing their dissertations will have an insignificant impact on practice in the long run. However, Lee Shulman (personal communication, 2008) suggested that the dissertation should be viewed simply as our graduates' "opening night." Here they demonstrate that they know how to use research to inform and lead change efforts. But he argued the reenvisioned doctorate would only truly make its mark if our graduates continued to act as scholarly practitioners through continued "performances." In fact, all of these graduates have continued to perform in leadership roles as a direct result of their degree completion. Equally as important are the ways in which these newly minted EdD graduates continue to use research to inform their work as change leaders, demonstrating their stance as scholarly practitioners.

The Carnegie Project on the Education Doctorate defines scholarly practitioners as individuals who know how to "blend practical wisdom with professional skills and knowledge to name, frame, and solve problems of practice. They use practical research and applied theories as tools for change" (CPED, 2010). Among the five co-author and former students, this role was most consistently enacted by them by using the research literature to inform decision making and change efforts and to help them make a

compelling case for a range of improvement initiatives with key stakeholders in their work contexts. For example, Tali said,

> I have learned how to look at problems in a new way...Now I will investigate
> what the research says to inform me on how to proceed. Moreover, I know
> how to find evidence to convince a parent or board member of an important
> point to help improve the school."

Cathy too, like Tali, has become an avid consumer of research. Not only
does she use it to inform change efforts, but she also sees it as part of her
mission to help other practitioners understand and appreciate its value for
informing change efforts. She said,

> Because I view both of these titles [teacher leader and scholarly practitioner]
> as one and the same, I see the need for studying research-based practices,
> availing myself of educational studies and then sharing what I learn with col-
> leagues, and having a wider view of how to tackle problems of practice that
> involve a step-by-step process inclusive of professional development.

Michelle is not only using her dissertation research to inform the design
of the professional development center she directs, but she has also done
her next "performance" by engaging in further research to address a problem of practice at her work site. When the teacher education program in
which she teaches shifted from a traditional student teaching experience to
a co-teaching model in response to identified deficiencies in the current program, Michelle jumped at the chance to evaluate the impact of this change.
In conjunction with another professor and the Director of Teacher Preparation, they secured a university grant to conduct a mixed methods study that
evaluates how the co-teaching model works for student interns. It is unlikely
the program would have been formally studied otherwise. She reports that,
"Perhaps before the EdD I would have just worked on shifting the model. But
since the EdD, I looked at how to study it and its impact on the experience."

KEY PROGRAM COMPONENTS

The faculty members who participated in redesigning the EdD at Rutgers
sought to build in multiple program components that they believed would
support the program goals. These included a core set of courses designed
with the intention of giving students different theoretical lenses through
which to view and analyze problems of practice and research methods
courses that prepared them to conduct applied, problem-based research.
However, from the perspective of the five graduate co-authors, the program components that contributed most to their formation of a scholarly

practitioner disposition were not necessarily tied to specific courses. Rather, they cut across their course experiences. This observation points to the importance of creating a coherent vision for the EdD program that is enacted by all (or at least most) faculty members and an overall program structure that supports and enhances students' ability to learn and develop.

Coursework Supports: Practical Skills for Scholarly Practitioners

The students felt that the program's early emphasis on choosing a meaningful dissertation topic that had the potential to address an authentic problem of practice, the encouragement to try out newly developed skills in their work settings, and the emphasis on applying coursework to the identified problem of practice so that expertise and focus could develop from early in the program were critical to their growth and development as change leaders who could enact program goals and the larger EdD vision of impactful research to improve educational outcomes. Not only did these program elements promote cohesion, but they also supported the accelerated time line (approximately 3.5 years) of the program.

Beginning with the new student orientation, the EdD students are encouraged to identify a research interest, and they are advised to use coursework, whenever possible, to pursue that topic by immersing themselves in the related research literature, designing and implementing pilot studies, and trying out new, relevant practices through a process of design and evaluation. In addition, the concept of problem of practice is now explicitly defined so that students have a clear and immediate framework for thinking about the type of dissertation work that is expected of them. This information is consistently communicated to them across courses, in the student handbook, and in the structure of the qualifying process which requires them to write a dissertation preproposal about 6 months before that process actually begins. Tali reported that the program's problem of practice orientation meant that she started thinking about a specific problem she was having from the start of the program. Because she had a clear and immediate focus on a problem that was extremely relevant to her work, she says she was able to use her coursework as an opportunity to begin solving the identified problem from the moment she began the program. Tara noted that being encouraged to focus on an "insider" problem meant that she immediately had a deep understanding of the problem, had a preexisting relationship with the participants, and was able to see concrete and actionable results. It also meant that she could hit the ground running with regard to implementing her study. Cathy also experienced the benefits of insider status.

A major contributing factor to my work as a teacher leader was that my dissertation study occurred in my professional context, my elementary school. I knew the participants in the study and they saw the changes that were happening to our traditional grade-level meetings from the beginning of the study and recognized progress.

This experience helped her view the dissertation as a means for teachers "to actively seek and solve problems of instruction that would begin with teacher learning and lead to an increase in student learning." Her dissertation work also gave her clear "wins" in her own work context, thus raising the visibility of her intervention and her capacity as a change leader. Her accomplishments eventually positioned to take up new leadership responsibilities in her district that would enable her to continue to be a change leader and scholarly practitioner.

While EdD students are clearly encouraged to develop a researcher's theoretical and analytical perspective on a problem of practice, they also gain practical experience as change leaders. For example, students in the Teacher Leadership concentration learn how to facilitate teacher-led, collaborative, data-driven professional development using protocols to structure professional discussions through a highly experiential process. First they take turns bringing data (e.g., assessment data, student work, or teacher-developed assignments) to class, using protocols to analyze, reflect on, and draw implications from the focal data, and then analyzing and reflecting on the process. They are required then to try out these strategies three times during the course of a semester with their school colleagues. They report back in class about their experiences and collaboratively troubleshoot issues and challenges they encountered, reflect on their experiences as a way to learn more fully from the experience, and engage in action planning to articulate how they might use these developing skills in the future. For many Teacher Leadership students this course is an important starting point for their dissertation work, as it was for Cathy. She explained that what enabled her to effectively use protocols with the participants in her dissertation study was the practical experience she gained during coursework.

Learning in a Community: The Power of the Cohort

All of the graduates emphasized the importance of the cohort model. Not only did it provide important emotional supports, but it was also a source of learning. Both aspects of the cohort contributed to the students' capacity to move forward as change agents.

The graduates talked about the value of the cohort model using words like "family" and "life-long relationships" and indicated that cohort members helped motivate and shore each other up when they needed it. It also gave them a ready sounding board. Working across concentrations in their core courses and in their dissertation groups gave them a range of perspectives from which to draw and gather constructive feedback. Especially in their dissertation groups, where they regularly shared their work and provided each other with feedback, they felt motivated to adhere to deadlines because they were responsible to each other. The cohort helped people succeed and thrive in the program, thus enabling them to graduate as scholarly practitioners with the credentials in hand and the skills ready to take up new leadership roles, get new jobs, and use their knowledge about research to effect change and advocate for improved educational outcomes.

The students also learned important skills and gained some tools from working in a cohort that they report continuing to use. For example, Michelle used the cohort model approach when she designed the professional development center in her new job. Others reported that working so often in groups and having to work across differences helped improve their communication skills and sharpened their abilities to work collaboratively on group projects. Tali reports that working in groups, as they so often did in each level of the cohort, helped her learn to communicate in distinctive ways, being responsive to the task, the co-workers, and the audience. "This has helped me professionally when I give presentations to the board or to faculty," she reported.

BARRIERS

Only Tali and Tara explicitly identified barriers that limited the potential impact of their work in the EdD program on their professional practice. Like all her co-authors, Tali did her research in her own worksite. However, unlike the others, she collected data and developed findings that created less than flattering portrayals of the research participants as Tali found that their ways of working together were not very collaborative or constructive. Learning that her faculty would need explicit supports and scaffolding if they were to engage in collaborative professional learning was extremely helpful in providing her with a leadership direction. However, Tali has felt constrained in documenting her findings publicly. As she said, "When you do research in/on your own setting, when findings are unflattering, it can be very difficult to know how to share what was learned." She has chosen to restrict public access to her dissertation, thus limiting its potential impact. However, she is now working on a manuscript she will submit to a scholarly journal in which she masks and blurs many descriptions so as to make the research participants more anonymous. She also did find a constructive way to share her findings with her teachers through a brief that highlights new protocols and ways to help them share their practice with each other as a tool for learning within their collaborative groups. Additionally, she hopes to be able to share her findings with a broader audience assuming her paper is accepted for publication.

Given the emphasis in the program on solving "local" problems of practice, the program would do well to recognize the possibility of sticky situations when students do research in their own worksites. Not only might "what's going on here" focused dissertations sometimes need to tell a less-than-happy story before real change can happen, but sometimes "what happens when . . ." focused dissertations might tell the story of failed interventions given that they can not all work. Still, much can be learned from either of these possibilities. Students need strategies for addressing these possibilities if faculty are to discourage a discourse of "happy talk" that is often the norm when practitioners share their work but which fails to address the real difficulties and frequent failures of teaching and leadership in educational settings.

Tara observed a different kind of barrier related to the value of the degree and Cathy experienced it firsthand. As a classroom teacher, Tara noted her doctoral degree brought her prestige and the respect of colleagues and administrators, but it did not offer a professional credential for any particular position within K–12 settings. While it made her eligible to apply for an adjunct faculty position in higher education, within the K–12 arena the EdD did not qualify her for any particular career advancement. Tara noted,

> During the three years of the program, I grew professionally and I was ready to take on new positions within the K–12 public school district. However, there was a challenge. The EdD enhanced my classroom instruction but did not offer any certifications toward professional advancement.

What this meant for her was attaining a doctorate "without any opportunity to gain a higher position within the K–12 system."

Cathy, another classroom teacher, struggled with this same issue. Although her district eventually recognized her with a new position, she struggled to move into something that seemed a good fit with her new skills. As she waited, somewhat impatiently, for a shift in her job responsibilities, she wondered if perhaps her district just did not know what to do with her. Her skills as a teacher leader were an imperfect fit for career structures in her district. Her self-advocacy and her efforts to demonstrate her skills eventually did pay off, but it certainly was not a clear path.

Given that the EdD at Rutgers is designed to train scholarly practitioners in the field, Tara's observation and Cathy's experience points to an irony about the mismatch between the degree and career opportunities for those who want to stay very closely connected to the school setting, especially as teacher leaders. Ideally, the K–12 system would recognize and reward the skills and dispositions that EdD graduates bring to school buildings, but the licensure culture makes this difficult. Perhaps it would be helpful to provide additional emphasis during coursework on how to navigate organizational structures in ways that promote scholarly practitioners and utilize their skills so that they can be in appropriate positions to lead change. They not only need to learn to be change leaders, they need to learn how to positions themselves within organizations so that they can have the opportunity to use their skills in this role.

From a faculty perspective, another challenge is balancing preparation for the dissertation with training to be a scholarly practitioner and change leader. Skill development in these two areas does not always overlap. Alisa observed that students are so focused on acquiring the skills necessary to complete their dissertations, that many of them considered any other skill development to be superfluous, even when aligned with clearly stated program goals. For example, a core course on adult learning is required out of the recognition that leading change often means engaging adult colleagues in a learning process and therefore that change leaders should have an understanding of effective practice for adult learners. However, students critiqued the course as a waste of time because it did not help them prepare for their dissertations. In an accelerated program, it can feel like everything should be about getting through and getting done, and anything that does not support this notion is a distraction of limited value; it is easy to lose sight of program goals especially given the enormous challenge of learning how to conduct and write about a dissertation study. The challenge then becomes finding ways to more effectively integrate these two aspects of the program by making expectations for dissertation work broader than completing a large-scale research task. If the dissertation process was also designed to be a demonstration of skills related to leading and sustaining a change effort, a broader array of courses and experiences may seem more relevant to students. However, as long as they are being evaluated on their ability to design and carry out a research task, the skills needed to do this successfully will be most valued by students.

CONCLUSION

Reenvisioning the EdD to make it a more impactful and valuable degree is a complex process with many components. One of the most high-leverage changes that can contribute to this goal is to reimagine the dissertation. To shift the dissertation from a PhD-oriented process designed to demonstrate that the graduate knows how to generate new knowledge and theory to the EdD-oriented process designed to show that the graduate knows how to use research strategies to address problems of practice and improve learning outcomes means rethinking the types of questions students pose, the types of research they conduct, and even the ways in which they report their findings. While not all faculty have easily made this transition and not all students conduct high-impact research, most are doing work that does "move the needle" on some meaningful aspect of teaching and learning.

At Rutgers we have made a number of changes that seem most relevant to accomplishing this goal. We came to understand that a clear articulation of what we meant by a "problem of practice" dissertation was probably a helpful first step in breaking faculty out of their assumptions and beliefs about what a dissertation is. Doing so also helped guide students' thinking about their dissertation work, and early and frequent exposure to it provided a framework for them within which to plan for it. We have also identified alternative dissertation formats that seem more likely to make dissertation work accessible to stakeholder audiences. Coursework that is designed not only to cover content but also is constantly encouraging students to focus on and engage with their problem of practice is also an important component. However, students may need help to understand how a wide variety of courses contributes to their development; explicit ties to program goals should be made clear. Finally, the power of the cohort cannot be emphasized too much. Not only does the cohort contribute to the development of scholarly practitioner skills, but also it provides the glue that helps hold the students together as they struggle and strive through the rigors of an accelerated and rigorous program.

EdD graduates can play an extremely important role in improving educational opportunities for all students. The skills learned and demonstrated to complete a problem of practice dissertation are key to training our students for this task. However, if faculty members stick to what is most familiar, and students are guided toward doing the traditional PhD-type dissertation, we will fail to realize this promise. Instead, a dissertation needs to be thought of as the first full demonstration of a scholarly practitioner's capacity to be a change agent, and EdD programs must rethink the dissertation expectations and processes to align with this goal.

REFERENCES

Belzer, A., & Ryan, S. (2014). Defining the problem of practice dissertation: Where's the practice, what's the problem. *Planning and Changing, 44*(3/4), 195–207.

Carnegie Project on the Education Doctorate (CPED). (2015). *Design concept definitions.* Retrieved from http://cpedinitiative.org/design-concept-definitions

Lovitts, B. E. (2005, November/December). How to grade a dissertation. *Academe, 91*(6), 18–23.

Rutgers University. (2015). *Education doctorate student handbook, 2015–2016.* New Brunswick, NJ: Rutgers University Graduate School of Education.

Ryan, S., De Lisi, R., & Heuschkel, K. (2012). Redesigning an EdD program: Reality and necessity engender new possibilities. In M. M. Latta & S. Wunder (Eds.), *Placing practitioner knowledge at the center of teacher education* (pp. 75–88). Charlotte, NC: Information Age.

SECTION III

IN THEIR OWN WORDS—EXPERIENCES
OF SCHOLARLY PRACTITIONERS

CHAPTER 11

COMMUNITY COLLEGE STUDENT PRACTITIONER

Pamela S. Campbell and Stephanie J. Jones

This chapter includes an overview of the CPED-influenced Higher Education program at Texas Tech University and the experiences of leading a community college from a current community college practitioner who is a student in the program. The chapter will provide future readers with an opportunity to vicariously experience the doctoral program through the adventures of a practitioner of higher education as she discovers research and scholarly substantiation for her many years of prior experience.

Texas Tech University (TTU) is categorized as a Research University (very high research activity) by the Carnegie Classification of Higher Education Institutions (Indiana University School of Education, 2016) and has also been identified as an emerging research university within the state of Texas. Its main campus is located in Lubbock, Texas. In fall 2014, TTU enrolled over 35,000 undergraduate and graduate students in 150 undergraduate, 100 master's, and 50 doctoral degrees (Texas Tech University, 2015). The University is composed of 10 independent colleges, a graduate school, and a school of law.

The College of Education is 1 of 10 colleges within the University. It serves over 1,900 students, a large percentage of which are graduate students. The

The EdD and the Scholarly Practitioner, pages 179–195
Copyright © 2016 by Information Age Publishing

college offers two undergraduate degrees, 12 master's degrees, and 8 doctoral degrees, as well as various specialization and certification options. It provides a large percentage of distance learning offered by the University.

The Higher Education program is a stand-alone program within the College of Education and is part of the department of Educational Psychology & Leadership. The Higher Education program serves over 180 students in both an onsite and online master's program, a CPED-influenced online EdD in higher education with an administration focus, and an onsite PhD in higher education research. The majority of the program's students are enrolled in the CPED-influenced online EdD.

ONLINE EDUCATION DOCTORATE IN HIGHER EDUCATION ADMINISTRATION

In fall 2011, Texas Tech University became a second-wave member of CPED. The primary program involved with this membership is the Higher Education program. CPED has six working principles that frame the design for the practice-based doctorate. The Higher Education EdD is well-grounded in these principles as a practice-based doctorate that "prepares educators for the application of appropriate and specific practices, the generation of new knowledge and for the stewardship of the profession" (CPED, 2014).

The CPED framework for the EdD focuses on developing scholarly practitioners, which is a cited need throughout the research for higher education leadership (Perry, 2012; Shulman, Golde, Conklin Bueschel, & Garabedian, 2006). Being part of a national discussion with like-minded individuals at CPED convenings enabled TTU higher education faculty to reflect on and explore how to redefine their existing EdD program. As part of the redefinition of the EdD, discussions by the faculty about the purpose of the EdD evolved with the information presented about the program to potential students and others at the university focused around the national conversation that was occurring about the value of the EdD.

As a result of applying the CPED working principles and concepts to the EdD program design, the existing EdD program was transitioned to an online EdD in Higher Education Administration, with the following trademark outcome:

> Graduates of the EdD in Higher Education will have exceptional skills in inquiry. Graduates will demonstrate the research skills and the creative modes of thinking that enable them to act as scholarly reformers who advance the field.

The online delivery of the program provides access and opportunities to a diverse student population who otherwise may not have access to pursue a terminal degree. It provides great flexibility for current higher education professionals who want or need to attain their doctorate degree, thereby increasing access to advanced graduate-level education (Li & Irby, 2008) for those who could not attend on-site programs due to geographical location, employment barriers, and/or family responsibilities (Freddolino, Blaschke, & Rypkema, 2009; Saleh, 2012).

Students are admitted to the program in cohorts and admittance is once a year in the fall semester. The cohort model was chosen due to its ability to bring together the experiences and expertise of our students who work in multifaceted higher education roles, into a collaborative doctoral learning environment (Aiken & Gerstl-Pepin, 2013, p. 172)—a community of practice. The cohorts are composed of representation from different types of higher education or affiliated institutions (e.g., community colleges, 4-year colleges and universities, public, private, and for profit), as well as is further diversified by the divisions that the students are employed within (e.g., academics, student affairs, administrative, operations, technology, among others). Students complete 21 credit hours per year for the first two years of the program—6 in the fall term, 6 in the spring term, 9 hours across the summer and 18 hours in the third year. Students are required to attend one week of intensive professional development each Summer I term for the 3 years of the program at the home campus of Texas Tech University in Lubbock. Residency is met by completing 21 hours in an academic year.

The curriculum for the program is sequenced in three phases: (a) Phase 1 is knowledge level, (b) Phase 2 is guided practice, and (c) Phase 3 is authentic practice. All Phase 2 and Phase 3 courses utilize embedded fieldwork projects to ensure students obtain the skills, knowledge, and competencies to be scholarly practitioners. Authentic applied projects are also incorporated into appropriate courses. All students enrolled in the program work in professional positions in higher education, and their institutions serve as their laboratories of practice where they engage in authentic environments for course projects. All coursework is designed to take advantage of students' access to authentic problems in practice at their institutions. Most courses have problems in practice components and require application of learning outcomes of the course in guided or authentic settings. Inquiry courses are instrumental in ensuring that students have these skills. The program has recently been revised to incorporate 18 hours of inquiry instruction, with specific focus on applied methodologies as well as assessment and evaluation. All students are required to complete a scholarly practitioner-based dissertation in practice, working in partnership with a higher education institution that has an identified problem of practice that needs to be resolved.

Milestones for the program are assessed in each of the three phases. In order to progress through the program, students must demonstrate skills and competencies throughout all phases and are assessed at the end of each semester and each year to determine if remediation is needed to ensure skills and knowledge are obtained. All students are evaluated once a year through a formal program evaluation process. Students who are deemed to need remediation, mainly in writing and critical thinking, are put on an academic plan designed to help them improve their skills and competencies in needed areas.

LIFE PRIOR TO THE DOCTORATE

The following is Pam's story. With 38 years of public education and higher education experience, one would think that a career educator would be reluctant to begin a doctoral program late in the game. However, I had a long-time, unfulfilled personal goal to earn a doctorate. As background, I began my first teaching assignment in 1974, just three months after completion of a Bachelor of Science in Secondary Education with teaching fields in mathematics and history. Within a year, I began graduate studies focused on K–12 curriculum and instruction, as well as guidance and counseling. Though I earned more than 36 graduate hours, no master's degree resulted. Additional components of those early teaching years included my service as an activities and student council sponsor, cheerleading sponsor, and magnet-program mathematics teacher.

Upon moving to a different part of the state with previously unknown community college opportunities, the emphasis of my graduate studies shifted to a master's degree in mathematics in order to fulfill the credential requirements for teaching academic mathematics courses at the postsecondary level. The semester after the completion of the degree, I had an opportunity to teach a trigonometry class as an adjunct faculty member at a community college. Fortunately, a full-time faculty position became available at the end of that semester, and I made the transition from K–12 education to postsecondary education.

After 10 years of teaching mathematics at the college, an opportunity was presented to me to oversee the creation of a dual credit program with the K–12 partners associated with the college, while continuing to teach mathematics. Using the 14 years of secondary education experience and the 10 years of experience at the community college, I had the opportunity to facilitate higher education opportunities to motivated high school students. This seemed like the appropriate next step in my career path.

Transition From Teaching to Administration

After 9 years of building the dual credit program and continuing to teach, the administrative position of Dual Credit Director was created on the campus. A short 4 years after that official transition to administration, I interviewed for the district-level position of Assistant Vice-Chancellor for Educational Partnerships. With 14 years of K–12 mathematics teaching experience, 20 years of college mathematics teaching combined with 14 years of midlevel administrative experience, and having worked collaboratively with school districts associated with the college since 1998, the position seemed perfect for me. There was no opportunity for a direct appointment into the position, so preparing for an interview process after so many years was significantly important. It was critical for me to focus my thoughts about leadership, change, and the college's vision, mission, and values. The first brick in the path to what would become my next educational journey was fired and laid by those musings.

The Scholarship of Leadership

As O'Banion (2012) noted, "Community colleges live and thrive in the crucible of change" (p. 1). In a 2012 report from the American Association of Community Colleges (AACC), one of the elements of institutional change is leadership, with this instruction: "community college leaders need to see change as their friend, embrace it, and then, indeed, lead it" (p. 17). According to Wallin (2010), change leaders should "remove barriers and free people to use their strengths to improve the organization, make it responsive to the community... [and] look with fresh vision on the landscape" (p. 5). Decisions in my new position would need to be informed with data and scholarly findings to face the changes and challenges of legislated collaboration, funding based on student outcomes, divergent levels of student preparation, core curriculum revisions, declining economic resources, demands for community and workforce needs, and requirements for additional faculty and advisors. Any change in culture requires changes in its people. In any setting, there is a moral and ethical component that seeks to create a culture of change in an institution. Rowley and Sherman (2001) observe that "change is not a one-time event—it is a continuous phenomenon" (p. 291).

Community colleges must be able to rely on their leaders to articulate and plan for visionary change. Change leaders, then, must be committed to living with change while remaining stable, growth-oriented, and ethical, authentic leaders. Was this philosophical notion of authentic leadership fully formed at the time of the job interview for the new position? No, it was not. However, gaining the wisdom from these important observations by scholars in the higher education field comprised a significant part of the EdD program in my future. It is only now that there is the scholarly foundation to what was innately known by this practitioner, yet was deepened by the scholarship, examples, and experiences of others.

The Value of Reflection

Studying leadership is an empty experience without reflection. Our EdD coursework not only encouraged but also required that reflection. Through the use of scholarly texts and contemporary research, we wrote, discussed, accepted, evaluated, rejected, and examined our own leadership styles, as well as those of others. We considered the question, "What is a good leader?" As I mused over that query, it was imperative in my mind to create my personal views about characteristics of good leaders:

- Good leaders must understand what they know and can do, and in what areas are there deficiencies.
- A good leader listens to the voices from all sectors and is able to filter wisdom from rhetoric.
- A good leader can back away from the fray and find a calm place in her brain and in her heart from which to make wise decisions.
- A good leader values reflection without second-guessing.
- A good leader knows when to invoke the "weekend rule" in order to gain perspective.
- A good leader is capable of acknowledging mistakes and learning from those experiences.
- Good leaders identify their core ethical principles and live by them.
- Good leaders strive to grow in their knowledge of new ideas, new challenges, new perspectives, and new opinions.
- Good leaders use that knowledge of what is new to evaluate what is past and present, tried and true, and what should be kept "as is," updated, or replaced.
- A good leader is creative and seeks unique solutions to common problems in order to strengthen partnerships within an organization.
- A good leader values all jobs, roles, and people within the organization and treats each individual with dignity and respect

Previous experiences in my midlevel administrative role provided opportunities for a broader view of college operations, legislative implications, regulatory agencies, financial planning, personnel decisions, and crisis management. As a former faculty member, transitioning to the administrative level was not without its challenges. It was apparent that there were good leaders to mimic and poor leaders to provide examples of behaviors and attitudes to avoid. Most faculty still recognized my leadership style as genuine; however, there were those who took the "Star Wars" mindset and referred to "going to the dark side."

Leading Self

Experiences from my past fueled my determination to be chosen for the administrative position for which I was applying. At the time of the interview in 2010, it had been 11 years since a breast cancer diagnosis that required surgery, chemotherapy, and radiation. My strength to fight and to flourish came from those around me—particularly my partner and my family—as well as from within. It was important that I was in control of the disease, not that the disease was in control of me. During the different stages of my treatment, there were only four absences from work. Drawing upon the lessons learned during that experience strengthened my resolve to make wise decisions and to live as an authentic leader.

In the process of preparing for the interview, it was important to draw upon the wisdom of mentors who have been great leaders for many years. One of those mentors, and my long-time friend, Dr. Hardy S. Clemons, PhD, ThD, offered his best bit of advice. When asked about his best thoughts about leadership, he said, "You have to decide . . . do you want to be somebody, or do you want to accomplish something?" This statement provided mission focus from that point forward.

FINDING THE RIGHT FIT

Though selected for the administrative position without a doctorate, that long-term unfulfilled personal goal came back to mind. After consulting with my family and supervisor, the search began for the right doctoral program. Finding a program that would allow a full-time community college administrator to complete a degree in a 3- to 4-year period of time was key. It was also important that the institution providing the degree was well-respected. As an alumnus of Texas Tech University, the Doctorate of Education in Higher Education with an emphasis on Community College Administration was the perfect choice. With 24 years of experience at the community college, this degree plan was the appropriate program for me. Though the information explaining a practitioner's degree was presented in our orientation, it did not become clear to me until a little later in the program just what solving a problem in practice really meant. Beginning the dissertation process solidified the importance of the difference in this focused, problem-solving kind of research versus the theoretical nature of PhD research. The selection of a case-study methodology honed my approach to solving the problem identified nationally as the dilemma of completing a college-level mathematics course as a component of earning a college degree. Again, student success was the ultimate focus for my work in my position and in the doctoral program.

The Cohort Model

One of the most valuable components of the program was the cohort model. Functioning as a professional learning community, this design allowed practitioners to learn from each other's diverse experiences across academic disciplines, administrative experiences, aspirations for future employment, and thoughts on leadership. Our cohort consisted of faculty from both academic and technical areas; student services personnel from counseling and disability services; institutional researchers and financial officers; academic administrators; and marketing and grant support personnel. This variety of roles provided valuable insight from a variety of perspectives as we participated in discussion boards and synchronous online sessions.

Residency requirements brought the cohort together for three consecutive summers, renewing and nourishing relationships initially established in person, yet cultivated at a distance. These weeks in the summer also created a face-to-face relationship with the university professors in the program. Our courses were taught by both full-time and part-time faculty at the university. Each of these professors provided an element of expertise in particular areas. Since some of those professors would ultimately serve on our dissertation committees, the time together was vital in beginning relationships that would encourage and support the completion of the dissertation and its defense.

The Challenge of Distance Learning

One of the biggest challenges was the role of distance learning in this program. After all, if the years of experience are summed, you will recognize a 60-year-old student beginning a doctoral program. I had no distance learning experiences in either my bachelor's or master's degrees. The learning curve was significant, but the program provided more than sufficient information to aid the novice distance education learner. Technical support was readily available for all students. During one summer semester, the Blackboard system became unavailable. The professors extended deadlines for completion of tests and submissions of papers. Challenges other than using Blackboard (Bb) as a Learning Management System (LMS) as a student, rather than an instructor, included work-focused travel that meant managing connectivity from all over the United States and the commensurate time zones for synchronous class meetings.

These online sessions enabled our cohort to support each other, to challenge thoughts and opinions, to provide insight from experiences beyond what some members had, to interact with the faculty in the program, and to simply hear each other's voices on a monthly basis. We worried if one of our members was not online. We communicated offline by text message, email, and cell phones to make sure that the missing link was found and connected. We built a network of a professional learning community that would continue to support its individual members through family challenges, new jobs, births of babies, raising of children, burying of parents, and yes, indeed, of the writing, proposal, research, more writing, and defense of dissertations.

The Curriculum

Courses in the EdD program were intentionally designed to prepare the community college practitioner as future leaders and to allow individuals to focus on particular areas of interest. Cohort members were faculty, staff, and administrators, in both technical and academic fields, from 2-year and 4-year institutions mostly in Texas. Assignments were focused, yet allowed for research that was applicable at one's home institution. Historical, legal, strategic planning, and institutional effectiveness perspectives, all necessary skills for administrators, were included. Seminal authorities (e.g., Cohen, Brawer, Kisker, Thelin, Kaplin, Lee, Northouse, Lincoln, and Guba) in the field of higher education provided years of background knowledge, as well as more recent research and observations by newer authors (e.g., Merriam, Creswell, Glesne, Bess, Dee, Eddy, Townsend, and Dougherty).

Early Exposure to Research

An initial introduction to the processes and structure of research was a component of our first semester in the program. Using a backwards design process (begin with the end in mind and construct the steps in a process), the Higher Education Research Seminar presented an approach to research that enabled us to build the pieces of a research proposal in a logical progression of steps. Tentatively identifying a research topic led to learning to use online databases such as EBSCO, ERIC, Google Scholar, and PsycINFO and to understanding the logic operators that would locate appropriate articles. Learning to write entries for an annotated bibliography and then to identify common themes and organizing them into a matrix became the foundation for writing a literature review. The subsequent construction of well-written research questions from the information in the literature review led to identifying a research methodology and study design. The culminating project came to form as a result of the learning associated with each of the steps in the process. This course provided the structure for every paper and ultimately for the first three chapters of the dissertation.

In addition to the mechanical aspects of the course, it provided me with an opportunity to pair scholarly resources with ideas that I already had, providing me with a theoretical foundation for addressing problems in the practice of higher education. As is noted on the CPED website description of an EdD program that uses their *Working Principles and Design Concepts*, "Scholarly Practitioners blend practical wisdom with professional skills and knowledge to name, frame, and solve problems of practice. They use practical research and applied theories as tools for change" (CPED, 2014, para. 2). Comparing the content of this first-semester course in my EdD program with the experiences of other colleagues in different programs made me realize the insightful planning of the program chair to include this instruction in the early stages of our studies. Without the benefit of this structured approach, the future semesters would have been filled with unclear expectations and ambiguity in the research process.

Qualitative and Quantitative Methods Classes

Our early introduction to the research methods class mentioned in the preceding section also initiated our first discussions regarding selection of a research approach, participant selection, data analysis, instrumentation, and measures of reliability and validity. Subsequent courses in qualitative research and in statistical testing and analyses were difficult for many of my cohort colleagues. With a strong background in mathematics, much of this information was an applied version of computational processes and concepts with which I am very familiar. Both courses were offered by faculty from the educational psychology department, which is separate from the higher education leadership part of the EdD program. Unfortunately for some of my cohort members, these two courses were taught with little instructor interaction, which proved problematic.

Having chosen a qualitative approach to the case study in my dissertation, additional self-study was needed, and references were sought to reach the level of understanding to conduct my research. Merriam's (2009) chapter on qualitative case study research was very helpful, as was the early, yet still insightful, writing of Lincoln and Guba (1985) in their text on naturalistic inquiry. Glesne (2011) provided detailed examples of interviewing techniques, field notes, researcher bias, trustworthiness, and the finer details of listening and questioning. In addition, her "Qualitative Research Spiral" (Glesne, 2011, p. 61) provided an organized diagram of the interrelated elements of the qualitative research process, which gave graphic meaning to the many elements and stages of this research design. Each of these authors provided their emphases on the rich, thick descriptions necessary for qualitative research to convey its findings.

The quantitative statistics course provided instruction in interpretation of certain measures and of their implications in reporting data. Though only using a questionnaire to guide the selection of interview participants in my case study, the ability to look at aggregate responses in comparison to individual responses was helpful in asking follow-up questions during my interviews. In addition, instruction in the details of quantitative analysis proved vital in reading quantitative research studies as part of the literature review and being able to understand the findings and their significance.

The Challenge of Being ABD (All But Done aka All But Dissertation)

We had all heard the horror stories of those colleagues who completed their coursework in a doctoral program but were never able to claim the elusive title of "Doctor" due to the abysmal black hole known as "The Dissertation." Determined to not fall prey to the ABD label, my first three chapters were completed in fall 2014, the first semester of our third year in the program. My dissertation topic dealt with student perceptions of their mathematical self-efficacy in a co-requisite model of developmental mathematics and college algebra. As noted in the introduction to the dissertation, completion of a college credit in mathematics is often the roadblock to successful completion of a college credential (Bonham & Boylan, 2011; Hall & Ponton, 2005). Because many students arrive at community colleges lacking college-level skills in mathematics, they find themselves required to enroll in as many as three semesters of developmental coursework prior to even attempting a college-level course in mathematics (Attewell, Lavin, Domina, & Levey, 2006; Bailey & Cho, 2010; Crisp & Delgado, 2013). Bailey, Jeong, and Cho (2010) found that in a sample of over 256,000 students enrolled in Achieving the Dream colleges, only 20% of students referred to developmental mathematics successfully completed the entry-level, credit-bearing college course in mathematics in 3 years.

To address this issue of students who languish in developmental mathematics, often never completing a college credential, my institution designed a co-requisite model in mathematics that simultaneously provided developmental coursework with instruction in the student learning outcomes of college algebra, all within one semester. The program, known as

AIM (Acceleration in Mathematics), was piloted in the spring and fall semesters of 2012. The program continues to produce completers with an A–C success rate of 64.1% (N = 1,660) over the time period from 2012 to 2015. This rate is 20 percentage points higher than students who place directly into college algebra.

According to researchers, self-efficacy in mathematics is an indicator of academic achievement in mathematics (Usher & Pajares, 2009). Specifically, students need to be coached to recognize that difficult problems in mathematics are not threats to their success but rather serve as challenges that can be met and successfully overcome with persistent, productive effort. The combination of the study of self-efficacy and the design of the AIM classroom through the lens of Bandura's (1997) social cognitive theory formed the basis for the case study in the dissertation. The dissertation proposal was heard, defended, and approved in early February 2015. Our program chair made certain that all requirements for the proposal to be approved were in place prior to the proposal hearing. She wanted to be certain that our work was in the correct format and our plans for research were solidly grounded in theory so that we would be successful in this process.

The subsequent approval from the Human Research Protection Program (HRPP) at the University came within a few weeks, but the Institutional Review Board (IRB) approval at the study institution took longer. The IRB at this institution only met every other month, so April 2015 was my earliest opportunity to submit the request. By the end of April, my approval was granted, a data request was submitted, an online link to the survey was created using Qualtrics software, available through the EdD program at Texas Tech, and the wording for the email to potential participants was created. My survey was used to identify a purposeful sample of former successful students for subsequent interviews. The initial email went out to over 1,000 students who had successfully completed the AIM program. However, the timing of these emails coincided with the spring commencement ceremonies at the college. Therefore, most of the students were no longer looking at their college email accounts. The response to the survey was minimal, with fewer than 15 students indicating an interest in being interviewed. Even fewer of those students actually responded to a request to set up interviews. The result only produced four interviews.

Feeling somewhat discouraged, I reached out to my dissertation chair to ask if I might request that the survey be resubmitted. She agreed, and indeed, timing is everything! In two weeks, I received three times the number of responses as compared to the earlier email. My interviews were completed by the first week in August 2015.

The results of my dissertation will be used to improve classroom teaching practices based on students' insights into the characteristics of the AIM classroom that helped them to be successful. In addition, future co-requisite models are in the design phase to allow for an option in statistics or quantitative reasoning rather than college algebra. These acceleration models will reflect data-informed components from interviews with the students in my study. Contributions to student perceptions of their self-efficacy in mathematics will be noted and classroom activities destined to fuel those improved perceptions will be designed and implemented in other sections of mathematics, as well as in the co-requisite models.

Writing the fourth and fifth chapters during the late summer and early fall accomplished the penultimate step in this journey, making it possible for me to meet deadlines to defend the dissertation in October and to ensure graduation in December 2015. My long-time, unfulfilled personal goal was achieved!

LIFE AFTER THE DOCTORATE

As noted in the earlier section entitled "The Scholarship of Leadership," the coursework, readings, research, discussions, and reflection informed and continues to shape my leadership style, my decision-making processes, and my vision of higher education from a broader viewpoint. The earlier reference to change as a way of life in higher education led me to explore perspectives on authentic leadership during my pursuit of the doctorate. As a practitioner in an administrative role, I continue to reflect on my experiences in the EdD program and the many scholars' writings that I read, reflected upon, and now apply in practice.

Authentic Change Leadership

Authentic leadership is not universally well defined; additionally, there are different viewpoints for various perspectives on authentic leadership (Northouse, 2013). One of those views is from an intrapersonal perspective. Those who take this position focus on a leader's experiences and on how those experiences shape the development of that person's leadership style (Northouse, 2013). Another approach is from the interpersonal perspective and views leadership as a collaboratively developed dynamic crafted by both leader and follower (Northouse, 2013). A third viewpoint defines authentic leadership from a developmental perspective. Walumbwa, Avolio, Gardner, Wernsing, and Peterson (2008) suggest four components required in the developmental process of authentic leadership: "Self-awareness, internalized moral perspective, balanced processing, and relational transparency" (p. 89). Relational transparency refers to presenting one's authentic self to others (Walumbwa et al., 2008). These components incorporate the tenets of leadership ethics.

Authentic leadership also highlights the need for leaders to be reflective, lifelong learners and above all people of integrity. George (2007) notes that "Leaders are defined by their values, and values are personal...Integrity, however, is the one value required of every authentic leader" (p. xxxii). In addition to the four components named above, other factors contribute to authentic leaders: "positive psychological capacities, moral reasoning, and critical life events" (Northouse, 2013, p. 264). Psychological attributes such as confidence, hope, optimism, and resilience, appear as positive traits and states for authentic leaders. Northouse (2013) notes that these attributes may preexist in a leader as a trait, but should be further developed through training and coaching as an enhanced state of being.

Considered a lifelong process for authentic leaders, moral reasoning development involves not only knowing what is right or good, but also requires acting upon that knowledge (Northouse, 2013). Authentic leaders must be able to survey the entirety of an issue in order to guide decisions that affect an entire institution. Their moral compasses must steer them beyond individual preferences or agendas to the greater vision of the institution, its people, and its community.

Critical life events compose the third factor related to the formation of authentic leaders (Northouse, 2013). Positive or negative, these events contribute to the shaping of a leadership style and personalized theory. Northouse (2013) notes that "Critical life events act as catalysts for change....By understanding their own life experiences, leaders become more authentic" (p. 266). According to George (2007), most all of the leaders he interviewed "found their passion to lead through the uniqueness of their life stories" (p. 8). This critical examination and introspection is a required component throughout one's leadership journey contributing to the self-awareness, internalized moral perspective, and balanced processing identified in the research of Walumbwa et al. (2008). The complex process of personal and professional development of authentic leaders yields characteristics that enable leaders to be seen as trustworthy and believable, fulfilling the final component of relational transparency as outlined by Walumbwa et al. (2008).

CONCLUSION

As Levy, Parco, and Blass (2010) observe, "Great leaders are those who have a refined ability to adapt to change. The greater your adaptive capacity, the more likely you are to develop creative solutions to complex and ambiguous organizational problems" (Preface, para. 1). Adapting to change requires leaders to have a well-developed vision for their organization and for themselves as a leader within that organization.

In order for these leaders to be prepared, they must be committed to a leadership style and theoretical perspective in which they believe. The ethical, authentic leader can be the visionary change leader that our institutions need. However, they must live the developmental perspective of authentic leadership, giving attention to personal and professional reflection, in order to articulate the vision they wish to enact. Searching one's life stories enables leaders to draw on experiences and insights gained from positive as well as negative outcomes. Examining the past often sheds significant light on the present and on the future.

In addition, current leaders, such as those of us emerging from the EdD program at Texas Tech University, bear the responsibility for identifying and encouraging future leaders. By creating environments of trust, nurture, empathy, creativity, and mutual respect, young leaders can grow and question the status quo. Northouse (2013) clearly states that authentic leadership can be learned, and authentic leaders must be lifelong learners. One crucial attribute that must be present in all authentic, ethical leaders of change is a clear vision of, and commitment to, how they treat other people. Typically divided into two categories, theories about ethics address conduct and character (Northouse, 2013). How a leader treats others is a reflection of both actions (conduct) and virtue (character), and must demonstrate respect and integrity in relating to all people within the organization. College leaders must attend to the well-being of themselves, their organizations, and their people by searching for those key components that need to be unfrozen, changed, and then refrozen, to bring about data-informed, thoughtful change in their institutions (Rowley & Sherman, 2001). They must do so with a lasting commitment to integrity as their strongest attribute.

REFERENCES

American Association of Community Colleges (AACC). (2012, April). *Reclaiming the American dream: A report from the 21st century commission on the future of community colleges*. Washington, DC: Author. Retrieved from http://www.aacc.nche. edu/aboutcc/21stcenturyreport_old/index.html

Aiken, J. A., & Gerstl-Pepin, C. (2013). Envisioning the EDD and PHD as a partnership for change. *Planning and Changing, 44*(3/4), 162–180.

Attewell, P., Lavin, D., Domina, T., & Levey, T. (2006). New evidence on college remediation. *The Journal of Higher Education, 77*(5), 886–924.

Bailey, T., & Cho, S.-W. (2010). Developmental education in community colleges. *Community College Research Center*. Retrieved from http://ccrc.tc.columbia. edu/publications/developmental-education-in-community-colleges.html

Bailey, T., Jeong, D. W., & Cho, S.-W. (2010). Referral, enrollment, and completion in developmental education sequences in community colleges. *Economics of Education Review, 29*(2), 255–270. doi:10.1016/j.econedurev.2009.09.002

Bandura, A. (1997). *Self-efficacy: The exercise of control.* New York, NY: Freeman.

Bonham, B. S., & Boylan, H. R. (2011). Developmental mathematics: Challenges, promising practices, and recent initiatives. *Journal of Developmental Education, 34*(3), 2–10.

Carnegie Project on the Education Doctorate (CPED). (2014). *Design concept definitions.* Retrieved from http://cpedinitiative.org/design-concept-definitions.

Crisp, G., & Delgado, C. (2013). The impact of developmental education on community college persistence and vertical transfer. *Community College Review, 42*(2), 99–117. doi:10.1177/0091552113516488

Freddolino, P., Blaschke, C., & Rypkema, S. (2009). Increasing access to graduate education: A blended MSW program. K. Swan (Ed.). *Journal of the Research Center for Educational Technology, 5*(2), 27–50.

George, B. (2007). *True north.* San Francisco, CA: Wiley.

Glesne, C. (2011). *Becoming qualitative researchers: An introduction* (4th ed.). Boston, MA: Pearson.

Hall, J. M., & Ponton, M. K. (2005). Mathematics self-efficacy of college freshman. *Journal of Developmental Education, 28*(3), 26–32.

Indiana University School of Education. (2016). News & announcements. *Carnegie Classification of Institutions of Higher Education.* Retrieved from http://carnegieclassifications.iu.edu/

Levy, D. A., Parco, J. E., & Blass, F. R. (2010). The 52nd floor: Thinking deeply about leadership [Kindle version]. *Amazon.com.* Retrieved from http://www.amazon.com/52nd-Floor-Thinking-Deeply-Leadership-ebook/dp/B0025KUEWW/ref=sr_1_1?s=digital-text&ie=UTF8&qid=1399236243&sr=1-1&keywords=the+52nd+floor

Li, C., & Irby, B. (2008). An overview of online education: Attractiveness, benefits, challenges, concerns, and recommendations. *College Student Journal, 42*(2), 449–458.

Lincoln, Y. S., & Guba, E. G. (1985). *Naturalistic inquiry.* Beverly Hills, CA: Sage.

Merriam, S. B. (2009). *Qualitative research: A guide to design and implementation.* San Francisco, CA: Jossey-Bass.

Northouse, P. G. (2013). *Leadership: Theory and practice* (6th ed.). Thousand Oaks, CA: Sage.

O'Banion, T. (2012, January). Change and the completion agenda. *Leadership Abstracts, 25*(1), 1–4.

Perry, J. A. (2012, September). To EdD or not to EdD? *Kappan,* 41–44.

Rowley, D. J., & Sherman, H. (2001). *From strategy to change: Implementing the plan in higher education.* San Francisco, CA: Jossey-Bass.

Saleh, A. (2012). A closer look at online graduate degree programs in public institutions. *Review of Higher Education and Self Learning, 5*(16), 155–163.

Shulman, L. S., Golde, C., Conklin Bueschel, A., & Garabedian, K. (2006). Reclaiming education's doctorates: A critique and a proposal. *Educational Researcher, 35*(3), 25–32.

Texas Tech University. (2015). *Texas Tech facts.* Retrieved July 26, 2015, from http://www.ttu.edu/about/facts/

Usher, E. L., & Pajares, F. (2009). Sources of self-efficacy in mathematics: A validation study. *Contemporary Educational Psychology, 34*(1), 89–101. doi:10.1016/j.cedpsych.2008.09.002

Wallin, D. L. (2010). Looking to the future: Change leaders for tomorrow's community colleges. In D. Wallin (Ed.). *Leadership in an era of change* (pp. 5–12). San Francisco, CA: Jossey-Bass.

Walumbwa, F. O., Avolio, B. J., Gardner, W. L., Wernsing, T. S., & Peterson, S. J. (2008). Authentic leadership: Development and validation of a theory-based measure. *Journal of Management, 34*(1), 89–126. http://doi.org/10.1177/0149206307308913

CHAPTER 12

PROBLEM OF PRACTICE DISSERTATIONS AS IMPROVEMENT EFFORTS

Implementing Research-Based New Teacher Induction

Nicole Petrin, Patricia Tartivita, and Alisa Belzer

There is an old African proverb that states, "A fish in water doesn't know it's in water." This proverb, and its inverse, which refers to "a fish out of water," aptly describes the mentoring and novice teacher experience. Experienced teachers often do not think about the everyday challenges of teaching. They swim along, flowing with the current of changing administrators, challenging students, and disappearing supplies. Novice teachers, on the other hand, may feel like fish out of water. They are looking in from the outside. As one novice teacher at Trish's high school reported, novice teachers "are afraid to ask questions" because they feel it may make them look incompetent. Instead, they struggle without asking for help. While they sometimes learn to "swim," many leave teaching before doing so (Weiss, 1999). At best,

The EdD and the Scholarly Practitioner, pages 197–216
Copyright © 2016 by Information Age Publishing
All rights of reproduction in any form reserved.

novice teachers often struggle more than necessary. We found the struggles of novice teachers we observed in our schools troubling, and as a result chose to focus on this problem of practice in our dissertations. The goal of our studies was to ease the difficulties we saw new teachers experiencing in our schools. In this chapter we detail our problem of practice dissertation work and its ongoing impact in the school district where we are employed as an example of EdD student research that can positively change the learning opportunities for both novices and mentors in schools. We connect the ways in which we learned how to address the new teacher induction problem of practice and others we encounter in our work to the training we received in our CPED-influenced EdD program.

Our dissertation research was well aligned with our doctoral program at the Rutgers Graduate School of Education, which is designed to "help future and current leaders develop the knowledge, skills, and dispositions to solve problems of practice and improve instructional quality" (Graduate School of Education, 2015). More specifically, a problem of practice dissertation as defined by the program "describes a challenge in educational practice, seeks empirically to investigate the challenge and/or test solution(s) to address the challenge, generates actionable implications, and appropriately communicates these implications to relevant stakeholders." Through our work, we planned to act as change leaders. Our training in the program had helped us learn how to identify an important problem of practice, select appropriate solutions from the research, lead an implementation effort, and then conduct a systematic inquiry to understand the barriers and opportunities of making the change to address the problem which could help us engage in ongoing program improvement. In the end, we hoped that our efforts would lead to systemic change in our district, thus improving the learning potential for our colleagues and students.

BACKGROUND TO THE PROBLEM

Between 40% and 50% of new teachers leave the profession within the first five years of entering the classroom (Ingersoll, 2012). This attrition rate is much higher for those teachers with less preparation and no mentoring (Darling-Hammond, 2000). Darling-Hammond (2011) also asserts that this trend will not slow until the needs of beginning teachers are adequately addressed. Making the situation even more difficult, novice teachers are often placed in the most challenging classroom situations (Cochran-Smith, 2004; Ingersoll & Strong, 2011). These conditions have been associated with many new teachers leaving the profession soon after they begin (Cochran-Smith; 2004, Lumdsen, 1998). Low rates of new teacher retention continually fill the teacher ranks with novices. Yet experienced teachers are often higher-quality teachers and are linked to improved student achievement (Darling-Hammond, 2000). Low teacher retention rates have an impact not only on school success and achievement, but also district finances. The cost of teacher attrition is estimated at $15,000, on average, per recruit who leaves (Darling-Hammond, 2011). This makes teacher retention critically important.

Researchers have found that the majority of new teachers who leave are unsatisfied with their career choice, feel unprepared, or believe that their expectations of what teaching would be like are not well matched with their actual experiences (Jandoli, 2013). Numerous novice teachers enter the profession each year lacking the skills that most experienced teachers have. Yet these new teachers are often left on their own to acquire the necessary skills to be successful on the job. This situation occurs because even the best preservice training cannot fully prepare teachers for the complex realities of the classroom (Sava, 2010). In many cases, the information and skills learned in preservice teacher preparation may not be transferable to classroom environments or there may be significant gaps between what was learned and what is needed to be an effective teacher. Preservice teachers may learn the theory of teaching and classroom management during their preparation, but rarely spend enough time learning how to assimilate into the culture of the school, communicate with administration, or appropriate ways to develop collegial relationships in the workplace. Certification requirements may include learning a wide array of general academic, subject area, and pedagogical skills (Darling Hammond & Bransford, 2005), but new teachers may not learn enough about how to address district specific needs. Novice teachers tend to be underprepared and lack the skills necessary to manage their classrooms or solve problems related to teaching and student learning (Jandoli, 2013).

The school districts that hire them should, but do not always, make up the difference between what novices learn in their preservice training and what they need to know to be high-quality teachers. Researches indicate that providing systematic structures through an induction program that includes an effective mentoring component (Ingersoll, 2012) within which novices can extend and enhance their knowledge of teaching, stay committed to the profession, and be successful teachers is essential. A recent analysis of large-scale national teacher surveys, for instance, revealed that the most important predictor of a teacher's ongoing commitment to the profession is the quality of new teacher mentoring, not the mere existence of the program (Darling-Hammond, 2011). This finding provides compelling evidence of the importance of carrying out a structured, systematic, research-based mentoring program.

Schools need to provide assistance to novice teachers from the time of hire through their first years of teaching to help them become more effective and able to meet the high expectations of the profession (Feiman-Nemser, 2001). Mentoring is viewed by many researchers as a key component of effective new teacher induction (Feiman-Nemser, 2001). New teacher mentoring is defined as the establishment of a formal relationship between a novice and a veteran teacher to provide the novice teacher with various kinds of support, supplemental training, and professional development (Washburn-Moses, 2010). In addition to providing mentoring and the training needed to help new teachers be successful, effective induction programs can include ongoing, collaborative, professional development, making it part of the culture of the school and the district and not an isolated, one-time or episodic event (Washburn-Moses, 2010).

PROBLEM OF PRACTICE

The Loop School District, the site of our dissertation studies, required novice teachers to have mentors as part of a state mandate, but we knew at the outset of our research that this district did not support the mentor program in any recognizable way and additionally did little else (such as providing an adequate induction program) to support the growth and development of new teachers. Loop is an urban district serving a racially diverse student population. The district consists of eight neighborhood elementary schools, two middle schools, and one high school. Each year, many novice teachers enter the district's schools, presumably with hopes of having a long-lasting career. Although statistics were not available when we began our research, there was no reason to believe that the Loop District's attrition rates would not be similar or even worse than the national average because of its challenging environment and an almost nonexistent induction program in the district. In fact, the difficulty of being a new, unsupported teacher was reflected by one departing first-year teacher who said, "I'm leaving. I'd rather dig ditches than work in this place."

Because of the high turnover rate, districts must constantly hire new teachers. However, implementing large recruitment efforts without providing proper training "is like pouring water into a leaky bucket instead of repairing it" (Darling-Hammond, 2011, para. 41). Prior to our studies, the Loop School District was doing just that. It had no structured mentoring program, including no clear guidelines that outlined the roles of mentors and novices, no mentor training, and no systematic induction procedure of any kind. There were mentor training manuals, but they were outdated and incomplete.

Although the district had provided mentor trainings and manuals in the past, no recent training had been offered and mentors went unsupervised and were not held accountable for assisting their novices. There was no systematic approach to or clearly articulated set of expectations for new teacher induction in the district. The only concrete procedure that was in place was that new teachers were assigned mentors who were expected to meet with them for 20 hours during their first year of employment (the state requirement). Other than completing paperwork stating that they had met, there was no accountability; there was no one in person or office to oversee new teacher induction. This resulted in a haphazard mentoring experience for novices and an ineffective induction program. The undefined mentor role and lack of accountability meant that teachers trying to be responsible had to guess at what was expected of them. Many simply did not complete the required components, and we knew, as long-term employees in the district, that there was a great deal of negativism about the program. This lack of structure and guidance made it questionable whether the Loop School District was actually meeting the state requirements. Even if the requirements were being met "on paper," it was tacitly understood by staff that the quantity and quality of mentoring experiences varied greatly for the novice teachers in the district.

Given the research that demonstrates its importance for improving new teacher retention and efficacy (Darling-Hammond, 2011; Ingersoll, 2012), putting a more systematic and research-based induction plan in place was of critical importance for our district. A well-executed induction program would ensure that novice teachers could gain the knowledge and develop the expertise to become highly effective teachers. The purpose of our dissertations was to respond to a clearly defined need in our school district by developing and then studying the implementation of a structured new teacher induction program based on best practice research and teacher input. While we both worked on improving aspects of new teacher induction, Nicole implemented a systematic, one-on-one mentoring program in her elementary school where she is a 1st-grade teacher, and Trish implemented ongoing professional development for novices and mentors that focused largely on helping new teachers learn to navigate general school and classroom culture issues in the Loop District High School where she is an English teacher and Department Chair. Nicole documented the mentoring that new teachers received and mentors and novices' perceptions of the program. Trish documented the collaborative, teacher-led professional development for both new teachers and mentors, which she facilitated.

Doing this kind of formative research was aligned with the Rutgers EdD program goals because of its value in furnishing information to guide improvement (Rossi, Lipsey, & Freeman, 2004) for the district's induction program. Our research identified the strengths and problems with the new teacher induction programs we had implemented. Although we addressed separate research questions that were relevant to the specific interventions we implemented and the contexts where we work, overall, our research questions focused on perceptions of research-based new teacher induction programs, implementation issues, and what could be done to improve similar efforts in future. Based on what we learned from this effort, we developed recommendations for improved design and implementation in the future, an extended new teacher orientation, new mentor training, created an induction and mentoring manual (which was adopted by the district), and are now facilitating ongoing professional development for novices and mentors throughout the district.

PREPARATION FOR OUR WORK AS SCHOLARLY PRACTITIONER CHANGE AGENTS: KEY EdD PROGRAM COMPONENTS

The Rutgers Dissertation in practice design helped us to understand how to implement change, even in areas where change agents might encounter resistance. We learned how to involve stakeholders, how to create a need for change, and how to deal with setbacks during the inevitable "implementation dip." Classes are designed to encourage doctoral students to become change agents within their own district.

We began our coursework by learning what is necessary for change to take place. To gain practical experience, we ran protocols in our classes that mimicked situations we might find when implementing change. Our classes at Rutgers also helped us understand how to avoid getting caught up in the negative responses and challenges we encountered, but rather use them to help us understand better how make changes in the future. We came to understand the importance of honest feedback. We also learned how to find and use research to support our process.

More specific to our particular studies, at Rutgers we were able to learn how to provide appropriate professional development based on research and teacher leadership classes. For example, we learned how to provide hands-on, relevant activities rather than the traditional and all too common lecture with PowerPoint. We saw professional development modeled effectively, and therefore we could implement those strategies in our workshops for new teachers and mentor training. These classes also taught us that being a scholarly practitioner is about taking the research and putting it into practice.

In preparation for carrying out our dissertation studies and as a first try at scholarly practice, we were required to run pilot studies in our own districts that allowed us to home in on a problem of practice that needed an intervention; in our case it was a focus on teacher mentoring. After identifying our problem of practice, classes focused on how to research our question, create a proposal, and submit the proposal for committee review.

After our proposals were accepted, support from the university shifted to one on one time with our dissertation chair who helped us refine our proposal, identify further areas of research, and run our studies. Rutgers also encouraged us to enlist the support of people in our district to help us implement change so that our work would be more collaborative. We wanted to use our studies as a platform to improve the district's induction program; the EdD program taught us a wide variety of skills that we could use to have an impact in our schools and bring about positive change. We no longer settle for the current situation but are constantly gaining feedback and researching to guide improvement. In our careers, we are change agents that seek out and spearhead initiatives to improve current situations in our district.

ADDRESSING THE PROBLEM OF PRACTICE: IMPLEMENTING A RESEARCH-BASED NEW TEACHER INDUCTION PROGRAM

Our response to the problem of practice was informed by two sources: change theory and the research literature on new teacher induction. As teachers in the Loop District, we recognized the need for change regarding the mentoring process and took concepts from Fullan's (2007) change model both to guide us as we initiated this needed change and as we analyzed the results of doing so. According to Fullan (2007), an overview of the change process includes three phases: initiation, implementation, and institutionalization. We attempted to follow this model to record what happens during the implementation of a research-based mentoring program. In order to gain support and buy-in from district stakeholders, we discussed the purpose and design of our studies with them. While implementing the changes to the mentoring program, we followed many concepts that Fullan suggested, such as staying in touch with the participants throughout the process to help them as needed. This is important because too often top-down initiatives with little guidance on how to implement them leave staff frustrated and unwilling to engage with new initiatives (Fullan, 2001). The findings from the implementation stage, as well as Fullan's concepts, offered many implications for practice that lead to institutionalization of certain components of our new teacher induction programs. We also researched best practices on induction and mentoring, asked novice teachers, mentors, and administrators what their perceptions were of the induction and mentoring process in the Loop schools, and then designed, implemented and studied a research-based induction program. Although our studies were thematically linked and we did share some resources, ideas, and problem-solving strategies, we conducted two separate studies, detailed here.

Nicole's Study

The goal of my study was to implement a research-based mentoring program in School Three, an elementary school in the Loop School District.

Two main areas of focus in my study were to provide more structure and direction to the mentor and novice relationship and to add a peer observation component. Research questions guiding my design study were How do the mentors and novices perceive a new research-based mentoring program? How do they use the program? What influences their implementation of the mentoring program?

According to researchers, regularly scheduled meetings with mentors who employ a specific structure and are responsive to novice needs prove beneficial for novice teachers (Tauer, 1996). When I began my study, mentors and novices had already been matched and the school year had begun. One of the first things I did was to ask the mentor/novice dyads about the expected frequency of their mentoring meetings; they all reported that they planned to meet on a weekly basis at a set time and place. All dyads seemed to have a schedule in place, therefore the next step was to help provide more structure for mentoring meetings. I created a protocol, "Cheers and Fears" (Ganser, 1992), that was designed to facilitate mentor and novice dialogue. The idea was that before each session, novices would reflect on their successes and their challenges or frustrations; writing them down in advance of meetings with their mentors could guide their meeting discussions. Another document given to the teachers to provide structure for the meetings was a Tracking Log that could be used to document dates and times when they met and topics they discussed. Although very basic, this log was created because the District did not provide the dyads with anything that served this purpose even though they were expected to provide this information to district administrators. I created these two documents to help structure mentoring meetings, but I also encouraged the dyads to follow whatever structure felt most comfortable to them so as to not interfere too much or unduly influence the data I could collect about implementation issues.

While both of us encouraged mentors and novices to participate in peer observation of their teaching, I made supporting this process the main component of my induction program design. This was a key element of my design because researchers have indicated that opportunities for peer observation that include recorded reflections, critical feedback, time for co-planning, and analysis of student work are components of a successful mentoring program (Barrera, Braley & Slate, 2010; Young, Bullough, Draper, Smith, & Erickson, 2005). It is important for novices to observe veteran teachers' strategies to broaden their knowledge of teaching methods and other classroom techniques and to receive the nonevaluative feedback based on observations of their own teaching that the peer observation by mentors affords. When teachers interact with colleagues in this way, they become more conscious of their own craft (Stanulis & Weaver, 1998), helping them to self-reflect and improve their teaching.

To support peer observation in my school, I helped with scheduling, provided coverage for the teacher doing the observation, and developed an Observation and Reflection Log to facilitate reflective dialogue during pre- and postobservation meetings. The observation procedures which I facilitated were implemented in both mentor and novice classrooms. The Observation and Reflection Log asked the teacher being observed to determine an area of focus for the observation, record teaching strategies implemented, and pose questions that arose during the observation. After the observation, the teachers were to use the log to help them debrief the observed lesson and establish a plan of next steps and support needed, then reflect on the plan. My hope was that this type of reflection would encourage novices to identify instructional areas they felt were weak and highlight those in need of improvement, and then seek relevant and responsive input from their mentors. Even with the supports in place which I provided, however, the number of observations conducted was less than I hoped for. My experience seemed to point to some of the challenges entailed in operationalizing a fully functioning peer observation program in a building. Without substantial focus and with more obstacles, the teachers at Trish's school did even fewer observations.

Early data analysis helped me understand some of the barriers. Although the first version of the Observation and Reflection Log encouraged rich dialogue, it was three pages long and took a lot of time for the teachers to complete. In addition to the time commitment involved in filling out the original log, teachers had difficulty just keeping their hands on copies of it, much less filling it out. The problem with the Log was highlighted when a veteran teacher approached me with the original observation form a week after she observed her novice and asked if she "had to" complete the form. Clearly, this teacher saw the log as just another requirement rather than a helpful tool. Because of the confusion and lack of response to the log, I created a simpler document, which was then completed by more participants. The revised document helped the mentoring pairs select a focus for the observation and provided a structure for writing a brief reflection after the observation was completed.

Despite the supports I put in place, mentors and novices found it hard to meet, and the frequency of meetings quickly dwindled. In addition they did not complete as many observations as I had hoped. This may have been due to competing demands on their time, having to complete too much paperwork for the district, scheduling changes, teacher absences, or other unforeseen events. At least as importantly, the principal was not able to allot time during the school day for mentors and novices to meet or observe each other. Although the study participants confirmed the value of regular meetings and peer observations, even with supports in place, they were not able to overcome many of the obstacles they encountered. Without the support of the principal and administration, the teachers were not able to fully engage in research-based, best practices for induction.

Trish's Study

My study was designed to help new teachers feel like "fish in water" by implementing a research-based induction and mentoring program at my high school that featured professional development aimed primarily at helping them learn the culture of the school and gain collaborative assistance from experienced mentors and other novices to address challenges they were facing. The research question for this study was How is a research-based new teacher induction and mentoring program implemented at Loop High School? Subquestions focused on how best to support new teachers and the challenges of implementation.

I facilitated monthly meetings, which focused on the immediate needs of both mentors and novices. Needs were determined by analyzing survey results and conducting "one-legged" interviews (Hall & Hord, 2006) before the school year began. The data I collected during this phase of the study indicated that high school teachers did not feel they had time to meet, did not understand what the state requirements of mentors or novice teachers were, and in some cases, were unsure of who to contact when they had questions about induction or mentoring. Consequently, the monthly meetings I facilitated created time for mentors and novices to discuss pressing issues, socialize outside of the classroom, and ask questions about classroom practices. The questions led to highly practical, specific, and concrete discussions on topics such as dealing with administration, how to respond to criticism, and how to use data to improve teaching practice.

Peer observations were encouraged, but very few mentors observed their assigned novices, and not one novice observed a mentor. Reasons included time constraints, since high school teachers only have one 42-minute prep period a day; feelings that they would be intruding in their mentors classrooms; and an unclear understanding of the purpose and positive effects of peer observation. While a few mentors observed novices, they subsequently offered little constructive help. This finding implied that mentor training, especially in the area of peer observation, was imperative for successfully implementing this important component of new teacher induction.

CHALLENGES TO LEADING SUCCESSFUL CHANGE EFFORTS

We both planned to implement a research-based induction program at our schools and although our district administration supported us in important ways, we both encountered challenges that detracted from our efforts.

The challenges of implementing the new teacher induction program were largely logistical, having to do with the mentor and novice matches; and contextual, having to do with mentor training and accountability. However, undergirding these issues was the challenge of being a change leader without full leadership authority.

Logistical Challenges

Although the research points to particular factors that lead to the most productive matches between mentors and novices, the matches in both schools were mostly based on who was available. This led to matches that were not always conducive to effective mentoring. In particular, they struggled to find time to meet, a problem that is echoed in the literature (Ingersoll & Smith, 2004). At Nicole's school, matches were made between novices and mentors in two noncontiguous grade levels, in two different buildings of the school, with opposite lunch schedules. When mentors and novices are not matched by grade level, it may be less likely that they will have similar schedules or common planning time when they could meet. This is exactly what happened; mentors and novices had difficulty finding meeting time. In addition, novices who were matched with mentors working in different grade levels had to seek help from their grade-level colleagues. This made time management difficult; the novices in this situation felt as if their time was spread too thin because they needed to meet with more people to get the help they needed.

Similarly, mentors and novices at the high school were neither matched based on schedules nor were schedules modified to accommodate the matches so that meetings could occur during the school day. Therefore, one-on-one meetings proved impossible for most pairs because they did not have some easily available time to meet. Because teaching schedules were created for novices and mentors before they were matched with one another, and thus without regard for common times to observe and meet, it became evident that this element of effective induction was going to be impossible to improve, much less implement. Mentors and novices alike identified this as a significant barrier to induction throughout the year. The peer observation component of the program was similarly compromised by scheduling difficulties and also by a lack of mentor preparation and prevailing school culture. Although we were leading an important change effort in our schools with the support of district and school administrators, neither of us could address the logistical issues that created barriers to implementation. Similarly, we could not hold teachers accountable for doing observations.

Our only recourse was to try to communicate values, standards of practice, and expectations regarding new teacher induction as a way to try to achieve the desired outcomes (Fullan, 2007). Communicating with the teachers often and conducting one-legged interviews with novices regularly allowed Nicole to monitor how the program was being implemented and modify it accordingly. However, without someone organizing and monitoring the program, some components could easily be overlooked or not included. When there is no one to hold teachers accountable for implementation, it is easy for initiatives to get ignored. This suggests the importance of someone being in place to oversee programs such as new teacher mentoring in general and peer observation in particular.

Role Challenges

Nicole observed that filling multiple roles as a teacher, teacher leader, and researcher also hindered the implementation process and led to obvious challenges, which would need to be addressed in order to improve and sustain the mentoring program. She could not always provide classroom coverage at the time requested by the novice or mentor to do observations because of her own duties as a classroom teacher. The multiple hats she was wearing also complicated her efforts. As their colleague, she did not want to push teachers to fulfill her expectations at the expense of jeopardizing healthy relationships or normal boundaries. Along the same lines, Trish did not want to pressure them to do extra work that took up valuable time that the teachers needed to fulfill their usual teaching duties. Had she done so, it might have caused resistance to the whole program. If teachers did things only because she pressured them, this would have compromised her capacity to understand implementation issues as well as the positive relationships she had with participants and the good will she had toward the new teacher induction initiative.

School Culture Challenges

Although Trish offered to provide coverage for observations, not one novice or mentor took her up on the offer. She observed that a significant challenge was the lack of training in the area of observation for mentors, and because of this, the uncertainty they had about the mentoring role when observing colleagues. In addition to the uncertainty over how to conduct observations, the norms of the high school proved difficult to overcome. Teacher feedback indicated that resistance to participating in peer feedback was, in part, because the veteran teachers were not used to or comfortable with the idea of peer observation. Novices too felt resistant as they were leery of being perceived of as incompetent. In general, at the high school, it was rare to have teachers entering one another's classrooms for any reason and most were resistant to it. Mentor and novice dyads were paired at the beginning of the school year, and though the veteran teachers were willing to participate in the ongoing professional development, the observation component of the new teacher induction program was so far outside the cultural norm of the school that the teachers found it almost impossible to overcome. As a leader without authority, Trish did not have the leverage to overcome this cultural barrier to positively impel peer observations.

Although district administrators were supportive of our efforts and were more than happy for us to improve the induction program, an ongoing challenge was that the district did not help make conditions conducive to a research-based approach. For example, not matching the mentors and novices until October hurt the facilitation process and meant that modifications regarding timing and scheduling needed to be made before our initiatives could even begin. The district did not allot time for meetings or observations so that supporting this process fell to us as the facilitators. Similarly, without any formal support, any paperwork Nicole asked the dyads to complete (not only for research purposes but to support the mentoring process) was potentially viewed as extra work that no one in a position of authority would be checking on. Therefore, it is likely that the teachers did not feel any real obligation to complete it, and many did not despite its potential to improve mentoring by providing structure and support.

Most theories of change are weak on capacity building—knowledge, resources, and motivation—and that is one of the reasons they fall short (Fullan, 2001). As we reflected on the findings from our studies, we found challenges regarding the knowledge, resources, and motivation that impacted the mentoring program. Perhaps the participants were not given enough knowledge or resources in order to complete the components successfully. As facilitators and change agents, we needed to provide the participants with all the tools necessary. Although we did the best we could under the circumstances, we did not supply all necessities and perhaps impeded the teachers' motivation. With that said, the Loop District institutionalized many of the new mentoring components derived from our studies.

IMPACT

Despite these challenges, our efforts led the Loop District to make specific changes to its new, research-based teacher induction procedures. Specifically, the new teacher orientation held every year in August was revised, and monthly professional development meetings for mentors and novices were instituted. In addition, Trish developed a new teacher manual as a direct outcome of her dissertation work, which included the Tracking Log and "Cheers and Fears" protocol developed by Nicole because her research demonstrated that they improved the substance of novice/mentor meetings and increased accountability. Additionally, as a result of systematically supporting the implementation of mentor and novice classroom observations and documenting their value from the perspective of participants, peer observation is now a required component of the district's mentoring program. Our joint focus has brought much-needed attention and improvement in the district to the new teacher induction program in general.

New Teacher Orientation

The expanded new teacher orientation was created to help better prepare novice teachers for the upcoming school year. In the past, there had been only a half-day training for new teachers, which mainly focused on the legalities of entering the school system, including sessions on health benefits, teacher-student sexual harassment, and other bureaucratic topics were offered. Now each new teacher is required to participate in two full days of professional development that we designed and facilitate. Contrary to new teacher orientations in the past, where presenters often shared outdated or impractical information, these new teachers are provided with information by peers—teachers from the district, who are knowledgeable about the most current curricula, standards, and methodologies. After covering the district-required topics, we are able to incorporate our findings regarding what new teachers need to know to be successful before the school year begins. We discuss in detail what to expect during their first year of teaching, including dealing with difficult students and classroom management, dialoging with administration, and understanding the district and school culture specific to their grade level. In addition, novices are introduced to the restructured mentoring handbook, which includes state regulations, mentor/novice guidelines, and materials to enhance their induction into the district, such as tips for classroom setup, the observation component, and topics to discuss with their mentors. We hope that giving the manual out at the beginning of the year will increase the chances that it will be used and that all the new teachers will have access to the same information. Based on the feedback gathered informally since we began the extended, teacher-driven orientation, it is beneficial. The district administration has committed to continuing this orientation in future years.

Ongoing Professional Development

Another important change that emerged as a result of our work was that the Loop District started providing mentor and novice teachers with monthly professional development activities and required that both novices and mentors attend. These meetings allow the teachers to gain one hour of professional development "credit" (they need 25 hours a year) and also meet the state's mentoring requirement of 20 hours if both members of a dyad attend. Beyond meeting requirements, as they did during the study, they provide a structured venue for teachers to share ideas, ask questions, and learn from one another in a nonthreatening atmosphere. Nicole facilitates the elementary school professional development meetings and Trish does the same at the high school. During the first meeting of the year, a needs assessment is distributed for each teacher to describe his or her strengths and challenges (Queeny, 1995). Because of our studies, we learned how imperative needs assessments were in matching participants' needs with meeting agenda. Therefore, each month, a friendly meeting reminder is sent to the teachers through email also asking them to make their facilitator aware of specific questions or concerns they may have. Additional needs assessment is conducted at the end of each session by way of an evaluation survey which asks participants to suggest future meeting topics. These also allow us to collect data about how to improve for upcoming years. As a result, we have made changes to the program. For example, last year we added a new teacher induction leader in the middle school. This year, teachers requested additional support on topics related to special education, specifically in the area of in-class support and co-teaching. We are now in the process of creating a special education component for the mentor and novice training next year that will take place before the beginning of the school year.

Mentor Preparation

An additional finding that emerged from both studies was that although the Loop District can take certain preliminary steps with novices to jump-start the mentoring process, mentors must prepare as well. Given that our research indicated that mentors did not know their responsibilities and roles, which may have been due to poor or infrequent training (no mentors had been trained since 2006), lack of awareness of state guidelines, and lack of time, it seemed clear that they needed (re)training. To help the mentors understand their importance in the first days of a new teacher and prepare them to support their assigned novices effectively, the district administration gave us the opportunity to (re)train all the mentors. The training, which took place during the 2014–2015 school year was mandatory.

During this training, we were able to incorporate new guidelines set forth by both the state and the district. At this session, the new mentoring manual was distributed and discussed and the specific mentor requirements and expectations were made clear in an effort to alleviate confusion and inconsistency in services offered to novices. Mentors participated in activities guided by our studies. For example, we discussed the importance of peer observation and how to implement it effectively. We discussed ways to enhance the mentoring relationship through communication and trust building. We instructed the mentors on what we learned from our studies about what the Loop novices need and expect from their mentors. We reflected on our own first years of teaching, and asked the mentors what they wished they had known when they were novice teachers. Many deplored the old "sink or swim" method of induction, and embraced the idea of a more collaborative approach, using the meetings and observations as a springboard for more open discussion about improving teaching practice. We also gave the mentors research which demonstrated the importance of mentoring. The purpose of this is to help them see that mentoring is not secondary to teaching. Rather it is another kind of teaching from which both mentors and novices can benefit.

We received very positive feedback from the mentor training. According to the evaluation we conducted, mentors were "grateful," "enthused," and "ready to help." These affirmations are a distinct change from what mentors had said about mentoring in past years when they had been more likely to talk about it as a burden or a question mark. Training will continue to be a mandatory professional development day for any teacher who would like to mentor a novice in the Loop District.

SUPPORTS

Although we could not have done our studies without our district's support, we would not have known how to do them without the benefit of specific coursework in our EdD program. Through our course experiences, we became knowledgeable change agents ready to restructure the Loop District's mentoring program. In particular, we took classes that focused on designing, initiating, and sustaining change efforts. We learned that we first had to focus on issues and challenges related to implementing the change. For example, in a class called Sustaining Practitioner Change we learned that an understanding of and ability to apply ideas of change are essential for those of us who wish to become change leaders. Models of change were presented and discussed, and as change leaders ourselves, we attempted to make sense of both the vocabulary and the skills needed to create those changes. We also looked at what challenges can create barriers to change, and attempted, using our own personal ideas about change, to create a toolbox to use as we moved forward in our inquiry. Our coursework gave us real-life experiences to help develop our understanding of how change occurs.

Not only did we study change theoretically, but we also learned experientially, and this gave us much to draw on. For example, in one course, we had to initiate and sustain a change in our schools; we then had to document, analyze, and reflect on what occurred. Throughout this process we observed challenges and resistance, which helped us be more prepared to deal with leadership challenges during our dissertation studies. These preliminary change leadership experiences helped better prepare us to carry out our dissertation studies more effectively. Our professors at Rutgers were able to guide us in implementing small change efforts and provide us with critical feedback so that we felt prepared to lead the larger-scale changes implemented for our dissertations with considerable success. By following examples we learned about and gaining experience before actually conducting our dissertation studies, we were able to initiate, implement, and institutionalize substantive change to the mentoring and induction process in the Loop District.

We also gained specific skills for facilitating meaningful conversations about practice that had the potential to improve teaching. In a course called "Models of Professional Development," we learned about a variety of protocols that can be used to structure and deepen conversations about teaching, learning, and students. For example, the National School Reform Faculty (http://www.nsrfharmony.org) provides several protocols that can be used to enhance the value of peer observations. This class provided us with the knowledge and skills to use these protocols by providing extensive opportunities to practice using them during class time. Perhaps more importantly, we were also required to practice using them in our worksites. This hands-on experience helped us understand the importance of peer observation protocols and prompted us to include protocol training during novice teacher orientation to help them understand not only the importance of observation, but ways to approach observation from the point of view of a "critical friend."

An important strategy for initiating and sustaining the new teacher induction program was to gain administrative support. Rutgers encouraged this by suggesting that the students in the EdD program have qualified stakeholders from their own workplaces on their dissertation committees whenever possible. This proved to be important to the success of our dissertation work and its "staying power" beyond the study period. We asked the superintendent of the Loop District to be a member of our dissertation committees so that he would be knowledgeable about and (hopefully) support the steps we were taking both at the elementary and high school levels. Indeed, his participation in the dissertation process brought a lot of visibility and support to our projects that might not have existed if our committees were composed solely of Rutgers faculty. A key factor in his interest in being involved was that he recognized the need to improve our induction program and bought in to our vision of implementing a research-based program from the start. The presence of the superintendent on our dissertation committees had far-reaching positive consequences for institutionalizing the new teacher induction program in the Loop School District. Although he knew that the district's induction program was weak, he came to understand the needs in a more detailed way as a result. For example, he learned that there was no mentor training in the district. Consequently, we were commissioned to develop and facilitate mentor training, and mentors were provided with coverage to attend. This was important to the mentors, because it alleviated some of the struggle of finding time to deal with mentoring responsibilities while maintaining a classroom just when the year is getting underway. He also provided coverage for us to facilitate professional development and resources to run mentor training, and he invited us to present our findings to stakeholders, including the Board of Education, our peers, and other administrators.

Administrative support trickled down and extended beyond the superintendent. After our studies were completed and presented, the assistant superintendent asked us to develop and facilitate our newly designed professional development for mentors and novices. Principals also demonstrated investment in our efforts by supporting peer observation with classroom coverage, allowing participants to be excused for new teacher induction professional development when necessary and allowing us to host meetings in their schools. This administrative support is also indicative of how the climate of the district is beginning to change with regard to new teacher induction. The district continues to move forward, improving in the area of induction and mentoring, and new teacher retention and satisfaction continues to be a priority.

CONCLUSION

The Rutgers EdD program encouraged us to find a problem of practice in our work sites and initiate an improvement effort focused on addressing it. As a result of what we had learned during our coursework in the program, we implemented studies that led to specific improvements in new teacher induction for teachers in our district. Finding a problem of practice relevant to our work and implementing an initiative that was research based and informed by change theory led to innovations that truly "moved the needle" on a problem that had been left unattended to in our district for years. As a result, our district now has a new teacher induction program with many research-based components, and we have become leaders tasked with facilitation and ongoing program improvement. Problem of practice–oriented EdD programs like Rutgers' which include hands-on, applied-learning experiences that are focused specifically on issues and challenges in actual educational contexts can truly bring about substantial research-based change for schools and districts. Not only can the graduates effect change in the locale where they do their dissertation work, but very practical, problem-solving type dissertations can provide change models which we think can serve as helpful examples for audiences dealing with similar challenges in other settings. Our dissertations provide compelling evidence of the potential for EdD programs to train change leaders who can use and consume research in ways to encourage specific and substantive change.

REFERENCES

Barrera, A., Braley, R. T., & Slate, J. R. (2010). Beginning teacher success: An investigation into the feedback from mentors of formal mentoring programs. *Mentoring & Tutoring: Partnership in Learning, 18,* 61–74.

Cochran-Smith, M. (2004). Stayers, leavers, lovers, and dreamers: Insights about teacher education. *Journal of Teacher Education, 55*(5), 397–392.

Darling-Hammond, L. (2000). Teacher quality and student achievement. *Education Policy Analysis Archives, 8*(1), 1–44.

Darling-Hammond, L., & Bransford, J. (2005). Preparing teachers for a changing world: What teachers should learn and be able to do. San Francisco, CA: Jossey-Bass.

Feiman-Nemser, S. (2001). From preparation to practice: Designing a continuum to strengthen and sustain teaching. *Teachers College Record, 6*(103), 1013–1055.

Fullan, M. (2001). *Leading in a culture of change.* San Francisco, CA: Jossey-Bass.

Fullan, M. (2007). *The new meaning of educational change* (4th ed.). New York, NY: Teachers College Press.

Ganser, T. (1992). *Getting off to a good start: A collaborative mentoring program for beginning teachers.* Whitewater: Wisconsin Department of Public Instruction, Wisconsin Improvement Program.

Hall, G., & Hord, S. (2006). Implementing change: Patterns, principles, and potholes (2nd ed.). Boston, MA: Allyn & Bacon.

Ingersoll, R. M. (2012, April 4). Beginning teacher induction: What the data tell us. *Education Week.* Retrieved from http://www.edweek.org/ew/articles/2012/05/16/kappan_ingersoll.h31.html

Ingersoll, R., & Smith, T. (2004). Do teacher induction and mentoring matter? *NASSP Bulletin, 88*(638), 28–40.

Ingersoll, R., & Strong, M. (2011). The impact of induction and mentoring programs for beginning teachers: A critical review of the research. *Review of Education Research, 81*(2), 201–233.

Jandoli, M. A. (2013). Goings and comings: Younger teachers join the profession in an era of rapid change. *New Jersey Education Association.* Retrieved from https://www.njea.org/news-and-publications/njea-review/april-2013/goings-and-comings

Lumdsen, L. (1998). Teacher morale. *ERIC Digest.* Number 120.

Queeny, D. S. (1995). *Assessing needs in continuing education: An essential tool for quality improvement.* San Francisco, CA: Jossey-Bass.

Rossi, P. H., Lipsey, M. W., & Freeman, H. E. (2004). *Evaluation: A systematic approach* (7th ed.). Thousand Oaks, CA: Sage.

Rutgers University Graduate School of Education, Education Doctorate (Ed.D.). Retrieved from http://gse.rutgers.edu/edd.

Sava, S. (2010). Select master teachers to mentor the novices. *Education Week, 29*(23), 25–25.

Smith, T. M., & Ingersoll, R. (2004). What are the effects of induction and mentoring on beginning teacher turnover? *American Educational Research Journal, 41*(3), 681–714.

Tauer, S. (1996). *The mentor—Protégé relationship and its effects on the experienced teacher.* New York, NY: American Educational Research Association.

Washburn-Moses, L. (2010). Rethinking mentoring: Comparing policy and practice in special and general education. *Educational Policy and Analysis Archives, 18*(32), 1–25.

Weiss, E. M. (1999). Perceived workplace conditions and first-year teachers' morale, career choice commitment, and planned retention: A secondary analysis. *Teaching and Teacher Education, 15,* 861–879.

Young, J. R., Bullough, R. V., Draper, R. J., Smith, L. K., & Erickson, L. B. (2005). Novice teacher growth and personal models of mentoring: Choosing compassion over inquiry. *Mentoring and Tutoring, 13*(2), 169–188.

CHAPTER 13

JOURNEY TO BECOMING A SCHOLARLY PRACTITIONER

Nancy C. Kline

This chapter describes my educational journey to obtain an EdD from Lynn University, a member of the Carnegie Project on the Education Doctorate (CPED). It highlights my personal passage from being a K–12 educational leader to becoming a research practitioner who solves problems in practice. In particular, I highlight my experience with and characteristics of my nontraditional dissertation. First, I provide an overview of the Lynn EdD program.

Lynn University is an independent, nonprofit institution located in Boca Raton, Florida. Lynn joined CPED in 2007 and was part of the original membership that developed the CPED principles and design concepts (Carnegie Project for the Education Doctorate, 2015). They promptly set out to redesign the EdD degree to include this framework. The Lynn CPED-influenced EdD consists of a 3-year program of study, which aims to equip graduates with the skills needed to connect research with practice, lead high-performing organizations, and contribute to students' learning (Lynn University, 2015a). The focus of the degree is Educational Leadership and includes four program themes: leadership, accountability, equality and diversity, and

The EdD and the Scholarly Practitioner, pages 217–224
Copyright © 2016 by Information Age Publishing
All rights of reproduction in any form reserved.

learning and instruction. Embedded in these themes is a focus on methods of problem-based inquiry (Lynn University, 2015).

To prepare students to understand problem-based inquiry, Lynn faculty members offer students the opportunity to engage research in collaborative ways that focus on solutions to real problems they face in their practice. The culminating project for this preparation is the dissertation in practice (DiP), which includes students collaborating on a common theme, using shared research to design solutions, and incorporating modern technology into their final products. Faculty selected this contemporary model after realizing that traditional methods of research and theory fell short of preparing students to identify solutions for immediate implementation. They now advocate for hands-on research that results in more immediate and relevant solutions. The workplaces of the EdD candidates—schools and classrooms—become their laboratories of practice where they can actively try out this project-based model. In their final DiP, the students work in teams to identify a common problem of practice and accept differing roles and responsibilities in researching and creating a final product (Lynn University, 2015).

My DiP was a product of this new method. My issue was the importance of regular school attendance and the opportunities associated with increasing attendance. As a result of this DiP process, I developed several products such as a user-friendly manual for schools, districts, or central offices; an interactive website; and a video that supported schools and district offices to address chronic absenteeism. In this chapter, I discuss my own experience of meshing theory with practice to develop a patented solution that improved school attendance and academic achievement (Kline, 2016).

THE ROAD TO SCHOLARLY PRACTITIONER

Currently, I work in a clinical faculty role as an assistant professor and coordinator of the Lynn University educational leadership master's program. Before taking on this role and during my EdD program, I was a superintendent of schools, school board member, nonprofit executive and teacher. While working toward my doctoral degree, I learned that theory combined with a practitioner's approach to solving problems is an effective way to impact educational change. I implemented this approach in my dissertation in practice which produced research that showed a school can increase student achievement through improved attendance. My DiP produced useable products and resources for schools including an attendance manual and a patented toolkit I call *Bring It 180*, which consists of interactive materials, and a website of downloadable materials, posters, and graphics, and a targeted video which teach and assist schools in increasing student attendance. This toolkit has been utilized by numerous Florida schools (Kline, 2013).

As a Guardian ad Litem and Educational Advocacy Trainer for Florida volunteers, I educate stakeholders regarding the importance of regular school attendance and its impact on children within the child welfare system. I also continue to consult with both school districts and colleges utilizing *Bring It 180* to increase attendance and student achievement (Kline, 2015). I believe my research and action on attendance can affect policy decisions regarding compulsory attendance at the state and national levels, and I aim to scale the program to influence positive changes in student achievement for schools nationwide.

Graduate School

I was motivated to get an advanced degree by my aspiration to affect positive change for children and families. By gaining additional theoretical knowledge and skills, I felt I could be a more effective superintendent, educational consultant, and now assistant professor. I chose the EdD because, to me, the degree clearly put research into practice. I also saw an opportunity to collaboratively work with my peers and wanted a face-to-face or blended model of instruction. Lynn's program offered both of these characteristics.

One aspect of my program that I found both attractive and ultimately crucial to my learning was the cohort model, which produced a group or community of individuals that became a strong component of my learning. My cohort consisted of 10 professionals working in varied positions at PreK–12 schools or higher-education institutions. Their collective capabilities and wide-ranging proficiencies offered me an exclusive opportunity to collaborate with and learn from their diverse educational experiences. This kind of experience helped all of us to explore problems of practice with greater insight and ultimately resulted in remarkable outcomes in our own research and solution creation.

Together we explored issues such as how to improve parent involvement at disadvantaged schools, types of gender equity policies that protects students' rights, digital gaming lessons, and core high school subjects. Each person brought their professional experience to these issues as we simultaneously read about them in the literature. We then cooperatively sought practical solutions for these issues to implement and then research. This cohort model was important to our learning not only because it involved us in both problems and solutions but also because we all had a stake in the outcomes.

Solving problems was important to all of us since we collectively pursued solutions to each other's challenges. The joint approach helped us gain knowledge and access to new ideas and solutions. Practicing scholarship, evaluating data, and analyzing implications, in this professional "think tank" supplied invaluable feedback and collaboration within the group. This practice exponentially increased our knowledge base of research methodologies and practical solutions.

A second important aspect of the program was the application of theory to practice. We received a rigorous foundation in understanding the literature and theory and in utilizing methodology to construct research designs. The result was our ability to assess scholarly information and combine this with practice to inform practical solutions.

These skills were enhanced by a group of faculty who were well versed in PK–12 educational challenges and opportunities. Most of them had been in leadership positions for decades. Their knowledge and expertise streamlined the problem-solving process because they had lived and experienced many of the same challenges we currently face and offered counsel for study and research. They offered scenarios which we debated regarding school policy and procedure, where cohort members and professors would bring forth unique solutions depending on their own experiences. I could freely discuss issues relating to compulsory attendance, how to meet the needs of at-risk learners, and the future of student assessment. Broad knowledge from a varied group of professors with both the theory and practical knowledge was central to my learning and developing my DiP.

My Study

While serving a 4-year term as the superintendent of a medium-size school district in Florida, I began the EdD program. As I mentioned, I wanted to understand how theoretical knowledge and research skills could impact positive academic change. My school district had remained stagnant for many years and was experiencing declines in some core academic subjects. I knew the district was capable of higher student achievement results. So I decided that the pursuit of an EdD would better equip me with the tools necessary to address this problem.

In my district, the graduation rate was not as high as I imagined it could be based on our population's demographics (Martin County School District, 2008). I noticed that attendance appeared to be part of the puzzle. As I investigated attendance both nationwide and in Florida, I learned of the influence attendance has on student achievement (Sheldon, 2007). This prompted my interest in studying the effects of attendance in my own district. I wanted to evaluate the relationship between chronic absenteeism and student achievement in my district. Through the literature, I discovered that when we determine why children are chronically absent, we could identify, prevent, and intervene with successful measures to reduce low attendance, therefore increasing student achievement (Balfanz & Byrnes, 2012). I then set out to see if this would help my district.

The Problem

The purpose of choosing to research student attendance rates compared to student achievement was to first determine the impact that attendance had on academic achievement and then design an inventive product and process that would increase attendance in my district. Based on a review of literature I was able to determine that other regions of the country had increased school attendance and improved overall student academic outcomes (Balfanz & Byrnes, 2012). As an educator I also knew intuitively that when you attend school regularly you are more likely to receive the instruction necessary to become academically proficient. Therefore I was interested in researching the number of days a student could miss school before it substantially impacted student learning. I also wanted to examine which core subjects showed the greatest decrease in achievement with lower school attendance.

The Research

My study compared attendance to academic proficiency in two Florida school districts. The study evaluated the hypothesis that a negative relationship exists between missing more than 11 days of school annually and demonstrating low proficiency on the Florida Comprehensive Assessment Test (FCAT) in reading and math at the elementary, middle, and high school levels. I collected data from the two districts and from the Department of Education's (FLDOE) website for the time period of 2011–2013.

The design and evaluation of this assessment provided correlational evidence regarding academic proficiency versus student attendance rates. The two main variables studied were attendance rates for students missing zero to 5 days, more than 11 days, and up to 20 or more days of school annually, and math and reading FCAT test scores from the same students (District Research and Assessment Department, 2003). The study investigated the relationships that existed between these two variables and the outcome of their cause and effect on student achievement and academic proficiency (Fraenkel, Wallen, & Hyun, 2011).

What I Learned

I asked the question, How do student absences compare to academic proficiency in two Florida school districts? What I found was substantial evidence of a causal impact regarding days absent and academic proficiency in both reading and math in elementary, middle, and high school in two districts (Kline, 2015). In the 2011–2012 school year, academic achievement was negatively influenced because of the number of student absences in both districts (District Research and Assessment Department, 2013). As students amassed more absences, the relationship of the negative correlation continued to grow. The large metropolitan school district recorded only unexcused absences, while the smaller school district counted all absences (District Research and Assessment Department, 2013). However, the results were remarkably similar with little difference, which is consistent with existing research related to little differences between excused and unexcused absences and student achievement (Eaton, Brener, & Kann, 2008).

Students absent 5 days or less in both school districts exhibited academic proficiency in reading and math between 70% and 76%. Students absent more than 11 days or between 11 and 15 days recorded proficiency between 28% and 57% in reading and math during the 2011–2012 school year. In the small school district, 2,613 students in high school scored 70% proficiency in reading when absent between zero-to-five days (Kline, 2015). During the school year 2011–2012, in the large metropolitan school district, 156,352 students with zero unexcused absences also scored 70% reading proficiency. The similarity of this analysis is noteworthy considering the difference in sample size (District Research and Assessment Department, 2013).

Throughout the study, the percentage of student absences compared to academic proficiency was similar in both districts. Reading and math proficiency declined with increased absences. Elementary math students who missed between 11 and 15 days in the small school district showed achievement levels at 57% nonproficient. In both districts, when students crossed the 11-day mark, their academic achievement declined dramatically. Students chronically absent with 20 or more days in high school logged reading scores at only 33% proficient in the small school district. In the large school district, high school reading students who missed 11or more days scored 28% proficient. Overall, the nature and degree of the relationship between attendance and academics is significant (District Research and Assessment Department, 2013).

My Action

The learning that resulted from my study prompted my thinking of different ways to improve attendance. With the support of my program and faculty, I developed an attendance campaign that relied on innovation and technology to present a simple message. The benefits of implementing *Bring It 180* are measurable with rich data results. Both school districts I studied in Florida have received professional staff development to educate faculty on the positive implications of increased student attendance rates, and they have implemented my program (Kline, 2014).

CONCLUSION

My EdD program taught me how to examine a problem found in practice and seek solutions by conducting research and evaluating results. These skills have become an integral part of my practice as a professional educational consultant. As an assistant professor, I also have the opportunity to teach this model to my doctoral students and to do so with firsthand knowledge of the process. At Lynn, we often talk about how students will flip the way they think about research after they enter and complete the program. The transformation in students' thinking and processing begins immediately with the initial coursework that includes the first steps of a literature review, and progresses with the program as the learners are encouraged to think beyond their practitioner knowledge and embrace the idea of becoming a scholarly practitioner.

My choice to pursue an EdD worked well for me. Experiencing an innovative and alternative model of a dissertation has changed the way I view research and theoretical knowledge. I now see how it can benefit practice and practitioners as they face the difficult problems on a daily basis. As a researcher and now as an assistant professor, I continue to value and engage in problem-based inquiry and combining theory and practice to improve education.

REFERENCES

Balfanz, R., & Byrnes, V. (2012). *The importance of being in school: A report on absenteeism in the nation's public schools.* Baltimore, MD: Johns Hopkins University Center for Social Organization of Schools.

Carnegie Project for the Education Doctorate. (2015). The Carnegie Project on the Education Doctorate is an international effort aimed at strengthening the education doctorate, Ed.D. *CPED.* Retrieved from http://cpedinitiative.org/

District Research and Assessment Department. (2013). *Student assessment and research department data, 2011–2012.* Fort Lauderdale, FL: Broward County Public Schools.

Eaton, D. K., Brener, N., & Kann, L. K. (2008). Associations of health risk behaviors with school absenteeism. Does having permission for the absence make a difference? *Journal of School Health, 78,* 223–229.

Fraenkel, J. R., Wallen, N. E., & Hyun, H. H. (2011). *How to design and evaluate research in education* (8th ed.). New York, NY: McGraw-Hill.

Kline, N. (2014). *Broward's Bring It. 180. A toolkit for Broward County schools. Public access.* Fort Lauderdale, FL: Broward County Public Schools.

Kline, N. (2015). *Two fabulous programs "On Time Graduation" and "Bring It" help schools and students succeed.* Retrieved from http://bringit180.com/Home.html

Kline, N. (2016). *Attendance vs. achievement—Bring It 180* [Video]. Retrieved from https://www.youtube.com/watch?v=7vknmQjcjjw

Lynn University. (2015). *Donald E. and Helen L. Ross College of Education: Doctorate of Education, Educational Leadership.* Retrieved from http://www.lynn.edu/academics/colleges/education/programs/edd-educational-leadership

Martin County School District. (2008). *State of the district 2008–2012.* Retrieved from http://ontimegraduation.com/uploads/state-of-the-district-2008-2012.pdf

Sheldon, S. (2007). Improving school attendance with school, family, and community partnerships. *Journal of Educational Research, 100,* 267–275.

Student Assessment and Research Department Data. (2013). *Public access.* Fort Lauderdale, FL: Broward County Public Schools.

ABOUT THE EDITOR

Dr. Jill Alexa Perry is the Executive Director of the Carnegie Project on the Educational Doctorate (CPED) and a Research Associate Professor in the Department of Administration and Policy Studies at the University of Pittsburgh.

Working with Dr. David Imig (Professor of Practice, University of Maryland) and Dr. Lee Shulman (President-Emeritus, Carnegie Foundation for the Advancement of Teaching), Dr. Perry began CPED in 2007 as part of her doctoral studies at the University of Maryland. Her research focuses on professional doctorate preparation in education, organizational change in higher education, and faculty leadership roles. Her publications have appeared in *Planning and Changing Journal, Journal of School Public Relations, Innovation in Higher Education*, as well as in several books and practitioner journals. She is co-editor of *In Their Own Words: A Journey to the Stewardship of the Practice in Education*, published by Information Age Publishing and will be the editor of the new online journal *The Scholarly Practitioner: The Journal for the Impact and Transformation in Professional Preparation in Education*, which will launch in spring 2016. Professionally, she has served as a consultant on the design and development of EdD programs at several universities around the United States and abroad. She is also the Board Chair of the Research & Innovation Advisory Board of the International Higher Education Teaching and Learning Association.

Dr. Perry is a graduate of the University of Maryland, where she received her PhD in international education policy. She holds an MA in higher education administration and a BA in Spanish and international studies from Boston College. She has over 20 years of experience in leadership and program development in education and teaching experience at the elementary, secondary, undergraduate, and graduate levels in the United States and abroad. She is a Fulbright Scholar (Germany) and a returned Peace Corps Volunteer (Paraguay).

The EdD and the Scholarly Practitioner, page 225
Copyright © 2016 by Information Age Publishing
All rights of reproduction in any form reserved.

CPSIA information can be obtained
at www.ICGtesting.com
Printed in the USA
FSOW04n2344280916
25519FS